The Calamity Form

The Calamity Form

ON POETRY AND SOCIAL LIFE

Anahid Nersessian

The University of Chicago Press CHICAGO AND LONDON

The University of Chicago Press, Chicago 60637
The University of Chicago Press, Ltd., London
© 2020 by The University of Chicago
Published 2020
Printed in the United States of America

29 28 27 26 25 24 23 22 21 20   1 2 3 4 5

ISBN-13: 978-0-226-70128-8 (cloth)
ISBN-13: 978-0-226-70131-8 (paper)
ISBN-13: 978-0-226-70145-5 (e-book)
DOI: https://doi.org/10.7208/chicago/9780226701455.001.0001

The University of Chicago Press gratefully acknowledges the generous
support of the University of California, Los Angeles, toward the
publication of this book.

Library of Congress Cataloging-in-Publication Data

Names: Nersessian, Anahid, 1982– author.
Title: The calamity form : on poetry and social life / Anahid Nersessian.
Description: Chicago : University of Chicago Press, 2020. |
Includes bibliographical references and index.
Identifiers: LCCN 2019053423 | ISBN 9780226701288 (cloth) |
ISBN 9780226701318 (paperback) | ISBN 9780226701455 (ebook)
Subjects: LCSH: Wordsworth, William, 1770–1850—Criticism and
interpretation. | Keats, John, 1795–1821—Criticism and interpretation. |
English poetry—18th century—History and criticism. | Romanticism—
England—History and criticism—18th century. | Figures of speech.
Classification: LCC PR571 .N47 2020 | DDC 821/.709—dc23
LC record available at https://lccn.loc.gov/2019053423

♾ This paper meets the requirements of ANSI/NISO Z39.48–1992
(Permanence of Paper).

So settle for knowing the approximate time
Because think of the alternative

And once you are actually in
the future, | pretend it's the present

KEVIN DAVIES, *The Golden Age of Paraphernalia* (2008)

Contents

Figures

Introduction

The life which surrounds us flows by from day to day in a familiar and accustomed channel. Even if it is broken, if its strongest dams are destroyed—our consciousness, our feelings invariably and inevitably lag behind in their development; they do not correspond to the new; we are still in the power of what has been before. Our eye is unable to discern, to make out what is being born amidst the rumble, in the flood, amidst all the change, or in the catastrophe.

ALEKSANDR KONSTANTINOVICH VORONSKIĬ,
"Art as the Cognition of Life," trans. Frederick S. Choate (1923)

Nach der damaligen Geisteslage mußte notwendig lyrische Poesie der erste Vorwurf . . . sein.

[Given the spiritual circumstances lyric poetry was the first resort.][1]

KARL MARX, letter to Heinrich Marx dated 10 November [1837]

This book has two ambitions, one modest and the other more intricate. The first is to describe how four figures—parataxis, obscurity, catachresis, and apostrophe—work in a handful of well-known Romantic poems. The second is to spend some lightly ordered time thinking about the limits of historical materialism for literary study.

What these objectives have to do with one another is a question I'm unlikely to answer to the satisfaction of even the most sympathetic readers. That they are connected or least adjacent the biography of criticism proves. The book leans often on that biography. It does so not in any reactionary spirit, nor to claim any sort of superlative status for the humanities. It simply assumes literary criticism to be the best way to understand literature and is interested in how people have managed to do so in the past. This is a far cry from saying that close reading, structuralism, or scansion is the best or even a good way to understand other aspects of the world. My discussion is grounded by the belief that the world's contents are ontologically plural—that they have different, sometimes overlapping ways of being. It is grounded likewise by the belief that any programmatic confidence in materialism as the theoretical ground of anticapitalist practice must also acknowledge that some things cannot be properly grasped and need not be contained by rigid or conventional projections of its reach.

This brief preface gives an overview of the book's themes and guiding principles. The themes are poetry, social life, and criticism. One guiding principle is the relative autonomy of aesthetic objects from the obligation to make sense of the world and, by extension, the relative autonomy of criticism from the obligation to explain its objects in evidentiary terms. To put it simply, art doesn't have to be about real things, and criticism doesn't have to pretend that it is. That sounds straightforward, but it's a claim backed, as we'll see, by complicated ideas about the nature and structure of reality.

Another guiding principle is that getting a grip on what is real is made harder by the historical emergence of capital, which renders the relation between nature and structure inaccessible, in excess of any synoptic perception. When the ambiguity and imprecision of the aesthetic object meet capital's phantasmagoria, strange things happen. They get even stranger in an era rattled by the runaway surrealism of climate change, which is both the progeny and the partner of industrialization and which finds its inflection point the same place this book does. That point is located close to the end of the eighteenth century; it is defined by "the separation of Nature from the facts of the labour that is now creating it, and then the breaking of Nature, in altered and now intolerable relations between men."[2]

The Calamity Form is interested not in what art writ large can and cannot do but in the peculiar position Romantic literature takes up vis-à-vis history conceived as a mode of explanation—that is, as a narrative form linking effects to their causes. My argument, which concerns poetry, is this: at the same exact moment in time when the ecological and human costs of industry were becoming palpable, some poets began actively staging their own works' competence, or rather its lack thereof, to the representation and analysis of the train of consequences set in motion by contemporary economic shifts. They did this, moreover, in the thick of an intensifying preoccupation with the difference between knowledge and imagination, facts and figures, the sciences and the arts—a preoccupation that cannot be written off as mere ideology or self-service. There are, it turns out, good philosophical reasons to believe a poem is unresponsive to the kinds of explanatory models proffered by biologists, statisticians, sociologists, and historians. And there are good philosophical reasons to believe that literary criticism might have something important to say about a poem that cannot be reduced to or clarified by the standards of other disciplines, particularly those driven by questions of *why* and *how*.

The phrase "the calamity form" plays on Marx's commodity form, the great prestidigitation by which capital disguises its logic. If the materialist conception of history tries to summarize the conditions that make up the basis of every transition between various modes of production, the commodity form—which causes "the definite social relation between men" to assume "the fantastic form of a relation between things"—sets a high hurdle between that effort and its chances for success.[3] In the Romantic period, before Marx helped articulate that conception though well within the cultural and intellectual framework on which it would be built, such a summation is emphatically impossible. It is always the case that the "Ovidian transformation of bodies into shapes of a different kind that leads in an unbroken thread from the wage relation down to capitalist modernity" cannot be appreciated from some point of view outside its saturation of life: it operates at too large a scale and across too vast a domain of activity.[4] This is plainly true in the dead midst of the Industrial Revolution, whose violent reorganizing of the world both depends upon and generates what I will call *nescience*, or unknowing, about it.

Geoffrey Hartman identifies this type of ignorance with trauma, the physiological disruption whose mental yield comes "as close to nescience as to knowledge."[5] He also views it as the informational output of literature, which, like traumatic experience, confounds rather than clarifies the world's order. In the 1971 preface to *Wordsworth's Poetry*, Hartman notes that both "the trauma of industrialization" and an "apocalyptic rate of change and nature-loss" are immanent to poems like those collected in *Lyrical Ballads* without being parsed or even really described by them.[6] To be clear, there is nothing especially new about this idea. The notion that poetry or works of art more generally are nonreferential or resistant to denotation, that they pick out nothing in the world or, in Philip Sidney's undying phrase, that they "nothing affirm . . . and therefore never lieth," is timeworn to the point of being trite.[7] It does not belong to 1971, nor to the Romantic period, nor to Sidney. It is, quite simply, a notion foundational to the history of Western aesthetics and to the history of Western philosophy. It also becomes newly salient in the context of industrialization's trauma, which, like all traumas, is an experience of phenomenological discontinuity, of the everyday match between what is felt, what is known, and what is actually true gone to irretrievable pieces.

The calamity form, then, names a secondary distortion laid over the cockeyed perspective so much mainstream or canonical poetry likes to say it gives on reality. Like the commodity form, it names a disfigurement that is at once sensual and cognitive: it effects changes in how we, as embodied beings, experience the material world, and it also makes those changes hard to grasp in explicative, let alone actionable, terms. What is to be done about a world whose complexity is so uncomprehendingly lived, whose harms are palpable and yet obscure, seeming to come upon us from everywhere and nowhere? Here "all things are full of labor" and yet "man cannot utter it: the eye is not satisfied with seeing, nor the ear filled with hearing."[8] To feel but not to get, to undergo but not to understand: this is the etiology of trauma and of the traumatic historical event. Nescience captures not just its rational but also its affective dimension. It is, you might say, calamity's unique structure of feeling.

Here is where it gets tricky. The calamity form, in this book, is *both* the Industrial Revolution and a poetics awkwardly responsive to or cooperative with it, working alongside though not necessarily in cahoots. It is a thing in the world with an objective character, and it is also an attempt to match up this thing in the world with a performance, habit, or style, an attempt to give the calamity a cultural expression. If "the Industrial Revolution" is shorthand for the total phenomenon of the transition to capitalism, which could not happen without the overturning of a certain set of social and metabolic relations, the poetry of this moment—tirelessly lyrical and telescopic—adopts formal strategies of abbreviation and foreclosure as it tries and fails to narrate that transition.

It goes without saying that industrial technologies move to increase productivity via the compression of time and space. Perhaps what we are used to seeing as Romanticism's exemplary inwardness may actually be this same compression returned *as an attitude*, a short-circuiting that aims to repossess the occult character of the commodity and sets it not against but beside the inscrutabilities of its historical moment. From Wordsworth's obsessive dismantling of stories into processes into things to Keats's experiments with the ode as a genre that, being at once descriptively terse and psychologically diffuse, is suspended between surfeit and longing, stillness and forward momentum, the calamitous forms of Romanticism make their history present precisely in its retreat from assessment or accounting. They do not, however, make it present just as they please.

This is a caution against taking the heroic possibilities of literature too seriously. Romantic poets are as limited as any other cultural producers—and any other historical persons—in their ability to challenge or subvert the status quo. Wordsworth is onto something when he tells the Whig politician and future prime minister Charles Fox that his poems might "cooperate, however feebly," with state-based welfare programs.[9] The feeble is lamentable, weepy. It is also weak, in the structural as well as the moral vein, and the poetry that interests me is likewise built to fray, twisted into a net that, sieve-like, sets loose more than it manages to hold.

There is no particular ethics to assign to this condition and no politics, especially if you believe that when it comes to emancipatory projects "culture itself" is nothing close to a silver bullet; as Huey P. Newton famously said, "We're going to need some stronger stuff."[10] Moreover, the poetry of calamity is not only feeble with respect to its object; it also renders its object feeble in the sense of faint or insubstantial, so overwhelming in its magnitude that its opacity becomes the most telling evidence of its significance. The poetics of calamity, then, is directed not toward an encounter with what is real but toward an encounter with the inaccessibility of the real. What it cannot diagnose, it cannot abolish.

When it comes to reading the symptoms of capitalist modernity, we are more used to turning to the novel, and particularly the high-realist novel at the center of Fredric Jameson's still-pivotal *The Political Unconscious* or his more recent extensions and refinements thereof. That book makes the case that realism, as a narrative mode, is in the best position to apprehend a "social order in the process of penetration and subversion, reorganization and rationalization" while also offering symbolically to resolve the social antagonisms that undergird and are provoked by that process.[11] Much has been said about this argument's dependence on plot, character, and other novelistic features that don't obtain or obtain differently in a poetic context. *The Calamity Form* might be said to invert the argument of *The Political Unconscious*, not because it concerns poetry instead of prose but because it does not believe that cultural artifacts treat symbolic phenomena in the absence of real phenomena—though life would certainly be easier if they did.

Rather, the book claims that the figurative, nonreferential, and antidenotative properties of aesthetic objects—here, poems—are longstanding, highly developed competencies well suited to a historical era in which the means by which life is reproduced become spectral. This account of what it is poems do, or what they can describe, sidesteps the crypto-psychoanalytic distinction between "real" and "symbolic" altogether, making a place for the disaffirmations of poetry as ways of turning absence into a curious kind of presence. It is the kind of presence against which nothing can be proclaimed nor achieved, and to which no harm may be definitively attributed. Again: what evades diagnosis evades abolition.

On this same note novels, at least the kind that are written in the nineteenth century, are built for teleology: they imagine, fix, and map how effects follow from causes in what George Eliot terms "those invisible thoroughfares" of human life, whether that life is seen as essentially free or tragically muted by its socioeconomic surround.[12] In this book, even the poetry that winks at narrative does away with forecasting. It does not estimate what is likely to happen based on what has already occurred; nor does it yoke what has already occurred to the outsize burden of the present instant. Still less does it claim to be able to assemble a causal network of actors and events capable of being translated into a predictive theory. This is a strike neither against poetry nor against theory. It is just a glance across the distance that exists between them, and a hint that criticism (whatever its aspirations) ought to be responsive and responsible to that distance.

Recent efforts to settle Romantic poetry within the crises of industrialization are bolstered by the proposal that the Anthropocene—a name for the geological era in which human activity is the dominant influence on the global mean temperature—has its point of origin around 1780, the same time James Watt's steam engine was enjoying wider use in cotton mills and collieries.[13] One might complain that this perspective assigns Romanticism a telos or trajectory that routes itself through the very visible thoroughfare of our own climate emergency. I would add that the shortcomings of this sort of presentism are not limited to the imposition of twenty-first-century ideas on eighteenth- and nineteenth-century texts. The issue, to begin, is that the social transformation we call the Industrial Revolution, and to which we compulsively assign dates coinciding with the invention of the steam engine, the power loom, the cotton gin, and so on, *is a version of Marx's commodity fetish*: it is a structure of unknowing underwritten by the commodity form wherein (again) real relations between human beings assume the fantastic form of a relation between things. In other words, it is a perceptual derangement that makes things seem other than they are and so produces a dilemma for the empiricist paradigms of the Enlightenment, which is ill equipped to understand the phenomena sprung up within it.

When the political economists of the age move to understand their new situation, the results can be "dazzling," but they are also fetishistic, for in their accounts value appears as a given even as the process through which value is generated while regulating social being "vanishes in its own result, leaving no trace behind" (*C* 1.187). We see the same logic subtending a great deal of scholarship that imagines Romantic-era literature as having privileged evidentiary access to the planetary conditions picked out by the word *Anthropocene*, which handily conceals the fact that capitalist enterprise, and not humankind, has caused climate change on the present scale. Even critics who dutifully point out that it is thanks to the social relations put in place *by* capitalist enterprise that we have a climate emergency at all nonetheless collapse those relations at once into the name of their cause (the Industrial Revolution) and the name of their effect (the Anthropocene). A literary criticism that subpoenas literature to testify to the existence and the experience of this cause or this effect merely applies one cultural form to another, investing these minimally descriptive, maximally tendentious categories, along with literature itself, with all manner of "metaphysical subtleties and theological niceties" (*C* 1.163). The messianic tenor of so much of this work gives some clue to how those subtleties and niceties make their way into something so tactile as style.

Throughout this book, I avoid reading texts as if to solve them; nor do I intend to pitch any part of its contents—from literature to my ideas about it—as an effective contribution to the global struggle against social and ecological catastrophe: "The purpose of literary commentary," as Hartman puts it, "cannot be simply amplifying the clichés of our predicament."[14] The claim that we learn something about the etiology of climate disaster from poems—cultural artifacts whose protocols limit their explanatory reach—is an amplification of this kind. It is also a breathtakingly false recognition, for it mistakes the charisma of both the Anthropocene and the literary text for the magnitude and potency of what subsidizes them.

To put it in language far afield from the critique of political economy, consider Eve Kosofsky Sedgwick's celebrated essay on paranoid and reparative reading. The essay opens with a conversation between Sedgwick and the activist Cindy Patton, about a particular conspiracy theory surrounding the HIV/AIDS crisis. Perhaps, offers Sedgwick, HIV is being deliberately spread among gay and African American communities by the United States government. This is Patton's reply:

> I just have trouble getting interested in that. I mean, even suppose we were sure of every element of a conspiracy: that the lives of Africans and African Americans are worthless in the eyes of the United States; that gay men and drug users are held cheap where they aren't actively hated; that the military deliberately researches ways to kill noncombatants whom it sees as enemies; that people in power look calmly on the likelihood of catastrophic environmental and population changes. Supposing we were ever so sure of all those things—what would we know then that we don't already know?[15]

The essay goes on to finesse Patton's comment into a reparative program that rejects critique as politically disabling. Where the paranoid reader is wildly unpleasant, reactive, and blustering, the reparative one is a road wide open to wonder and, beyond wonder, epiphany. Rather than confirming what we already know—the world is a terrible place—she makes things bearable, gracing damaged life with a new plenitude in the hope that from this enrichment of our (to put it mildly) imperfect state of being, new ways to imagine life will make themselves available.

But is this what Patton has in mind? Do her remarks really clear room for moving from skepticism to hope, and is she really wondering, as Sedgwick is, how best to navigate the turbulence of information overload? Perhaps, on the contrary, Sedgwick's frequent return to the trope of movement betrays her will to dislodge Patton from her deflationary carriage, which is no better suited to conjuring plenitude than to the ambulance chasing of paranoid scrutiny.

Sedgwick is after kinesis, but Patton is embodying an impasse. To be impassive in this sense is to put oneself in a position from which to sublate—to suspend, cancel, and move past—the hysterical form of political realism that views the status quo as impossibly diabolical and therefore impossible to beat. Patton's withdrawal of even the baseline commitment required by "getting interested" suggests anything but ambivalence or neutrality. Hers is a hot boredom, and it scorns those who need to believe in some Manichean melodrama before they can act to destroy a way of life whose evil is beyond dispute. The ethos of the shrug is not, as Sedgwick mistakenly suggests, pessimism but single-mindedness. The shrug says: it is neither paranoid nor poignant to struggle, it is simply necessary.

Here is the flip side of nescience understood as the cognitive and emotional imprint of the social experience of capital. Nescience can also be a recognition that all the knowledge we need is already behind us and that, when we act, we act in and across a void of uncertainty. What's the point of reading a poem as a record of verifiable social and historical processes? What will that tell you that you don't already know? To answer these questions by shrugging does not abnegate responsibility but exaggerates it. The shrug says: do more with less.

The poets and handful of visual artists I discuss in this book are fixated on the poorly representative and even misleading qualities of their work. This is true even when they advertise alertness to the world and its problems. Pulled between an eagerness to produce knowledge and a fear of devolving into abject mimesis or cliché, they organize their ambivalence around what we call tropes and figures: rhetorical devices that, while far from being the exclusive property of literary utterance, nonetheless anchor and exemplify the distance between it and ordinary communication.

It is a critical commonplace to say that figuration is always disfigurative, that it deflects language away from assertion. All the same, it is this evasive capability that specially allows Romantic poetics to recognize and render the disfiguration of the social without interpreting it, **much less** drafting plans for its amendment. How such a poetics makes and manages its own epistemic and analytical constraints; how it presents those constraints as a mode of countercognition or alternative processing; how it variously valorizes, eroticizes, strains against, and surrenders to the decision to be poetry instead of another kind of practice, specifically one with a systematic and penetrating relationship to crisis—these are the questions that guide my discussion.

When I had written about half of this preface, I asked a friend what he thought about the claim that literary objects aren't fully available to materialist methodologies. Maybe, I said, it's not that helpful to use a poem or a novel to take the measure of a theory of causation pertinent to social relations as a provisional totality. "None of this," I added, "would pose a challenge to a basic explanatory framework according to which the mode of production of material existence at any point in time is understood to direct the processes of social, political, and intellectual life. We know that just because the methods of biology aren't generative for theoretical physics doesn't mean biology is wrong or physics doesn't exist. Couldn't you say the same thing about literary criticism—that it might respond to the sort of data a Marxist theory of history isn't designed to handle, without that being a strike against either literary criticism or Marxism?" I wanted to know: Was I in error?

"I don't think it's an error or a nonerror," he replied. "It is a thought experiment with a potentially interesting yield."

This book is my version of that experiment.

* * *

In his 1993 book *The Disorder of Things*, John Dupré draws on numerous examples from the philosophy of science to argue that "there are many equally legitimate ways of dividing the world into kinds," and that "only a privileged and restricted set of entities and kinds could make it plausible that everything could occur in accordance with a unified and universally applicable set of principles."[16] This is a doctrine of ontological pluralism or, as Dupré sometimes puts it, promiscuous realism. The idea is that different kinds of things have different modes of being: the existence of a person isn't like the existence of an algorithm; the "form" in "formal semantics" isn't the same form operated on by evolutionary processes. And yet persons and algorithms both exist, and linguistics and the theory of evolution both produce legitimate knowledge in comparatively legitimate ways. Not only do these disunities have consequences for the way we study the world; they are *borne out* by the way we study the world. In other words, different fields or disciplines attend to distinct kinds of objects in distinct kinds of domains, and are no less cogent or persuasive for doing so. To want all these objects to boil down to one kind of substance, or to yearn for one single disciplinary framework to contain them all, is unreasonable. Such desires simply defy the evidence at hand. (Whether or not that is the nature of desire is another conversation entirely.)

No matter what the word *pluralism* might suggest, this view doesn't entail any kind of political affiliation. Still, it is nonetheless the case that people who would like all the world's objects unified under a single umbrella often claim a politics. John Dewey thought that the unification of the sciences was the best defense against fascism; E. O. Wilson and Steven Pinker have recently made similar pronouncements, while Bruno Latour intimates that a holistic ontology might be the cure for climate change. We might think, too, of the so-called new materialism, a broad church of critical movements that invert Dupré's "metaphysics of disorder" to say that everything in the world is made up of a single substance, and that all methods of inquiry might consolidate themselves in its elucidation. The new materialists often tag their work as radical and yet, much like the conspicuously anti-Marxist Latour, they leave aside the obvious similarities between that work and an older materialism whose revolutionary character is without a doubt better defined.

That would be dialectical materialism, which (contrary to popular belief) is neither Marx's coinage nor his idea. As the geneticist and evolutionary biologist J. B. S. Haldane wrote in his preface to the 1939 edition of Friedrich Engels's *Dialectics of Nature*, "Dialectical materialism is not merely a philosophy of history, but a philosophy which illuminates all events whatever from the falling of a stone to a poet's imaginings"; published one year after Joseph Stalin's policy-setting *Dialectical and Historical Materialism*, Haldane's preface hews to its rule that all of nature is "a connected and integral whole" and represents an only slightly fanciful boosting of the claim that, as Engels put it, dialectics is "the science of the general laws of motion and development of nature, human society and thought."[17] It comprehends, that is, not just social relations, not just their economic basis and their cultural forms, but—in its broadest application—the deep, daedal laws of the physical universe.

You might say that the new materialism, along with other trends in the humanities, leverages a slipshod version of dialectical materialism in order to reject the power of a specifically historical application of dialectics, and with it the baggage carried by communism's specter. For me, the challenge lies not in trying to restore diamat (to invoke its Soviet exemplum) to its rightful place in literary theory or cultural criticism. Far from it, since, as I've said, this book aligns with the ontological premise that the world's contents are plural, and so does not at all agree that the falling of a stone is anything like the poet's imaginings. Rather, *The Calamity Form* keeps time with the nonreferential effects of figurative language, and thus with the notion that works of art have an ontology distinct if not wholly divided from other kinds of things in the world. This relieves them of having either to prove or be rationalized by the soundness of large-scale explanatory models. It also gives them a peculiar kind of hold over categories like *explanation* or even just *aboutness*, in a way that is doubly vexed when the work in question claims to be thinking hard and important thoughts about history or, to use Engels's term, human society.

If an aesthetic object, like a poem, can talk about real people and real life, if it can make use of the resources of narrative and exposition, if it can represent historical events or versions of them, all without disclosing anything in particular or being held to standards like "true" or "false," what is it doing in the world? Sidney will tell you that the poem "labors not to tell you what is or is not, but what should or should not be"—a secular rewrite of a founding principle of early Christian and medieval hermeneutics, namely that the richly figurative discourse of Scripture has both historical and prophetic content, revealing both what *has* been and what *will* be.[18] By the eighteenth century, a nascent philosophical pragmatism is trying to ground a sentiment like Sidney's in the nuts and bolts of language itself. The imaginative expression of poetry, David Hume explains, corresponds to no "geometrical truth and exactness" and so "can never submit to exact truth"; the point is not really what poetry does but how it does it by virtue of the kind of thing it is, out of mimetic or descriptive alignment with the rest of the world.[19] This is of a piece with Alexander Baumgarten's Leibnizian account of poetic representations as "clear and confused," lacking the intensive clarity of concepts but considerably less muddy than mere perception.

While Hume emphasizes poetry's semantic idiosyncrasies and Baumgarten its impact on the reader—the poem, he writes, is "a perfect sensate discourse," "more perfect the more its parts favor the awakening of sensate representations"—both are part of a historical trend toward thinking of works of art as things that *do* but do not *denote*.[20] It's easy to define this doing in purely affective terms: the poem makes you feel something, think something, be pleased or disgusted. It's easy in part thanks to the long shadow Kant's *Critique of Judgment* casts backward over the earlier part of the eighteenth century, making it seem as though the philosophy of this period always centers the subject of aesthetic experience and not the object that produces it. And yet, as Tzvetan Todorov argued more than forty years ago, the most influential thinking about aesthetic representation during the Enlightenment was happening not in the rarefied atmosphere of transcendental idealism but in the workaday realm of the how-to manual. From well-known treatises like Hogarth's *The Analysis of Beauty* to an enormous, disaggregated body of books intended for use in schools, a consensus emerges that "all rhetoric, or nearly all, boils down . . . to a theory of figures," and that it is to the figure and not its audience that any philosophy of art—and, for that matter, of language—ought to attend.[21]

Eighteenth-century rhetorical theory is heavily indebted to classical models of figuration, for which the figure is always an instrument of divergence from some more precise or perspicuous meaning; this is what Hume means when he suggests that poetic language is not geometrical, that it swerves away from the body against which we would want to measure or compare it. Figures are intransitive, and their organizing presence in a work of literary or visual art corrals that work into their own oblique mode of representation—and yes, there lies behind all this a hypermetonymic understanding of the work of art itself such that, as John Guillory somewhat derisively puts it, "literature = literary language = rhetoric = trope."[22] Throw a rock anywhere into the emerging discipline of criticism during this period and you will find versions of Hume's statement, but the most memorable ones are those that freight indirection with the melancholy air of dissemblance.

Take, for instance, César Chesneau Du Marsais, in his influential 1730 volume *Des tropes ou des diférens sens*, on figurative expression as "the exterior form of a body" that borrows a costume not natural to it, or Dénis Diderot (in his *Encyclopédie* entry for *encyclopédie*) suggesting that the relation the work of art bears to the world is like the relation the portrait of his mistress bears, for the lover, to his description of her.[23] Unable, for unspecified reasons, to show (*montrer*) the mistress to any painter, the lover wrote down

> the exact proportions of her head as whole; he then moved on to the dimensions of her forehead, her eyes, her nose, her mouth, her chin, her neck; then he went back over all these different features and spared no effort to make sure that his words would engrave on the mind of the painter the same image he had before his eyes. . . . When his description seemed to him complete, he made a hundred copies that he sent to a hundred painters, enjoining each one of them to execute exactly on the canvas what they read on his paper. The painters went to work, and after a while our lover received a hundred portraits, all of which rigorously resembled his description, and not one of which resembled another, nor his mistress.[24]

This is no praise for word over image but a sympathetic suturing of the problem of representation to the plight of love, which, like writing, clasps experience in vain and prolifically falsifies what it imagines to be true.

It's common enough to characterize this view of figurative representation as one that privileges absence over presence, but this irons out the theoretical complexity of eighteenth-century rhetorical theory. More useful are the tropes of debt, demurral, and even avoidance whose downbeat energies suffuse this passage from Diderot and anchor even the most mundane discussions. In Hugh Blair's *Lectures on Rhetoric and Belles Lettres*, the language of poetry is said to correspond to "no precise expression" and to refuse to be "appropriated to the purpose" of denotation; rather, it is made up of "substituted forms of Speech" like metaphor and other devices that pad out the identity of a thing by giving it another name.[25] This padding neither belongs to what is being described nor has any richly meaningful association with it. It is, Pierre Fontanier writes in his *Figures du discours*, "loaned for the moment" to its object, "nothing more than borrowed."[26]

Like debt itself, the figure has an objective existence obscured by the indifferent relation it constructs between some thing and what is taken to be that thing's value—between, as Annie McClanahan puts it, "our vital needs and our economic capacities," and it's worth pointing out that, for Blair, figuration is exactly the mode of speech that allows human beings to economize by overextending, to use "one name for many" and thus to communicate over and above their actual semantic capacity.[27] This way of conceiving aesthetic representation as perpetual deferral may seem to belong to or terminate in poststructuralism and especially in the work of Paul de Man, whose readings of Romantic poems rely so heavily on eighteenth-century ideas about rhetoric and grammar. Without casting that work aside, I would suggest that an equally and perhaps more relevant genealogy in which to situate those ideas is the analytic tradition that grows directly out of Hume and Locke but owes much—and much undiscovered—to the Enlightenment rhetoricians. Here, we find good grist for the view that some representations are nonreferential without being nonreal, and that what such representations teach may lie outside the domain of epistemic evaluation without being devoid of epistemic significance.

By way of an example, take Donald Davidson's essay "What Metaphors Mean," published in *Critical Inquiry* in 1978. In a series of elliptical paragraphs, "What Metaphors Mean" identifies nonreferentiality as the essential attribute of metaphor, which, Davidson insists, "has [no] content or meaning (except, of course, its literal meaning)" and "convey[s] [neither] truths or falsehoods about the world"; the notion that it might convey one or the other is simply a "mistake" with a prestigious history. In fact,

> when we try to say what a metaphor "means," we soon realize there is no end to what we want to mention. If someone draws his finger along a coastline on a map, or mentions the beauty and deftness of a line in a Picasso etching, how many things are drawn to your attention? You might list a great many, but you could not finish since the idea of finishing would have no clear application. How many facts or propositions are conveyed by a photograph? None, an infinity, or one great unstatable fact? Bad question. A picture is not worth a thousand words, or any other number. Words are the wrong currency to exchange for a picture.[28]

Notice, again, the language of an incomplete transaction, where the bond between the figurative object and what it might plausibly pick out is always one of indebtedness or liability. With Davidson, there is also the ghost of an impasse: the metaphor, the map, the etching—these simply exist outside ordinary communication and can't be made to flow through its channels. The figurative relation is insoluble, stuck. Whatever it carries it does not convey, much as the debt does not actually facilitate, let alone entail, its clearance.

Davidson uses the language of propositions—of statements capable of being either true or false or, more loosely, of statements that offer to organize the real world in ways responsive to alethic assessment. It is a morally neutral language, but it maintains the temporizing logic of the figure, which is always attached to something whose name it can't supply. Davidson's map may not be Diderot's mistress, but when it comes to propositional payoff they model the same kind of deficit. More to the point, however, they also model *attention* to this deficit, so that if the figure or the object replete with figures does not provide any good data about the world, it also makes clear that this is what it is doing—if, that is, we read it correctly.

To be clear, not all genres, schools, movements, or tendencies in the history of art operate like this, not even in the context of Romanticism. The poetry of Thomas Spence or even (in some complicated cases) John Clare can be nakedly referential. Nor for that matter is a figurative representation good or interesting only when it does an end run around explanation, giving little to no account of the world but rather flaunting the standoff between our belief that representations represent something and the simple fact that not all utterances, gestures, pictures, sounds, or signs work that way. The argument I want to make about mainstream

Romantic poetry, in particular, is that it is self-consciously trained on the difference, which it has learned from rhetorical theory, between propositional and nonpropositional forms of speaking and writing—the difference, in other words, between language that makes a claim about how things are, and why, and language that insists on its own estrangement from positive knowledge.

To bring this discussion full circle, figures are structural devices that create disorder in Dupré's sense: they are and they also generate distinctive objects, along with distinctive modes of thought by which to apprehend them. As Dupré tells us, there are many equally legitimate ways of dividing the world into kinds. Propositional and nonpropositional forms of speaking and writing may be divided from one another in just this way; they each *belong* to different parts of the world and have different sorts of obligations to the contents of those parts. A newspaper article reports, or ought to report, on aspects of reality and is, or ought to be, subject to evaluations like "true" or "false." A poem has no such responsibilities. This is partly what d'Alembert, in an early version of Dupré's hypothesis, means when he says criticism inquires into "the reasons of things that have none," which is to say, into aesthetic objects that, by definition, have no fact of the matter to justify, explain, induce, antecede, or prove by their existence.[29] This is in contrast, he insists, to both the sciences and theology: the former squares causes with effects, the latter deals in pure speculation, but criticism, given the curious nature of its objects, is something else altogether. It is not a midway point between a discipline that explains reality and a discipline that supersedes or invalidates it. It has instead the special challenge of elucidating entities that obviously exist but whose figurative elements make them impossible to construe in evidentiary terms.

After all, what do you know if you know a poem? The question drives Plato's *Ion*, in which Socrates gets the titular rhapsode to admit that even if he knows Homer backward and forward, he doesn't know how to do any of the things Homer's poetry talks about—nor, for that matter, does Homer, because it turns out that writing a poem that includes chariot-building does not necessitate knowing how to build a chariot. "Art," Socrates concludes, is therefore not knowledge but a "divine dispensation [to] say many fine things."[30] For Plato this is an ethical as much as a metaphysical claim: if art is not knowledge, it is beyond the domain of truth and falsehood and thus likely to cause people confusion about which is which. By the eighteenth century, it is a philosophically promising platform on which to experiment with new ways of divvying up the world in a way that reflects that world's complexity. By the Romantic period, it is additionally a testing ground for art's and especially poetry's changing relationship to its historical circumstances.

If Plato thought the poets should be banished from his republic because of the threat they posed to rational order, the poets of this age have another problem entirely. Their skillset is defined by its inadequacy to an exegesis of the present; what they make is defined by a skeptical and beleaguered relationship to information. Now, in the rising heat of capital's disfiguration of the social, the figure finds its mirror and meets its match. If it is, as I've said, a condition of capital's flourishing that its own socially regulative and organizational processes remain obscure, how does a poetics that understands itself as constitutively cryptic and unable to scrutinize or spell out its own conditions, let alone the conditions by which modern life is reproduced, live with itself—which is to say, live, and not only with itself?

Despite its reputation for inwardness, Romantic poetry wants very much to live with others. To put a finer point on it, it wants very much to account for the uninhabitability of modern life—for the circumstances that make it impossible and yet mandatory to endure. This desire tends to be treated with suspicion in the poems themselves. "What benefit canst thou do, or all thy tribe,/To the great world?" Moneta, the goddess of memory, sneers at the poet-speaker of Keats's *Fall of Hyperion*; only those "to whom the miseries of the world/Are misery" are granted access to perfect historical knowledge, and without perfect historical knowledge there is, or so she implies, no hope for an end to immiseration.[31] Both *Hyperion* poems, with their postclimactic structure, insist that poetry and perfect historical knowledge do not mix. That is why, despite promising to tell the story of the Titans' overthrow by the Olympian gods, they're set in the doleful aftermath of this particular revolution. It is why Wordsworth, whenever he winds himself up to deliver a parcel of narrative about his childhood, political events like the French Revolution, or social-economic transitions like enclosure and urbanization inevitably bears out his own fuzzy axiom that "we see but darkly/Even when we look behind us."[32]

These are poems in which big moments get lost; just think of Wordsworth's oblivious crossing of the Alps. And yet this tendency toward aversion or avoidance proves something of a red herring. The problem here is that the miseries of the world Keats, Wordsworth, and others have in mind—"the increasing disproportion between the price of labour and that of the necessaries of life," for example, or "torched mines and noisy factories," or "A thousand men in troubles wide and dark"—aren't the result of a single cataclysmic incident but the inevitable upshot of manifold protean transformations of social existence, driven or enabled on multiple levels by technological advances, political legislation, and metabolic contingencies.[33] If these are poems in which big moments get lost, they are also poems using those losses as stand-ins for the unrecognizability of much larger processes, as well as for the frustration of the idea that poetry could ever account for any of this in the first place, much less make it better. Again we see the utility of Hartman's association of Romanticism, negative knowledge, and trauma, which likewise involves mistaking a situation for an event, a childhood for a day.

The rise of capital was never just one thing. The specific cognitive challenge that defines the poetry of this period is how to represent the experience of not understanding the present when the present is the very thing the poem wants to understand. Of course, this isn't only the case for poetry: as Mary Favret has shown, Jane Austen's fiction is decisively formed by the experience of war at a distance and the globalization of military-imperial campaigns. What Romantic poetry has that the Romantic novel does not is a long institutionalized tradition of thinking about figures—about the building blocks and grinding gears of the poem—as elements anchored to a world that is adjacent to, at times embedded in, and yet nonidentical to the social world whose violent transformations that poetry would, in theory, like to explain. When William Cowper begins *The Task* with "a historical deduction of seats" before launching into a dizzying survey of the movement of global capital, he is counting on an uneven fit between what his pocket-size epic can plausibly relate and the moral urgency of his effort.[34] This imperfect calibration is part of the poem: it is the very thing it has to offer to a new but rapidly developing vocabulary for representing capital—or rather for representing its capacity to evade representation, to enforce its presence through a set of behavioral compulsions that both require and produce nescience about them.

It has lately become fashionable to argue that disciplinary divisions did not exist before the nineteenth century, and that the absence of such divisions reflects a broadly monist picture of the world as ontologically indivisible and flat. I recently heard a historian suggest that because John Goodsir used a passage from Coleridge's *Aids to Reflection* as the epigraph to his 1845 book about cellular metabolism, we should think that the people of this period understood biochemistry and poetry to be univocal pursuits, trained on the same kind of phenomena (never mind that Coleridge's *Aids* is in prose). This is an especially unsophisticated version of a complex argument, but it's not quite a reductio ad absurdum. In its most benign form, what it reveals, in Christopher Nealon's adroit diagnosis, is the longing for a "wide-open, ontologically pure poemworld" in which organic life and literary text are seamlessly conjoined.[35]

At the institutional level, the end of this otherwise starry-eyed rhetoric is a well-funded turn to interdisciplinarity—something I've written at length about elsewhere.

Now, the fact that a poem might lay claim to scientific subjects, or a treatise on chemistry make use of figures, tropes, or literary quotation, does not entail that literature is science and science literature. Theme is not ontology. For the purposes of this discussion, I am concerned by the ways in which a dogmatism grounded in the idea that disciplinary divisions are in violation of some subatomic concord bypasses the hard problem so much Romantic poetry sets out for itself: how to balance a belief in the partial autonomy of figurative representations from other parts of the world with a commitment to explaining the parts of the world that contain the greatest misery for the greatest number. Jameson famously tells us that history is what hurts; the specific ache Romanticism nurses comes from the sensation of its own disengagement from that hurt and the attempt, which always fails, to correct it. To be clear, this is not a moral failing; it is a metaphysical consequence. That doesn't make it any easier to bear.

The following chapters of this book, with the exception of the epilogue, are each organized around a specific figure: parataxis, obscurity, catachresis, and apostrophe. That is because, as my brief but I hope persuasive survey of eighteenth-century rhetorical theory and its afterlives has shown, it is the figure that holds the poem back from referential extension into the world or, at the very least, slows down their interchange. Each of the figures I've chosen does so in a unique and, in some cases—especially the case of apostrophe—a well-established way. The chapters do not represent wholesale renovations of existing ways of thinking about how these figures work and what they do but attempt to follow their logic in a way that opens up the poem at hand. You might ask, opens it to what; the answer is, to a recognition of its own insufficiency. You might ask, its insufficiency to what; the answer is, to the analytical task it sets out for itself, namely to explain why things are the way they are in the historical moment to which the poem belongs. You might ask, finally, who says poems want to explain anything about their historical moment; the answer is, not all poems do, but these poems do, desperately, and reading them uncovers a lot about other poems knuckling under to the same unanswerable passion.

The figure, in this book, is always a site of misalignment—not just with the world but, more locally, with the prospect of serving as *evidence* for something. One of the challenges in writing the book has been to evolve and inhabit a criticism capable of remaining faithful to this moment in the history of poetics. The style of reading and interpretation I offer is at best agnostic: it does not massage facts out of objects that don't contain any but tries to flesh out a suspended mode of intellection sensitive to the uncertain content of the literary text. Like the figure itself, it aims not for naïveté but to capture the active and in-depth knowing of nothing, and the peculiar achievement of being on close terms with incomprehension. Always in the background of my argument is the claim that Romantic poetry is at once attracted and allergic to historical analysis in a manner that breaks with earlier, more conventionally humanist ideals about poetry's exemption from telling the truth. If, in the sixteenth century, Sidney could assure us that the poet "citeth not," that slantwise relation to the world has new meaning when the world itself undergoes a drastic diremption from its own social-ontological ground.[36]

The Calamity Form, too, is attracted and allergic to historical analysis. I'm extremely wary of any attempts, including my own, to say that a poem is *about* something, or capable of giving information on it. Obviously there's a contradiction here: on the one hand, I want to say these poems tell you nothing; on the other, I want to say that they tell you what it is to know nothing, under social conditions where the knowing of nothing becomes instrumental to the reproduction of unlivable life. But contradictions, as we know, are not sinkholes. When we investigate them more deeply, when we walk around their borders and extend their edges, we find that they hold the only way forward.

Each chapter of the book undertakes this kind of investigation, where the social conditions at issue are in the main those of early industrial capitalism and the mushrooming sum of its harms. Some chapters distribute their focus across multiple authors or works of art—mostly poems, other times examples from visual media—while others tarry largely with a single writer. That said, because I'm less interested in authors than in figures, I end up looking for the latter across a good number of cases. Readers may notice that a sizeable number of these cases hail from the domain of postmodern and often conceptually driven art. Like Davidson, who collaborated with Robert Morris, I find the art traditions of the mid- to late twentieth and the twenty-first centuries helpful in thinking through questions of denotation from the perspective of poetics—often more helpful, incidentally, than any poetics that labels itself "conceptual." Thus in these pages Helen Mirra and Robert Barry as well as the avant-garde filmmaker Derek Jarman crop up alongside the Romantics, pulse points in the body of the figure as it is put to work across historical and cultural contexts.

The first chapter is called "Parataxis; or, Modern Gardens." It takes the idea that, in Susan Stewart's nimble phrase, "a garden is the wresting of form from nature" as a point of departure for asking how an eighteenth-century poet might judge the activity of capital, which wrests in much the same way from the same source.[37] After outlining the rise of paratactical or disjunctive syntax and considering how it plays out—and has been said to play out—in the poetry of Friedrich Hölderlin, I turn to the less illustrious pages of Cowper's *The Task* and his short lyric "The Rose." Completing the triad is Jarman, the filmmaker, poet, and gardener in whom I find an heir to Cowper's melancholy noncoordination between poetic thinking and social critique. Framed by an understanding of parataxis as a Pindaric leap over a pit, my discussion finds in this figure a poetic rehearsal (of sorts) of what Marx calls "the commodity's *salto mortale*" and ends by speculating about some alternative situations in which this kind of incautious exertion might find itself cut loose (*C* 1.200).

The next two chapters represent something of a compare-and-contrast, or, in less banal terms, an opposition elemental as the one between Blake's Los and his fearsome Spectre. First, in "Wordsworth's Obscurity," I find a poetics that is spectral in both the idiomatic sense and in Blake's: elliptical and indefinite and ballasted by "stern despair."[38] The historical argument here is that Wordsworth—in "Michael" and *The Prelude*—marries classical to modern views of *obscuritas* to show how it is impossible for poetry to make arguments about history. The more literary claim is embedded in a personal, perhaps idiosyncratic reading of Wordsworth as a poet estranged from life, stuck in a relation of incremental access to it that, paradoxically, never adds up to a whole. The connection between these two parts of the chapter lies in a claim about poetics: there is, I think, a clear and consistent set of things Wordsworth does with language in order to make totality, both historical and existential, look impossible and life at best intermittently worth living.

The movement from "Wordsworth's Obscurity" to my third chapter, "Keats and Catachresis," is diacritical. It is meant to bring into relief a set of differences between himself and the elder poet that Keats was extremely keen to uphold but never managed to phrase convincingly. This isn't about a familiar stone-throwing distinction between what Keats called Wordsworth's egotistical sublime and his own Negative Capability but rather about what separates a poetry of half measures and ragged, unsought possibilities from a poetry distinguished—and often damaged—by its excesses. If a catachresis is, etymologically speaking, a *down-use*, Keats's catachreses try to find the upside of degradation, the material potency of being a thing that lives in, is hurt by, and passes defiantly out from the world. Collating catachresis from poems including *Isabella*, "Ode to Psyche," and the two *Hyperions*, this chapter considers Keats's oft-derided sensuousness as an elective affliction, a way of making language strain past its breaking point. The result is a full-blooded weakness set against the program of embodied inexhaustibility that Keats, in *Isabella* especially, associates with factory and enslaved labor.

In my final chapter, "Apostrophe: Clouds," I use the colloquial expression "under climate change" as a prompt for thinking about Romantic renderings of aerial phenomena, and particularly of clouds, as a form of apostrophe—as, that is, an address to a nature in the process of disappearing. This is, I suggest, one way of defining the action of Romantic lyric, which thrives on making attenuated moments or regimes of existence hyperbolically intense. Picking up my discussion of the *Hyperion* poems from the previous chapter or, rather, turning the poems to hit a different light, I move from Keats to the cloud studies of John Constable, and to their own apostrophic features. The chapter ends with Helen Mirra's 2001 installation *Sky-wreck*, and the encounter between real and ideal forms on which its imagination of an ecologically devastated but still open future rests. A brief epilogue follows.

This is a book about, and not in praise, of vanishing. We all have to go back to the world sometime, especially to its disappearances. Courting the forms of loss and bewilderment that inhere in a poem does not teach us anything about what is to be done; nor does it let us off the hook for doing it. What else, then, is the poem good for? What does it tell us that we don't already know? These aren't enigmas with answers; for those, we will have to look elsewhere.

1

Parataxis;
or, Modern Gardens

Now there, said he, pointing his finger, I make a comma, and there, pointing to another spot where a more decided turn is proper, I make a colon: at another part (where an interruption is desirable to break the view) a parenthesis—now a full stop, and then I begin another subject.

HANNAH MORE, journal entry for December 1782

Hic Rhodus, hic saltus. . . . Hier ist die Rose, hier tanze!
[Here is Rhodes, here the leap. . . . Here is the Rose, dance here!]

G. W. F. HEGEL, Preface to *Elements of the Philosophy of Right*, 1821

Parataxis, like history, is one damn thing after another. "Somewhere, some there, disorder out, entangled in language." It is a figure of insubordination with no respect for dependency or the logic of causes. "I was reading several books at once, usually three. If faster, then more." You expect syntax to explain things to you, to say how one thing follows upon or comes out of the thing that came before it, to build a thought upward as the sentence moves onward. A paratactical sentence, however, tells no stories and makes no arguments. "The typewriter at night was classical." The size of things stops mattering: no sequence, no rank. This makes it hard to divine the expository purchase of the words sitting side by side. What comes first; what is more basic, primal, effective, or co-efficient; which event sets off the others; which others could not have happened without it? "As the storm approached it was as if the blue slowly evaporated from the sky, leaving the sky merely a pale shadow of itself." Where in a parataxis should we stand to see the whole picture? "Why isn't the reflection in the mirror flat, since the mirror itself is flat."[1]

This chapter takes parataxis as a variation on what John Dixon Hunt calls garden syntax, the winding, seemingly hodgepodge arrangement of discrete particulars in a designated space. Like the paratactical sentence, the garden's syntax is neither casual nor conjunctive. Every element has

been chosen and thoughtfully arranged, and yet none obviously follows
from, is attendant upon, or is regulated by any other: what goes on in a
garden is, as Marvell's Mower puts it, uncertain and adulterate, strange
and unauthorized. If there is some significance to be retrieved from
the insistent procession of one thing after another, it lies in the formal
technique of disjunction itself. Over the course of the eighteenth century, modern poetry learned from modern gardens habits of looking and
thinking trained on the experience of the present as a regime of juxtaposition, the leftovers from the demise of a more integrated social order.
In the midst of economic stratification and imperial metastasis, writing
paratactically becomes a means of exploring both this mosaic condition
and poetry's inadequacy to it. It becomes, that is, an expression of life up-
rooted and transposed, a dark inverse of the garden as "heaven's centre,
Nature's lap,/And Paradise's only map."[2]

Not all the poems I discuss here are about gardens, but they are all by
gardenists, Dixon Hunt's word for writers who adapt the garden's form
and phenomenology to their own purposes. For them, the garden is the
flip side of an everyday chaos felt as perceptual derangement or lapse.
Capability Brown, the grammatical gardener in my first epigraph, punc-
tuates his landscapes with breaks and cutoffs, not joints. Alexander Pope,
writing about his day traipsing through the backyard of Sherborne, drifts
through "sudden Rises, Falls, and Turns of Ground" of which "tis very
hard to give an exact idea"; a hill leads to a grove followed by an arbor,
after which erupts "a natural Cascade . . . from whence you lose your eyes
upon the glimmering of the Waters under the wood, and your ears in
the constant dashing of the waves."[3] As "an increasingly prominent and
crucial feature of the century's aesthetic patterns," the garden sets the
standard for cognitive as well as syntactical incohesion.[4] Often pitched as
the antithesis of the turmoil of the world outside its walls, it is nonetheless the proving ground of an emergent set of compositional techniques,
a dialect of fracture that will come to be called Romantic.

The analogy between gardens and parataxis is useful in making head-
way from the gardens of Marvell and his Mower to William Cowper's
late eighteenth-century greenhouse to Derek Jarman's late Romantic pots
of "sempervivums . . . with the nuclear power station as a backdrop."[5]
We might play at framing this sequence in terms similar to those offered
by Joshua Clover, who identifies riot, strike, and riot prime as forms of
class struggle corresponding to different phases in capital's development.
Without mapping the early modern *hortus conclusus*, the greenhouse, and
the nuclear garden onto the historical forms of mercantile, industrial, and
finance capitalism, I would nonetheless like to experiment with asking

how a gardenist poetics confronts the collective immiseration erupting just within its sightline and yet never (or so it would seem) in full view.

To be specific, I'm interested in the capricious nonalignment between poetic thinking and social critique that parataxis brings to the fore. My claim is that by understanding parataxis as a trope of disruption—specifically, of orthodox modes of explanation, where events follow sequentially from the events that precede them—we may begin to see its simple besideness or underexplained contiguity as a proposition, an attempt to make a plan for "mediat[ing] between is and ought."[6] This would be in keeping with the well-known account of parataxis given by Theodor Adorno, who claims it as an invocation and working-through of dialectics, by which Adorno means the assertion that concepts coproduce with the forms of physical things.

Because it rejects the linear norms of discursive thought, parataxis is able to effect a "constitutive dissociation" within language such that language can "evade the logical hierarchy of a subordinating syntax."[7] In suspending hierarchy at the level of the sentence, parataxis—or so Adorno has it—figures the possibility of its real-life abolition. More to the point, it renders the transcendence of what Marx describes as the historical contradiction between essence (what it is possible for a human being to be) and existence (what a human being is forced to be) on the page, with ought and is brought suddenly, enigmatically together. This is a tall order and, for Adorno, nothing less than the task of poetry. What we are looking for in parataxis is "the qualitative leap that in responding to fate leads out of it," for the momentum of a poetics capable of projecting thought and language beyond their own historical limitations ("P," 113).

You could call this a Pindaric leap, the *saltus dithyrambus* that moves from one topic to another in response to some higher logic. The term *Pindaric leap* alludes to two things: to the fact that the Greek poet Pindar was known for his parataxes, which is to say his rocketing from clause to clause without the use of grammatical connectives, and to a line in one of his poems that reads like a compressed ars poetica in defense of that method. "Dig a long pit for my jump from here," he writes in the fifth of his Nemean odes; "I have a light spring in my knees." Pindar has just been saying a few words in praise of Pytheas, the young victor of the athletic games at Nemea, when suddenly he decides he's got something else on his mind, namely "wealth or strength of hands or iron-clad war." It's a sudden shift in focus and a long way to go: he'll have to jump.[8]

Why does the jump, the Pindaric leap, require a pit? In *Nemean* 5, the pit measures the distance between where the poet stands and where he wants to end up. It appears as a promise of success and as a threat of failure: imagine falling into the trench meant to gauge the magnitude of your achievement. It's the same threat faced by William Cowper when he, like Pindar, sets his mind to speak of wealth, war, and power. In his highly paratactic poem *The Task*, power means not the "strength of hands" but their products—it means, in a word, commodities. To sing the sofa, as Cowper says he will, comes to demand a terrifying leap of its own, a replication of the commodity's *salto mortale* that can only end either in apocalyptic fantasies or in the airless retreat of the greenhouse.

Cowper is my primary case study here, although the chapter touches, first, on the Pindaric experiments of Friedrich Hölderlin and eighteenth-century parataxis more broadly. Following that discussion, I turn to pulling parataxes out of Cowper's *Task* and showing, simply, how they work—how they upend the expository procedures of epic and push toward a turbulent view of a dissociated present. In this poem, the comforts of suburbia are tucked inside a larger frame of planetary suffering, and as Cowper shuttles between detailed scenes of domestic happiness and the murkier, grimier panoramas of world history, it becomes harder to say what is central to *The Task* and what peripheral to it. Is this a poem about the quiet life or about its toxicity? Do its experimental energies inhere in its cheeky, chatty blank verse or in its sprawl, its distension of the line across well-organized entropy?

Cowper's parataxis accommodates all these investments while refusing to present itself as a triumph of world-making or realist inclusivity: *Paradise Lost* or *Middlemarch* his poem is not. Compelled to make both plain and poetic the saturation of consciousness by what Cowper would call *trade*, *The Task* takes linearity off the table to sketch moods of unstructured anguish that cannot be gotten past, not even by Pindaric leap or escalation. Similar in this regard are the syntactical experiments of Derek Jarman, the filmmaker, diarist, and poet for whom the antagonisms of the present literally concretize in the nuclear power plant whose shadow looms over his Dungeness garden, a parataxis made possible only by a "capitalism . . . on its last legs" (*MN*, 234). In the wild collision of images that propels both these gardenists' work, various forms of life appear at once far-flung and brutally consolidated. Their poetry, in particular, beats out a crucible of apprehension in two senses of the word: it coughs up unities where none could previously be recognized, and it is exceptionally nervous, anxious and indefinite and unquiet.

To some degree, what *The Task* longs for is a bird's-eye view of the present, an Archimedean vantage on capital's global structure. The awkward and abrupt shifts between topics, between tones, and between lyric and epic registers that make *The Task* such difficult reading express the pathos of this longing, and how it feels to receive the agony of others as news we cannot grasp but cannot help absorb. For Cowper, the capacity to take in pain on the edges of his own existence is precisely what the greenhouse, with its exotic plants and illusion of sanctuary, tests. Inside this most artificial of gardens, there is a retreat from the call to understand everything, to find meaning in it all. And yet it is also here that the possibility of an unexpected convergence between private consciousness, social totality, and moral judgment startles into view, whatever good it does Cowper, his poem, or us.

Two centuries later, Jarman uses his garden as an extension of his filmmaking and its pop-punk ethos—a middle finger to the nuclear power plant that "hiccoughs" fewer than two miles from his home, and to the erratic weather patterns that alternately nurture and spoil his flowers from one day to the next (*MN*, 302). The garden is an act of persistence and grieving, for the countryside, for the seasons, for an unthinkable number of friends lost, along with Jarman's own eyesight, to the AIDS epidemic. The asyndetonic list of prescription drugs that ends *Modern Nature*, a collection of his journal entries from 1989–90, plainly echoes the catalogs of flowers strung beside accounts of gallery openings, fundraisers, visits and phone calls and frustrations with his film *The Garden*. Each inventory marks an effort to render the concatenation of crises we now tend to herd under the awkward aegis of neoliberalism: crises of health, of energy, of the planet, and what Jarman would unapologetically call culture. From his vantage point at "the end of the globe," in a house fittingly named Prospect Cottage, Jarman follows Cowper in offering a locodescription of capital as a poison in the bodies of living things. It's a project that is upfront about its informal reworking of Romantic genres "almost 200 years," as Jarman says, "since Dorothy Wordsworth wrote her journal in Alfoxden" (*MN*, 68).

Jarman's work is highly digressive, in a way that can sometimes approach an accidental parody of art-house sensibilities. In what follows, I'll argue that his paratactical drifts are, in fact, polemical; more specifically, that they rehearse the supersession or overriding of evidence by insistence. In this, they imagine a pose like that of Cindy Patton's agnostic militancy, an impassioned indifference regarding the causal logic of harm. For Jarman, the power plant on the front lawn is literally, figuratively, and politically adjacent to the man dying of AIDS inside the house when the weather in England in November is already much too hot. Someone is responsible, or something: Thatcher, capital, the cops. It's not all one, but it is beside the point. Parataxis is the figure matching this pose because it simply does not care *how* things happen; it cares merely that they are happening and about the obligation that they be stopped.

What does wild mint have to do with AZT? What do canaries have to do with "Ritafer, Pyroxidine, Methamine, Folinic Acid, Triludan, Sulpha-diazine, Carbamazepine" (*MN*, 313)? The linkages are inconvenient and also inexplicable. They emerge from Jarman's own position of depleted vitality, his anger a deathbed charge to no one in particular. This perhaps undermines its effectiveness, and it is an interesting feature of parataxis that the expansive, hyperbolically omniscient poetics it enables tends to insist upon the extreme isolation of the poet, who stands amid a world of things but not among them. We shouldn't forget that the pathos of being unable to understand the present in a serious way, to discern it as a consequence of the past and not just a prophecy of the apocalyptic future, is also the despair of the bourgeois subject. Cowper represents its early fortunes, Jarman its latter-day. This is not a complaint but an observation about the performance of social self-discovery that their work represents. That performance is not really born of the consciousness of class. It is born, instead, of a desire to translate an economic bearing into an emotional one.

* * *

In Adorno's "Parataxis: Zur späten Lyrik Hölderlins," parataxis is defined in opposition to "the syntactic periodicity à la Cicero" of logical argument. It is typified by the curveballs Hölderlin throws to his reader, who is led up close to one conclusion only to be sideswiped by something that does not follow—unless it does, but only according to the highly unorthodox, not at all ratiocinative logic of dialectical thinking ("P," 135).[9] This seems intuitively right to me. It is not, however, supported by Adorno's readings of Hölderlin's poems. If Adorno succeeds in producing a definitive analysis of the poet as "the master of the intermittent linguistic gesture," he tenders little in the way of a discussion of rhetoric ("P," 113). Here, statements like "All poetry protests the domination of nature with its own devices" are often followed by block quotes that have at best a logogram-matic relationship to argument ("P," 140). Funnily enough, Adorno is most attentive to Hölderlin's language when he's exploding Heidegger's claims about it, a task that takes up a good chunk of the essay's first half and reaps its best rewards, as when Adorno confronts a racist gloss on the brown women of "Andenken"; philology, he intimates, is a tool of white supremacy, a dull gadget used by a "right-wing German cult" to turn Hölderlin's poetry against its anti-identitarian ambitions ("P," 119).

Perhaps Adorno thinks the implications of lines like the following are so clear they don't need to be stated, in which case I hope my own reader will humor me as I try to tease them out. Or perhaps Adorno knows that parataxis—an undoing of the expectation that subordinate clauses will always lie in rhetorical as well as grammatical servitude to main ones—is after something less obvious than giving dialectics a home in poetic form. Take this sequence from "Andenken":

Wo aber sind die Freunde? Bellarmin	*But where are the friends? Bellarmin*
Mit dem Gefährten? Mancher	*With his companions? Many of them*
Trägt Scheue, an die Quelle zu gehen;	*bear shyness, to go to the spring;*
Es beginnet nämlich der Reichtum	*Riches, that is, begin*
Im Meere.	*In the sea.*[10]

Adorno's brief gloss on this passage is that it reflects the "historico-philosophical conception that spirit can only attain itself through distance and detachment" ("P," 119). Maybe so. But that's not an insight derived from any parataxis; it's just an inference based on the poem's genre: our lyric speaker is alone, and from this solitude something meaningful (and also this poem) will come.

But the essay gives us these lines as an example of parataxis, so let's find one in them. The semicolon points us to the lines "Mancher / Trägt Scheue, an die Quelle zu gehen" and "Es beginnet nämlich der Reichtum / Im Meere" and suggests that the latter clause is subordinate to the former. But parataxis isn't just a matter of grammar; it's also a matter of sense. As Adorno says, parataxis has to put words together in a manner that draws out their latent strangeness. If these lines have a totally straightforward relationship to each other, we can't consider them paratactical. Indeed, the presence of *nämlich*—which means namely, that is, or viz.—seems to insist that they're not, because *nämlich* is a connective and parataxes, by definition, don't use connectives. So what is going on?

Adorno is onto something; he just doesn't follow it through. The key to what's paratactical about these lines lies in "Mancher / Trägt Scheue, an die Quelle zu gehen," an ambiguous phrase whose opacity arises from its unusual use of the verb *tragen*, to wear, carry, bear, yield, or even to be pregnant. Depending on how you take the verb, the meaning of the line varies to the point of suggesting two entirely incommensurate things. Richard Sieburth's stately translation gives "There are those / Who shy from the source": some people are not going to the source; in fact, they're avoiding it.[11] However, and as Katrin Pahl suggests in her meditation on shyness as a "speculative transport that draws lovers together by pulling them apart," the more literal "bear shyness" not only conserves the haziness of the line but also perfectly renders the dialectical synthesis they compose but don't actually complete.[12] On this reading, we can see resistance (shying away) tussle with endurance (bearing, putting up with), but neither is able to pass into free movement. Where we might expect synthesis we get a non sequitur: "Es beginnet nämlich der Reichtum/Im Meere," or "viz., riches begin in the sea."

So here is our parataxis—or is it? Again, *nämlich* trips us up, for it invites these lines ("es beginnet nämlich der Reichtum/Im Meere") to clarify what's been said in the main clause. Sieburth's translation obeys precisely this logic: Some people shy away from the source since, after all, wealth has its origin in the sea, so why look elsewhere? Actually, what it obeys is not just logic but logical fallacy, the connective figment of *post hoc ergo propter hoc* that assumes causation where there may be only co-incidence.

Let's be clear about what's happening, since it is by no means self-evident. There are two ways to read the pairing "Mancher/Trägt Scheue, an die Quelle zu gehen" and "Es beginnet nämlich der Reichtum/Im Meere." Each of these ways has its little cues or alibis. On one reading, *nämlich* suggests an explanatory relation, and it requires shaving the two meanings of *tragen* down to one: no one goes to the fount because riches begin in the sea. On another, *nämlich* is a red herring, the subordinate clause as a whole is matter out of place, and the relation at issue between the subordinate clause and the main one, which itself comprises two rival meanings, is parataxis. This second reading is not so easily paraphrased, because the paratactical framing of the first and second clause prevents the meaning of the former from terminating in the latter. If there is, as I've said, a sneak preview or teasing of transcendence here, of an abolition of the antipodes of turning bashfully away and moving reluctantly toward, it remains strictly hypothetical. The last line does not bear it out, either in form or in content, but floats free as an isolated proposition. The conditions for dialectics have been set up, but they are not cashed out.

This may seem like a minor footnote to Adorno, for whom parataxis must mime the dynamism of dialectical thought. But on my reading of these four lines by Hölderlin, parataxis lays out the path of a dialectical progression only to leave it dangling in the air, subject to the petty dictatorship of conjunctions. If *tragen* only has one meaning (to shy away from), the lines are not paratactical and the brute strength of normative logic wins the day. If *tragen* has at least two meanings, the lines are paratactical and normative logic must coexist with a more speculative hypothesis, acting as a significant drag on speculation's momentum but unable to stymie it completely.

Words, of course, can have more than one meaning in everyday speech, but it matters that this second interpretation depends on being aware of the poetic frame of Hölderlin's sentences, of the fact that they are poetry and more likely to be ambiguous than not. One of the things these lines do is identify poetry as a form of reasoning that is *more than fallacious*, not the opposite of causal reasoning but evidence of its limits, as well as a procedure for jumping to conclusions that might be visionary instead of just false. Parataxis localizes that jump, clips it to a specific moment in the text or a specific leap from line to line, clause to clause, thought to thought. As "Andenken" indicates, parataxis will always contain the possibility of true randomness, the threat of the non sequitur that can't be overcome even through the most creative close reading.

I've spent this time with Adorno's famous essay in order to lay out some essential premises for my discussion. Among these are that parataxis is a dialectical provocation and not a dialectical achievement: even as it creates a space inside of which seemingly discrete terms become mutually intelligible as contradictions, it nonetheless constrains the scope of their movement, so that the paratactical poem is never quite able to synthesize a new perspective or concept from the ones it has already laid out. This suggests another premise, namely that parataxis is a location of bourgeois tragedy, which is to say that it sustains—even grimly celebrates—a certain paralysis of both thought and action. In "Andenken," the poet may merely "establish what remains" ("Was bleibet aber, stiften die Dichter"), a phrase that suggests ingenuity exhausted in the task of cultural curation. To this I'd add Bob Perelman's claim that parataxis generates an "unresolved pressure for [social] narrative," an account of how things are that parataxis, insofar as it resists the linear precepts of narrative while also failing to complete a dialectical jump from here to there, will never really supply.[13]

For Perelman, this aggressively indecisive poetics is specifically postindustrial. It belongs to a world of thundering randomness and dissonance, where our brains are constantly assaulted by "bursts of narrative-effect" that are, at best, "local totalities," never gathering themselves into "more permanent, meaningful" analyses of our condition. A paratactical poetics does not escape this state of affairs; nor does it simply copy it: rather, "the tension between symptom and critique is constant."[14] Without overstating the affinity between Perelman's view of the late twentieth century and Cowper's view of his own, I want to suggest that if *postindustrial* flags the heterogenous background of global militarism and multinational capital, consumer culture and its throttling of existence, the eighteenth century is as good a place to start as any. The new sentence, it turns out, is not quite so new.

* * *

The word *parataxis* wasn't used for a grammatical form until the late 1820s, when the classicist Friedrich Thiersch worked it into his third edition of *Griechische Grammatik*. Before then, a sentence lacking conjunctions would, in Europe and in the Anglophone world, have been tagged as an example of style coupé, the nimbler alternative to the ponderous style periodique. "The Style Periodique," explains Hugh Blair, "is, where the sentences are composed of several members linked together . . . so that the sense of the whole is not brought out till the close." In "Style Coupé," by contrast, "the sense is formed into short independent propositions, each complete within itself." What Blair could not anticipate in the 1780s, when his *Lectures on Rhetoric* was first published, is that his association of style coupé with "the French method of writing, [which] always suits gay and easy subjects," would soon take on a political charge.[15] In the wake of the Revolution, style coupé became the format of democracy, the syntax of Diderot and Voltaire set against the formality of seventeenth-century prose and court culture. By 1810, a coursebook put out by the École Polytechnique is positing sentence structure as social allegory: with the widespread adoption of style coupé, we learn, the French "language has become more clear . . . though perhaps it's lost some of its nobility."[16]

Coleridge, in the midst of his conservative turn, seals this pact between style and the spirit of the age. Having defended the "entortillage" of his own prose, he goes on to sneer at "the present illogical age, which has, in imitation of the French, rejected all the cements of language, so that a popular book is now a mere bag of marbles."[17] It's an image he'll use years later, in a complaint about "modern books, [in which] for the most part, the sentences in a page have the same connection with each other that marbles have in a bag": "They touch without adhering."[18] That a historical age could model its atomization on a corresponding form in literature, that it could come loose from a linguistic heritage that stabilizes the culture as a whole, that the popular presents a threat of chaotic kinetic unrest—the French word for marbles is *meubles*, "movables"—these are sentiments Coleridge imbibes from Burke, who, in his *Reflections on the Revolution in France*, likewise uses metaphors of "cementing" to criticize revolutionary departures from convention; these, he predicts, will condemn the French republic "infinitely to dissociation, distraction, and confusion" as a whole and "with relation . . . to the several parts within."[19]

This peek at the context of Romantic parataxis suggests, I hope, that there is or at least once was something compelling about the idea that abandoning transitions has the capacity to stylize historical crisis. If a poet like Hölderlin adapts style coupé for his own purposes, he also exploits in order to rebuff its association with a canting storyline in which stuffiness gives way to lucidity and kingdoms give way to republics. His method is one of scarification, an exorbitant cutting into the pseudo-egalitarian promise of the shorter sentence. The result is a poetic line that gives the appearance of having been grievously wounded, the syntactic equivalent of Wordsworth's Discharged Solider, "Forlorn and desolate, a man cut off/From all his kind, and more than half detached/From his own nature."[20] These lines—later abandoned by Wordsworth—vividly document the human wages of the Revolutionary and Napoleonic Wars. They too belong to the Romantic critique of modernity, and to the rhetorical stratagems of annihilation and decay that, as Hölderlin says, encode and console a world that "never looked so motley as now," dyed in "a huge plurality of contradictions and contrasts" ("die Welt noch nie so bunt aussah, wie jetzt"; "eine ungeheure Mannigfaltigkeit von Widersprüchen und Kontrasten").[21]

The other model for parataxis in this moment is more obvious, if less politically freighted. It is the Pindaric or irregular ode, the principal motor for the development of the greater Romantic lyric. There have been countless discussions of Pindar's influence on the poets of the seventeenth and eighteenth centuries, and on writers like Shelley, Keats, and Hopkins. And yet it's seldom observed that, as Susan Bernofsky points out, the Pindar to which these poets had access was a Pindar in paratactic overdrive. Not until 1821 (a few years before Thiersch put parataxis in the critical vocabulary) was Pindar's much-haggled-over colometry understood to have been sorted into periods at all. The edition of Pindar Hölderlin used for his experimental word-for-word translations maintained "the faulty division of Pindar's lines into short, often choppy lines[,] based on the failure to recognize the system by which his odes were organized." As a result, those translations place an outsized onus on each word in a line, where the idea of the line is already "pared down to a stark minimum of elements," "massively compressed" in the way Hölderlin's own verse would become. And, as a result, Hölderlin learns to find "in the Greek language[,] with its freedom of syntax," a poetics that is "inherently paratactic" even when it may originally have operated according to a different standard.[22]

Adorno is terse when it comes to Pindar, probably because he wants to emphasize Hölderlin's spiritual allegiance to Hegel's prose, with its expressive as well as philosophical fondness for the leap.[23] It's a connection that's meant to lend historical credibility to the picture of Hölderlin as dialectician, for whom parataxis can serve as a critique of what Adorno jarringly calls "the division of labor" ("P," 113). And yet, just as Hölderlin's work is unthinkable outside the aesthetic and ideological development of style coupé, so too is it significantly engaged in using classical texts to hone a technique for those contradictions and contrasts that make the post-Revolutionary present: "Old and new! Culture and barbarity!

Malice and passion! Egotism in sheep's clothing, egotism in wolf's clothing! Superstitions and unbeliefs. Bondage and despotism! unreasoning wisdom—unwise reason! mindless feeling—unfeeling minds! History, experience, heritage without philosophy, philosophy without experience!"[24] Through an adoption of paratactical extremes, Hölderlin finds a way to tug these unruly antagonists "resonantly together," "absolutely," as he renders the elliptical lines of Pindar's second Olympian, "though that which interpreters requires."[25] So much for Hegelian prose.

The case of Hölderlin is instructive because it brings the flashpoints of eighteenth-century literary culture together with a burgeoning approach to composition curious about the possibility of a dialectical poetics, at a time when dialectics is just beginning to bud off of Enlightenment materialism. Recent studies have shown the significance of the Lucretian revival on that philosophical constellation, which receives the Latin poet's atomist metaphysics with excitement, or at least good cheer. The seventeenth- and eighteenth-century turn to Pindar is as important and, when it comes to manifest changes in poetic form, of considerably more consequence. To understand parataxis, we need to hold in mind the Pindar whose irregular and overlacerated odes offer what looks to the postclassical reader like a phenomenology of fissure. The preoccupation with ruins, fragments, and other crumbs from the ancient world marking so much of the literature of this time becomes, in the neo-Pindaric mode cultivated by Cowley, Congreve, Dyer, and Gray among others, a prismatic material through which to filter the present as the long futurity of the antique past. Since that past comprises so many moments of civilizational collapse, it is thematically well suited to imagining the "ferment and dissolution" ("Gärung und Auflösung") out of which a "new organization" ("ein neuer Organisation") of the world must necessarily be born.[26]

Like style coupé, the Pindaric ode had a mixed reputation. Both meant syntactic aberration, and both attracted notice for the ways in which their disjunctive structure produced the effect of words being, in Samuel Johnson's phrase, "shaken together." In his "Life of Cowley," Johnson offers a rundown of flaws—thriving on "uncertainty and looseness," the ode is "lax and lawless," contagious and juvenile ("all the boys and girls [have] caught" the Pindar bug), and unfit for "the highest kind of writing in verse"—before grudgingly allowing that "the Pindaric Odes have so long enjoyed the highest degree of poetical reputation, that [he is] not willing to dismiss them with unabated censure." Nonetheless, the point stands: in neo-Pindaric, "the greatness of one part is disgraced by the littleness of another; and total negligence of language gives the noblest conceptions the appearance of a fabric august in the plan, but mean in the materials."[27]

These are defects of scale, propriety, and medium, and they are defects of sense. By mixing together long lines with short ones, serious intention with impoverished execution, Pindar's followers transgress the formal and generic conventions that allow poetry to be read, as Johnson thinks it must be, for its argument.

Johnson's complaint comes at a transitional moment for English poetry, between the assumption that good writing can be easily understood and the emergent experimental principle that it has to be difficult—difficult to read, grasp, and like. Interestingly, and as Johnson suggests, some of the strangeness of modern Pindaric comes from its affinity to prose, which is also metrically irregular, and from its roots in speaking into the air (Ancient Greek poetry being, of course, a performance art). Recounting the rise of paratactical constructions in eighteenth-century writing, Sylvia Adamson notes that the "speech-based model of literature" favoring an absence of conjunctions and herky-jerky relationship to rhetorical order suffers from "an information deficit" not present in spoken language. "When parataxis occurs in speech," she writes, "intonation normally tells us where the links are," but on the page these inroads are blocked.[28] The result is an ambiguity that wrests form from content; the poem becomes graphically visible as a physical object, a fabric (to use Johnson's word) behind which little to no referential significance may be discovered.

From Johnson's ode-as-fabric to Hölderlin's construction of the poetic sentence as a thing the poet breaks with his own two hands, the eighteenth-century Pindaric ode lures forth the critical intuition that the most provocative poetry asserts its continuity with a world of things. Because the irregularly abbreviated line is hard to understand, and because the poem's paratactical arrangement makes its rationale hard to retrieve, the poem affronts the reader with its own substance, which, far from inert, threatens to take flight. As George Woodward has it in his 1730 satire "The English Pindarick," the form's short lines are "like Dwarf[s] behind a Giant-Man," each of its "long-tailed" ones a "Thing/ . . . that swells, and foames with Rage" before it "leaps beyond the scanty Page," "thundr'ing on in frantick strain."[29] In his magisterial study of Pindar, John Hamilton will say that the insistent carnality of the ode forestalls the ideological passage of thought into common sense. By the time we get to Hölderlin, he writes, that preemption may be explained by an appeal to "the transit between two thoughts . . . infinitely hanging on to a third, which may be the poetry to come," an "unheard melody" that belongs to the future more than to any one language or tradition.[30]

In the historical absence of that possibility, parataxis might register mere midstness, as being in the thick of discontinuous experience. This is what Joseph Addison seems to have in mind when, in a 1712 issue of the *Spectator*, he jokes that his personal "Compositions in Gardening are altogether after the Pindarick Manner"—a phrase that seesaws pleasantly between poetic and horticultural idioms. "I think," he opines, "there are as many kinds of Gardening as of Poetry: Your Makers of Parterres and Flower-Gardens, are Epigrammatists and Sonneteers in this Art: Contrivers of Bowers and Grotto's, Treillages and Cascades, are Romance Writers." The Pindaric gardener, for his part, strives for "a Confusion of Kitchin and Parterre, Orchard and Flower-Garden, . . . so mixt and interwoven with one another, that if a Foreigner who had seen nothing of our Country should be convey'd into my Garden at his first landing, he would look upon it as a natural Wilderness." This is tongue in cheek, since even an ornamental hedge overgrown with herbs or an orchard in a field of flowers will never be taken for "an uncultivated Part . . . of [the] Country"—something Addison's identification of types of gardens with genres of poetry makes clear.[31] More sincere is the hint that the Pindaric garden is a place of social isolation, a hinterland in which one can neither comprehend nor be comprehended.

This passage from Addison returns us to the garden, and to its syntax. Dixon Hunt writes that the informality of the eighteenth-century English garden, which lets plants and buildings encounter one another free from the symbolic strictures of the *jardin à la française*, trains an entire generation of middle-class writers to see the world differently: as a collection of objects and experiences threaded through the couplet of art and nature. There is no prospect poem without Addison's Pindaric garden coming before it, nor any Wordsworthian gaze that moves through the green everything, green to the very door.

What happens in a garden, writes Thomas Whately in his *Observations on Modern Gardening*, should seem to have "irresistibly occurred," should "have the force of a metaphor, free from the detail" and narrative sequencing of allegory.[32] A garden, that is, should have a sense without having a story, even if that sense might be turned toward a more analytic reflection on historical existence. This is partly what Dixon Hunt means when he says that the "Pindarick manner" of the eighteenth-century garden helps refine a poetry built on a disjunctive series of impressions that arrive with a unified *bang*. It is a poetry corkscrewing away from any fixed subjective center even when the speaker's voice is, if anything, overamplified, for that voice too is absorbed into a world whose defining feature is that it is loud.

A parataxis is not a metaphor, but it has metaphoric heft: because it comes in pieces that fail to add up logically to some whole, and because this failure prompts an alternative means of deriving sense from sense-data, it tropes the belief that creative thought has power even in a moment of hyperattenuated *Erfahrung*. To borrow Miriam Hansen's gloss on gardening and other arts of "bewildering and hidden correspondence," parataxis wrings the sentence from its "ostensibly linear, instrumental destination and reconfigure[s] [it] according to a different logic—not unrelated," crucially, "to the aesthetics of collage, bricolage, and montage." These are also the aesthetics of parataxis, whose classical heritage allows it to represent, like the garden, "the return of archaic, cyclical, mythic time in an accelerated succession of the new."[33] Dragged into a very different modernity, it becomes "multidimensional, contradictory, simultaneous, contrapuntal, stereoscopic.[34]"

Cowper never joined his contemporaries in the full flush of the Pindaric revival, but he nonetheless strives for and achieves a poetics of "boundless contiguity," openly indentured to capital and struggling to escape from its various pollutants.[35] In the next section, I cull parataxes from *The Task* in order to limn what Coleridge called its divine chitchat as an experimental excavation of a self-consciously middle-class *dispositif* from that most highborn of genres, the epic. Cowper's parataxis is a corridor along which the contradictions of late eighteenth-century society rattle and pulse, their sound that of "a world that seems / To toll the death-bell of its own decease" (*T* 2.50–51). I do, however, have two cautions before proceeding. The first is simply to note that my focus will be on the first two books of *The Task*, for it is here—and not in book 3, temptingly called "The Garden"—that Cowper elaborates his paratactical method. The second is to warn that my reading of the poem cannot be called eco-critical, at least not dogmatically.

There has been much comment lately on *The Task* as an environmentalist poem, and on Cowper as a poet who understands before others can that eighteenth-century capitalism, the plantation economy, and a sudden uptick in the frequency and severity of natural disasters are the conditions for one another's calamitous reproduction. These discussions are welcome, but they force connections where Cowper is at pains to assemble adjacencies, to string topics along his poem's semi-mock-epic wire in such a way that they are obviously related and troublingly discrete. Troubling, because the moral ambition of *The Task* is—as Kevis Goodman has impeccably argued—to indict a present it can't really see, to unify phenomena whose crowded interconstitution it can suspect though never name. This is the positional pathos of its desire and parataxis is its figure, the technology by which a history "beyond lived experience and sense perception" appears both absent and immanent.[36]

* * *

The first line of *The Task* is so memorable it's easy to forget that the poem doesn't really begin with "I sing the Sofa" but with a prose synopsis that announces its first subject as a "historical deduction of seats" (*T* 1.1, p. 129). The phrase chimes with the poem's Advertisement, which offers "the history of the following production" as a digressive pursuit through "train[s] of thought" and "turn[s] of mind" (*T*, 128). Remember that Coleridge saw this sort of tangent-driven writing as "marbles in a bag," a collection of *meubles* or moving parts with no logic or order to them. Of course, *meubles* is not only the French word for marbles; it is also the French word for furniture. In *The Task*, furniture moves or launches the poem; it is the tracer the poem pins on capital, which Cowper identifies with the evolution of commodity culture and the circuit of trade around the globe. Insofar as it is movable, moreover, furniture—the sofa, the seat, the armchair, even the rabbit pen—is also an unexpected emblem of the poem's style, which is crafted to match capital's drama of high-speed perpetual displacement of one thing by another.

From poetic production to the commodity's deduction, these twin histories, like Cowper's title, expressly characterize *The Task* as an effort and as an artifact. Compare some other celebrated poems of the so-called Graveyard poets, among whose number Cowper is generally counted: *The Seasons, Night-Thoughts, Elegy Written in a Country Churchyard, The Deserted Village, The Hop-Garden*. The list isn't complete, but it is representative. These are poems about places and times and their imagination is topographical, even when the lay of the land concerns the shape of a feeling. They promise an experience of *presence*, as though by reading Gray or Goldsmith we are brought close to a gravestone or empty house, pulled toward ruins and twilit fields.

Cowper's poetic undertaking is of quite another order, and the world it paints is marked, first and foremost, by the poet's estrangement from what happens there. By estrangement I mean a specific psychic and structural pattern by which Cowper knows himself to be in collusion with crimes against humanity and against the natural world, crimes to which he vociferously objects. That objection, repeatedly associated with the figure of retreat or suburban quasi-hermitage, pitches itself as ethical, even a bit saintly, but Cowper also seems aware that it functions as a denial of what is, in a word, objective: "the pangs/And agonies of human and of brute/Multitudes" whose suffering is so distant from and yet so much a part of his own (*T* 2.105)

Coleridge's oft-quoted description of Cowper's poetry as chitchat is a good gateway to thinking about the older poet's style, or rather about the appearance of its absence. According to Hazlitt, Coleridge nominated Cowper as the best modern poet, and in the *Biographia Literaria* he makes the offhand remark that Cowper "combined natural thoughts with natural diction" in a manner that substantially altered the generic expectations of English poetry, which henceforth would be judged by its capacity to "reconcile . . . the heart with the head."[37] It's a surprising scaffold on which to build Cowper up, since the remarks on *Lyrical Ballads* that follow a few chapters later might lead one to believe that if there's one thing Coleridge doesn't like in poetry, it's the sound of people talking, in a cadence unmoored by prosodic discipline.

It's surprising, too, given Coleridge's distaste for the "intercourse" of "uneducated men," marked as it is by a "disjunction and separation in the component parts of that, whatever it be, they wish to communicate." This arbitrary progression, this suspension of "order," betrays "a want of that prospectiveness of mind, that surview, which enables a man to foresee the whole of what he is to convey . . . [and] so to subordinate and arrange the different parts according to their relative importance, as to convey it at once, and as an organized whole."[38] Chitchat seems to be evidence of precisely this want, even if the people chatting are as erudite as Cowper.

In order for Cowper to make his chitchat divine, he needs to make it metrical, which is to say, stressed. And stressed it is, for despite Coleridge's picture of Cowper as a mild country moralizer, his poetry, including but not limited to *The Task*, adopts disconnected discourse for the purpose of jeremiad. The most obvious target of Cowper's wrath is the Atlantic slave trade, which the seemingly innocuous opening of *The Task* rivets to the history of class society as a history of the social relations of production. A more general target is the paralytic condition of wrong life, about as natural as the greenhouse Cowper, with not a little irony, calls his "blest seclusion from a jarring world" (*T* 3.675). Blank verse has a lot to do with the elaboration of these concerns. Once fireside chat billows into the meter of epic, the effect is not merely "mock"; it is also critical, an invitation to consider why the apparent triviality of bourgeois life might be significant to a poem whose very title tropes work.

More significant, however, is the poem's management of images. I've implied that this management is essentially paratactical, since it relies on the juxtaposition of disparate elements. Coleridge helps us see, too, that Cowper's inability to subordinate is enmeshed in his development of an explicitly political poetics, for which being modern means feeling ourselves to be "agonizingly self-divided" in relation to "present reality," in which we "can only find . . . the grave of [our] life."[39] A syntax that divides and digresses brings that self-division to the page; it also gestures at the possibility of organizing what can seem like a random assortment of topics and themes, disquisitions and digressions into an actually existing social totality, even if there is no point from which that totality might become available to Coleridgean surview.

Suspending hierarchies of significance at the level of the page may not deliver "the concrete unity of interacting contradictions."[40] Nonetheless, there is something about packing things closely together that hints at the wish to grasp *some* unity as a whole dominant over its parts, even if the deep structure of that domination remains obscure. Cowper's coy defense of his poem as an accident of running on, of moving so quickly from one thing to the next that his "trifle" soon piles up into "a serious affair—a Volume!," belies the poem's central surmise, woven into its ungainly shifts of register and many muddled perspectives: the present is so flat it might press you to death (*T*, 128). The muddle is also the substance of history, seen from the perspective of a body that passes through and is helpless before it. By inlaying a carefully crafted figurative register within a poem whose topicality flirts with mere reportage, Cowper holds *The Task* back from simple documentation. And yet there is no heroism here, no triumph of the aesthetic. What speaks most loudly is the style of historical experience washed over historical fact.

To sing the sofa is to give its biography as a consumer object. The poem spends its first hundred lines mapping the sofa's family tree, from rocks to stools with three legs and to stools with four legs and soft, embroidered cushions to chairs of "cane from India" to settees, chaises, and finally the sofa itself. "So slow/The growth of what is excellent!" Cowper crows: "[N]ecessity invented stools,/Convenience next suggested elbow-chairs,/And luxury th' accomplished SOFA last" (*T* 1.86–88). If, by even the most optimistic standards, the paradigm of exchange governing political economy in the eighteenth century turns human beings into "product[s] of multiplying relationships . . . between things and persons," it likewise allows Cowper to present his sofa as a historical actor, or to suggest that commodities have thickened into agents like the persons with which they are also interchangeable.[41] And yet, and as the poem's first four words suggest, the epic protagonist of consumer culture is disjoined from even a prosthetic relationship to other forms of life. The poet sings not of arms and a man but of the products of men's hands, loosed from the social body of which they are the most bona fide remnant. Not for nothing does this history of seats proceed either in the passive voice— "joint-stools were then created," "the frame was form'd"—or by attributing their manufacture to abstract causes (*T* 1.19, 1.56).

Still, the sofa soon drops out of the book to which it gives its name, making its last appearance in line 137 just as Cowper begins to reminisce about his boyhood, when "No SOFA then awaited [his] return" from school, "Nor SOFA then [he] needed" (*T* 1.126–27). In its place is the tree, since, like his contemporary Oliver Goldsmith and John Clare after him, Cowper sees in the fate of the English tree proof of the dispossession of life by trade. In his unfinished "Yardley Oak," Cowper looks backwards at "those thriftier days," when "Oaks fell not, hewn by thousands, to supply/ The bottomless demands" of politicians and profiteers, making hay off the imperial wars of the late eighteenth and early nineteenth century.⁴² *The Task*, having hinted at a "fear" of "want of timber . . . /in Albion's happy isle," is likewise incensed by the deforestation that has turned England into "an Indian waste without a tree" (*T* 1.57–58, 1.261). Of course, we already know where some of India's trees have gone, namely into those cane chairs "smooth and bright/With Nature's varnish; sever'd into stripes/That interlace . . . each other" (*T* 1.39–41). And we know where the "fallen avenues" closer to home are headed: toward whichever newly discovered place lies beyond the "boundless oceans," waiting to be "plough'd perhaps by British bark again" (*T* 1.338, 1.629, 1.631).

Like the fibers of a cane chair, these and other figures of ecological devastation and colonial adventure interlard the reveries of book 1, without winding into an explanatory convergence of trees, sofas, boats, and islands. What develops is a motif of the present likewise severed into stripes, a striation that may well echo Phillis Wheatley's grisly pun on "Cain" in her "On Being Brought from Africa to America."⁴³ The stripes are parataxes, ways of "transcoding an orchestra of spatial, cultural, and political developments," including the emergence of London's poetry "mart,/So rich, so throng'd, so drain'd, and so supplied . . . opulent, enlarg'd, and still/Increasing[.] (*T* 1.719–22).⁴⁴ They are also "nice incision[s]" "plough[ed] [into] a brazen field" of poetry itself, for which there is no "soil/So sterile" that it can't be catachrestically "clothe[d]" in "the richest scenery and the loveliest forms" (*T* 1.708–11). These lines of partial or abandoned commentary build in excoriating energy until they collapse, in the last line of this first book, on the seat of "empire['s] . . . mutilated structure, soon," Cowper adds in a superlatively ominous pitch, "to fall" (*T* 1.773–74). If the modernist parataxis, as Ruth Jennison proposes, makes room for those "deep, spatialized histories, the knowledge of which is . . . part of any truly emancipatory trespass," Cowper's use of the figure is less directed.⁴⁵ At the end of book 1, parataxis sags under its own burden, part of an imperial quantum it cannot shift nor squeeze past.

The sofa, it turns out, never went away. It simply dispersed into the poem's hidden correspondences: felled trees, urban centers, tropical islands, Indian wastes, "a serving maid" and the "one who left her, went to sea, and died," "vagabond and useless tribe[s]" of gypsies, gout, Bacon and Reynolds, and all of the fine and mechanical arts, to name a few (*T* 1.537–38, 1.559). This is a theory of global economic and social complexity so expressive and yet so compact that Jane Austen, in her *Mansfield Park*, summons it to weld the proximate threat of Mr. Rushworth cutting down the trees at Sotherton to the distant horrors of Sir Thomas's plantation at Antigua. "Cut down an avenue!" mutters Fanny Price. "What a pity! Does it not make you think of Cowper? 'Ye fallen avenues, once more I mourn your fate unmerited.'"[46] Edward Said famously argued that Antigua is just Mansfield on a larger scale; still, for Austen the instinct to "think of Cowper" points at the suspicion that synecdoche or allegory of this sort hardly absolves the novel of its wrongs, namely the nurturing of local and intimate concerns at the expense of the world-historical ones it raises only to swaddle in "a dead silence."[47] This offhand nod to *The Task*, in other words, doesn't invite an imaginative laddering up and down magnitudes. It merges empire and home in the shape of a generic intrusion, a poetic jut into a narrative whose instinct is to draw down to the head of a pin.

Back to mutilated structure. Those two words end the poem's first book, and "boundless contiguity" begins its second. The longer you sit with them, the more synonymous those turns of phrase become, especially since Cowper, in an intervening prose text that gives the argument of book 2, tells the reader directly that this part of *The Task* "opens with reflections suggested by the conclusion" of book 1. This is an unusually overmanaged direction to the reader, and what it implies is a sequential logic that is, etymologically speaking, brought up from below—the literal meaning of *suggested*. Hauled like a broken body from the bottom of book 1 to the top of book 2, an image of structural impairment reconstitutes itself in an image of infinite expansion that is also a snare. This sequence is long, but its protraction is doing real rhetorical work:

OH for a lodge in some vast wilderness,
Some boundless contiguity of shade,
Where rumour of oppression and deceit,
Of unsuccessful or successful war,
Might never reach me more. My ear is paine',
My soul is sick with ev'ry day's report
Of wrong and outrage with which earth is fill'd.
There is no flesh in man's obdurate heart,
It does not feel for man; The nat'ral bond
Of brotherhood is sever'd as the flax
That falls asunder at the touch of fire.
He finds his fellow guilty of a skin
Not colour'd like his own; and, having pow'r
T' enforce the wrong, for such a worthy cause

Dooms and devotes him as his lawful prey.
Lands intersected by a narrow frith
Abhor each other. Mountains interpos'd
Make enemies of nations, who had else
Like kindred drops, been mingled into one.
Thus man devotes his brother, and destroys;
And, worse than all, and most to be deplor'd,
As human nature's broadest, foulest blot,
Chains him, and tasks him, and exacts his sweat
With stripes, that mercy, with a bleeding heart,
Weeps when she sees inflicted on a beast. (*T* 2.1–25)

Boundless contiguity of shade. Consider how odd a figure this is, this whorl of adjacencies, a chain looped into a logarithmic spiral. I make the comparison because book 2 wants me to, because, in its explicit attack on the Atlantic slave trade, it takes the chain as a sort of objective correlative both for the abolitionist movement and for the formal ambitions of *The Task* as a whole. In its long first verse paragraph, book 2 is littered with chains or versions of them, from the real "chains" and "bonds" and "shackles" "fasten[ed]" on "the slave" to metonymic "sinews bought and sold" to more fanciful pictures of empire's "veins" and the "flax" that is "the nat'ral bond/Of brotherhood," so easily severed. By the time Cowper attacks the trade explicitly in lines 12–15, it's impossible not to see his boundless contiguity of shade as a transposition of black bodies—with "skin/Not colour'd like his own"—into the poet's opening exclamatio. Even as he announces his wish for the life beyond the "reach" of "report/ Of wrong and outrage with which earth is fill'd," densely philological and free-associative urges get the better of him, dragging into the light the foundation of that dream and the conditions of having it.

It is therefore not quite right to call *The Task* an instance of sensibility discourse, a satiating, lightly penitent, and highly self-satisfied performance of moral compunction. As the introductory argument to book 2 makes clear, Cowper is writing this poem as an exercise in subliminality, and in its politicization. *The Task* is hyperconductive, designed to effect an irregular and arrhythmic transit within and between images, "threading . . . the[ir] conflict through a whole system of planes" until this "chain of bifurcations [is] gathered into a new unity."[48] That is Eisenstein on the work of montage, and Cowper's chain is also his chain, an organizational principle whose name and form make it absolutely clear that the poem's unity belongs to a social horror whose full outline it can never quite make out: not just slavery, but slavery as a source of the surplus population whose labor produces the various modern miseries Cowper tallies and the means by which those miseries are forgotten or made light of, the sofa and its song. Like the figure of the wake, furrow, or disturbance upon the water in which Christina Sharpe discerns "a dysgraphia of disaster" trailing "slavery's continued unfolding" in the twenty-first century, Cowper's chain tows nearly to the text's surface the knowledge that rural retirement is not an escape from the world but a spatial "dimension . . . of Black non/being."[49] The wish for a boundless contiguity of shade is a wish to manacle one body to the next in perpetuity and almost in secret; the instruments of captivity are poetry's instruments too.

Perhaps the idea that *The Task* is reaching for a dialectic of reprise and expansion, one that allows single words (*cane, stripe, task, plough*) and undercover synonyms to elaborate a partial critique of a "world that seems/To toll the death-bell of its own decease" assumes a diagnostic acuity the poem cannot sustain. And that's true: the poem cannot sustain it. Wherever *The Task* seems to build toward a historically particular indictment, it tends to dissipate into tone, to solubilize contradiction as affect. This is nowhere more obvious than in the passage that picks up immediately after Cowper's abolitionist plea, unequivocally apocalyptic in its tenor and promise. "Sure there is need of social intercourse,/ Benevolence, and peace, and mutual aid," Cowper pleads, when "the props/And pillars of our planet seem to fail,/and Nature with a dim and sickly eye/To wait the close of all" (*T* 2.48–49, 2.62–65). For the next 150 lines *The Task* unspools a list of recent natural disasters, among them the Calabrian earthquakes of 1783, the giant ash cloud that sprang up after the eruption of the Laki volcano that same year, and the Atlantic hurricanes of the 1780 season, the deadliest ever recorded. All this peaks with a bizarre wheedling of the *beatus ille* topos: "Happy the man who sees a God employ'd/In all the good and ill that chequer life," and who may thus discern that such convulsions of the earth and its weather systems are "furious inquest[s] . . . /On God's behalf" into the cruelty of his children (*T* 2.161–62, 2.135–6).

Like the paratactical title of J. M. W. Turner's painting *Slavers Throwing Overboard the Dead and Dying—Typhoon Coming On*, this passage moves from slavery to ecological disaster without quite saying one is the consequence of the other.[50] To be sure, both Turner and *The Task* are working overtime to imply precisely this kind of consequential relationship between human evil and divine reprimand. For Cowper, natural disasters mean that God is smiting the wicked. For Turner, the gray blotch rising steadily up the left-hand side of the canvas, toward which the slave ship is beelining with full force, seems to promise that punishment will follow crime. And yet both Cowper's poem and Turner's canvas defeat the providential commentaries they invite. Like the absence of grammatical suture between Cowper's first verse paragraph and his second, the composition of *Slavers* repeals any attempt to turn the painting into explanation or allegory. Turner's audience reads left to right, but the ship is sailing right to left, into a storm whose full body lies beyond the frame. If this is a moral it is illegible, or at the least what it teaches is unavailable to conventional interpretive means, which seize upon the appearance of linear conjunction only to realize this story is moving into its future backward. That Turner exhibited *Slavers* with an excerpt from his poem "The Fallacies of Hope" gives grist to this mill, for the pairing arrays the progressive movement of the English poetic line against the inverted pathway of the ship on its way out of sight.

I am aware that this take on book 2 could seem to pass up a golden opportunity to make plain just how serious and smart Cowper is about eighteenth-century capitalism and its ecological fallout. *The Task* would seem, after all, to have it exactly right. When carbon dioxide and methane begin to saturate the atmosphere, as they did near the end of the eighteenth century, "crazy earth" does get crazier, though it will take a bit longer for "the waters of the deep [to] rise" and "make [man's] house a grave"; at the very least, Cowper guesses correctly that meteorological disruption will be a regular feature of our times as well as his, which are not not-ours (*T*, 2.60, 2.143, 2.147). Verses like these could be an irresistible provocation, and many scholars have received them as an evidentiary object, an up-to-the-minute narration of sea-level rise, fracking-induced earthquakes, and turbocharged hurricanes (Katrina, Irene, Harvey, Maria . . .).

Still, I hesitate over the prospect of reading *The Task* as a poem about the weather, to say nothing of climate change. For one thing, Cowper has no inkling of climate change in any scientifically meaningful purport of the term—no inkling, that is, of an anthropogenic rise in global mean temperature and its runaway consequences. For another, his disasters have absolutely nothing to do with anthropogenic climate change; at best, they are of the Anthropocene, but not about it in any natural or denotative sense. Finally, it's worth noting that the section on natural disasters in book 2 never invokes temperature nor any kind of natural periodicity; Cowper even mocks "the spruce philosopher" who goes on about cause and effect and claims to have "found/The source of the disease that Nature feels" (*T* 2.189, 2.193–94). God, not gas, is Cowper's "genuine cause of all" (*T* 2.205).

To read *The Task* prophetically is to impose what we know now onto a text whose preoccupations are quite distinct. More troublingly, it is also to make too-quick recourse to the interpretive protocols of "the end of the world and the end of history," which are, as Christopher Fan says,

"two of our most familiar tropes for thinking through the impasses standing between late capitalism's crises and its uncertain futures."[51] "A stall-
ing out between two positions," Fan's impasse nicely addresses what's
happening in *The Task* at the level of figuration, which is where Cowper
is trying to make capital present as a problem for the world and as a
problem for poetry. The parataxes driving the poem's sideways rundown
of the barbaric relation between human surplus and the sofa's surfeit
cannot have prophecy as their horizon. Instead, they make a demand for
social narrative that the turn to apocalypticism, like the sentimentalist's
recourse to tone, can defuse but never satisfy.

Of course, it's not as though parataxis satisfies that demand either. As a
figure of dim concurrence, its duty is to advocate for and then to surren-
der the possibility of pinpointing the specific dynamic that fuels at once
the insipidities of bourgeois convenience and the transnational traffic
in people and things. As Cowper guesses, no extant eighteenth-century
rubric of causality is a match for the field of baroque overdeterminations
in which he finds himself, and in which his poem finds him. "What solid
was," he writes, "by transformation strange/Grows fluid"—or, as others
have put it, "all that is solid melts into air," a phase change by which all
"train[s] of ancient and venerable prejudices and opinions," including the
surety of providential annihilation, "are swept away," where "all that is
holy is profaned, and man is at last compelled to face with sober senses his
real conditions of life" even if he can't quite see them, yet (*T* 2.98–100).[52]

Another way to put this would be to say that Cowper leans on parataxis
because he doesn't have a more fine-grained technical vocabulary in his
arsenal, a vocabulary that might match the seething complexity of how
things happen. This seems unfair; it also voids the work of parataxis in
calling for something outside it to integrate its disjunctions, to make them
part of an unpredictable but undeniable unity no parataxis, and no poetic
text, could ever get just right. Poetry will inevitably stutter and stumble
when faced with the question of how to get there from here, of how to
grasp at the lineaments of a future that must be nascent in the present
and that the present almost utterly conceals. And yet, to abandon the
desire for poetry to be better at history might be to unlock a frightening
prospect: the necessity of action against a background of ignorance.

* * *

On the day the Laki volcano blew, Cowper sent his friend William Unwin
a poem in the mail. It would be a few weeks before the toxic cloud of
ash released by Laki would cover England and Europe in a red haze, a
few months before Cowper would tell Unwin of "such multitudes [be-

ing] indisposed by fevers . . . that farmers have difficulty gathering their harvest, the labourers having been almost every day carried out of the field incapable of work, many" of them to die.[53] It would, meanwhile, be centuries before anyone would venture to read Cowper's report as a glimpse into an anthropocenic future.

"The Rose" rests at a crossroads. An easygoing ballad about incaution and its consequences, the poem dilates a moment in time when the idea that such consequences might be planetary and permanent is just on the cusp of being available:

The rose had been wash'd, just wash'd in a shower,
Which Mary to Anna convey'd.
The plentiful moisture incumber'd the flower,
And weigh'd down its beautiful head.

The cup was all fill'd, and the leaves were all wet,
And it seem'd to a fanciful view,
To weep for the buds it had left with regret
On the nourishing bush where it grew.

I hastily seiz'd it, unfit as it was,
For a nosegay, so dripping and drown'd,
And swinging it rudely, too rudely, alas!
I snapp'd it, it fell to the ground.

And such, I exclaim'd, is the pitiless part
Some act by the delicate mind,
Regardless of wringing and breaking a heart
Already to sorrow resign'd.

This elegant rose, had I shaken it less,
Might have bloom'd with its owner awhile,
And the tear that is wip'd with a little address,
May be follow'd perhaps by a smile.[54]

These five pithy quatrains are not of the same order of achievement as *The Task*; nor do they engage thematically the "portentous, unexampled, unexplain'd" phenomena that make that poem so, well, portentous (*T* 2.58). Instead, "The Rose" tells a story about upset and adjustment so minor as to embarrass the poet who would write as searingly as Cowper of a world on fire. The world of this ballad is still green, but the rose, once cut, won't bloom for long. It begins to die when Mary plucks it; the speaker just finishes the job. The poem shifts incrementally to accommodate this modest act of destruction, letting the barely audible half-rhyme between "was" and "alas" imply something both awry and all right. It's a light sonic comment on the narrative of lost time and alternative futurity, in which one might have done something different but only to trivial effect. Hence the weak aphorism that closes the last stanza, wrapping the episode up with an aggressively banal remark on how best to persuade a woman to smile.

"The apparent resignation to aphorism and parataxis," writes Paul de Man, "is often an attempt to recuperate on the level of style what is lost on the level of history." It is, in other words, a poetic refuge for a "dialectical summation" more conventional historical discourse cannot achieve, because unlike that discourse poetry has room for "breaks and interruptions."[55] Although de Man doesn't say so—and he wouldn't—the implication is that there is a special capacity inherent in poetic language and the unassuming systematicity of style that doesn't obtain for more linear modes of analysis. It's a capacity to accommodate disruptions, deviations, or (to use this word again) impasses as part of the substance to which historical materialism applies itself.

Cowper's closing aphorism, which considers hypothetical sequences and our desire to secure them in advance, is motivated by resignation of exactly this sort. As the last word of the penultimate stanza, "resign'd" suggests not simply forbearance or failure but the specter of a cancellation, of some mark being struck out by another. The word's legacy is one of keeping accounts, of adding and subtracting and balancing sums: plus, minus, zero. In this poem, resignation sits between the poem's diegesis and its loosening into a series of hypotheticals, themselves recuperated as the general constituency of a future cast in the optative mood. If something "may" happen, its conditions are already almost all present. This is the claim of the aphorism, and it is also its point of similarity with parataxis: both capture the space between fact and hypothesis, where things in the world unevenly graze the thinner stuff of speculation.

Another name for this space, or for its epistemic intension, is nescience. A standoff between experience and conjecture, nescience can never quite mend their split. Instead, it contemplates the impossibility of knowing how behaving differently in the past would have made a difference in the present, and receives this impossibility affectively, as a barbed uneasiness about what is still to come. Consider the fait accompli of being "already to sorrow resign'd" hovering over the notional optimism of the poem's last four lines. The self-assurance of *already* and the doubtfulness of *had, might have, may be,* and *perhaps* place the poem in the otherwise uninhabitable time when the rose was still around and the equally uninhabitable future when it might have bloomed a little longer. It is a poem about the concept of an aftermath, about how it outlives itself over and over again and so perturbs our faith in the very idea of a next step. This is what trauma does too, and nescience is, as we know, the cognitive output of trauma. In "The Rose," the trauma at issue announces itself as the failure of poetry to capture history's aftershocks, to conceive the grief that belongs to us long before we know how to name it.

Environmentalists often ask us to picture a world without people. In our inevitable failure to uphold this suspension of disbelief, we're meant to confront the limits of our grossly flawed anthropocentric thinking and to balance what we cannot manage imaginatively with what we can grasp emotionally: a vertigo of dread that will always dissolve in the realization that we're not there yet. Without sounding a single apocalyptic note, "The Rose" may be even less forgiving. Not an allegory but an example, the poem documents what it's like when the compressed temporality of accelerating loss is forced to absorb alternative pasts and barely viable futures. By foregrounding the indeterminate link between actions and consequences, this minor poem produces a compelling argument about form in general: it is only through the "little address," the subtle lift and thrust of linguistic devices and generic frames, that accidents seem significant or prophetic. Form exerts the contextual pressure that can turn an event into a signal, from an uninformative to an informative occurrence, from snapping the neck of a single flower to one of those countless, cumulative acts of destruction whose effects can't and won't be kicked down the road forever.

Sometimes events are signals only in hindsight. In an essay on disco and the AIDS crisis, Walter Hughes observes how certain lyrical motifs— "the 'night fever,' the 'boogie fever,' the 'tainted love,' and the 'love hangover'"—became "rife with proleptic ironies" after the epidemic began in earnest. Today, "The Rose" has a proleptic cast all its own, the result of a climatological rather than epidemiological state of affairs forcing its metaphors to "pass . . . into literalism."[56] Interweaving these strains of crisis is Derek Jarman, whose devotion to parataxis or (to use his term) the cut-up discloses the morphological principles by which literal and figurative modes are made materially copresent. In his indispensable study of Jarman's "lyric film," Steven Dillon cites the cut-up as a technique of oblique association that disappoints "academic requirements of objectivity or argument," and as a skill Jarman puts in service of his own experimental historiography.[57] If disco's vehicles broach the tenors just beyond their periphery, Jarman's films splice together moments in time from a distance of centuries, rendering English history a field of near-simultaneities. Thus the Elizabethan world of Edward II, in Jarman's retelling, gets gatecrashed by gay-rights activists holding signs that say "Liberté/Egalité/Homosex/ualité" and "No Prison for Flirting"; thus in his adaptation of *The Tempest*, the order of Shakespeare's scenes is rearranged and its early modern iconography annexed by Disney, the oak in which Prospero threatens to imprison Ariel switched out for Snow White's glass coffin.

Jarman's ultimate cut-up, however, is his garden, from which the Dungeness B nuclear power station remains visible today. Here, the garden syntax of the eighteenth century finds new life, even at the verge of what will soon be known as nature's death and in the distended middle of Jarman's. "[I] came here," he writes, "after the discovery of my seropositivity. . . . I water the roses and wonder whether I will see them bloom. I plant my herbal garden as a panacea, read up on all the aches and pains that plants will cure—and know they are not going to help. The garden as pharmacopoeia has failed" (*MN*, 179).

In this "dying sunlight," the garden defines a weakening to which life implausibly continues to cling. Dungeness is sometimes referred to as England's only desert, and Jarman regularly finds his plantings "scorched by the continuous wind" or battered by icy rain (*MN*, 179, 26). The garden is also up against the increasingly volatile climate and who knows what kind of poison seeping from Dungeness B. "Ministers attend a seminar on global warming," Jarman snorts, and "say the answer is more nuclear power stations." Meanwhile, a "menacing sunset" fills the sky with "livid yellows and inky blacks [and] a deep scarlet gash" (*MN*, 67). And yet Jarman is committed. "You've finally discovered nature, Derek," a friend tells him, though when he demurs she changes tack: "Ah, I understand completely. You've discovered modern nature," the kind always faced with some novel unpredictable threat (*MN*, 8).

In the diary by that same name, "modern nature" is contemplated in variously elliptical ways, and often by a disjointed collection of lineated verses that crop up across the volume. "Power hums along the lines/to keep the fish and chips a-frying,/ . . . I've brewed my nuclear tea"; "to whom it may concern/in the dead stones of a planet/no longer remembered as earth/ . . . I have planted a stony garden"; "The garden is built for dear friends/Howard, Paul, Terence, David, Robert, and Ken,/And many others, each stone has a life to tell/I cannot invite you into this house" (*MN*, 13, 16, 178). I understand these poems in much the same way Dillon understands Jarman's films: both exploit the referential indeterminacy of lyric to present "a subjectivity more broadly social and historical than any particular, individual self."[58] This is a lyricism that rolls the most personal meditations outward, with an awkwardness that comes with the territory of being (in Jarman's words) "passionately militant."[59]

Parataxis puts things together; it does not explain why they should be so organized, nor tell some tale to justify their contiguity. For Jarman, it models militancy as a commitment to building abrupt, seemingly irrational linkages between discrete objects of knowledge. The alchemical meeting of anger and inelegance defines his form as much as Cowper's. Jump-cutting between discrete temporal frames, the vaunted lyric subject plays the role of a collider. He flings disparate particles at one another and as close as they can come, often with effects that border on the ridiculous. There are many things in Jarman's films that make you want to avert your eyes, not because they are obscene but because they are so self-serious, and thus often absurd. Still, the films earn their shambolic coordination of high art, pop culture, pornography, camp, punk, and sober invocations of heritage figures like Shakespeare, Milton, and Blake in a way the poems don't, quite. Perhaps that's why Jarman is so invested in Dorothy Wordsworth, whose journals, like his own, find that the disruption of the solitary subject by the historical present regularly expresses itself in the maladroit.

We've seen this in Cowper as well, in the yo-yo effect of his tonal gyrations and topical shifts, but for Jarman it is more obviously an avant-garde routine. In Jarman's diary entry for April 27, 1989, a bit of Dorothy's Grasmere journal prefaces a ballad of Jarman's making. Wordsworth's passage records a glittering stretch of parataxis, an outdoor document of near but impossible conjunctions: "I never saw such a union of earth, sea, and sky: the clouds beneath our feet spread themselves to the water, and the clouds of the sky almost joined them." Jarman seizes on this image of a dissolving margin between figuration and description and adds this to it:

> I walk in this garden
> Holding the hands of dead friends
> Old age came quickly for my frosted generation
> Cold, cold, cold they died so silently
> Did the forgotten generations scream?
> Or go full of resignation
> Quietly protesting innocence
> Cold, cold, cold they died so silently
> Linked hands at four AM
> Deep under the city you slept on
>
> Never heard the sweet flesh song
> Cold, cold, cold they died so silently
> I have no words
> My shaking hand

Cannot express my fury
Sadness is all I have,
Cold, cold, cold they died so silently

Matthew fucked Mark fucked Luke fucked John
Who lay in the bed that I lie on
Touch fingers again as you sing this song
Cold, cold, cold they died so silently
My gilly flowers, roses, violets blue
Sweet garden of vanished pleasures
Please come back next year
Cold, cold, cold I die so silently

Goodnight boys,
Goodnight Johnny,
Goodnight,
Goodnight. (*MN*, 69–70)

There are many Romantic echoes to hear in "I Walk in This Garden"—of
"To Autumn," "La Belle Dame sans Merci," "Ode to the West Wind," "The
Masque of Anarchy" and, of course, "I Wandered Lonely as a Cloud," with
its host of golden daffodils. Together they sound Jarman's attempt to improvise a poetics for the comorbid but categorically distinct calamities of
AIDS and global warming, and the fate of the earth beneath glowering
skies. Romanticism of this horticultural stripe, with its nearly rote images
of flowers as humans and humans as flowers, feels a heightened obligation
to use poetry to body forth the invisible (a project strongly simpatico, by
the by, with the critique of political economy). The labored artificiality
and inconstant rhyme of Jarman's poem cue us into its struggle to generate ontological presence by means of its figurative extension, to bring
men and seasons back from the dead and so to ring the alarm of several
crises lurching into others, "linked hands" whose affinity is mysterious
but obstinate, impossible to shake off.

"I Walk in This Garden" is a ballad of victimhood rather than victim-
ization, its shaking hand not the seizing, swinging, snapping hand of
"The Rose" but the palsied limb of a sick man for whom death is first and
foremost a muzzling. Jarman may be thinking of the SILENCE = DEATH
poster campaign that began in New York City in 1987, his rhyme of *cold*
with *old* sifting somatic through temporal screens to hint that the poem's
narrative drive is essentially entropic. The body cools, the world cools,
and time tilts everything forward unto its last. We can now add yet another caveat to the idea that lyric postures are necessarily antinarrative,

a claim that doesn't quite accommodate the macroscopic awareness, in a poem like this one, of the headlong march of thermodynamics or contagious disease.

At the same time, however, Jarman is careful to fold a refrain of disruptions into the future-oriented movement of energy and illness. "Cold, cold, cold" is the slogan of decline but also an impasse of its own, a drag on death's momentum. It is the motto, too, of Jarman's own resignation, which joins Cowper's as an anxious pose of inhabiting the no-man's-land between knowledge and conjecture, between the certainty that people have died and the savage question of how many more will too.

The status of what has and has not happened is vividly questioned in Jarman's fourth stanza. Did Matthew, Mark, Luke, and John lie in Jarman's bed for certain, or does he mean to ask "who lay" there before him? The query concerns status in a very specialized sense. Depending on how we read these lines, the bed is either a voluptuous memento or the figure for a history of transmission, a pandemic in miniature, and, of course, it is both. The Four Evangelists pass on a deadly virus as they pass on the good news. HIV seems to come to rest in the speaker's body, but it surely has passed beyond the barrier of the poem, handed down along innumerable bloodlines. The logic of contagion ensures that the sentence beginning in the past (lay) and ending in the present (lie) will resolve in the future tense of terminal illness, with the speaker's body lying low, prone and stiff. Jarman's lines dramatize the impossibility of separating the homophobic rhetoric of so-called risk groups from the anecdotal reality that everyone you know is dying, of slipping free from "the statistics which hedge the modern world about like the briar that walled in the sleeping princess" (*MN*, 151).

The John who closes the first line of the fourth stanza and the Johnny who closes the poem represent these two modes of knowing: the episteme of public health and the episteme of sociability, perhaps of solidarity, and don't forget that *Johnny* is slang for condom. When these meet, pull apart, and meet again, they generate what the poem encodes as political paralysis, a condition in which silence and death collude. The epidemiological perspective is also the forensic one, divulging in the circuit of male bodies a trail of infection and transmission. It is well-meaning and it is also mean, mistrustful, and prurient; it asks, "Who else lay in this bed? It was these four people, wasn't it?" Meanwhile, the speaker's sexual history limns an experience so distant it seems positively biblical. The fourth stanza also rewrites the prayer known as the White Paternoster, while the fifth turns to nursery rhymes: "The rose is red, the violet is blue / The gillyflower is sweet, and so are you." This is the only stanza where the subject of Jarman's refrain changes from *they* to *I*, as members of the speaker's frosted generation undergo a transmigration of souls into "gilly flowers, roses, violets blue" even as the declarative confidence of the child's rhyme vanishes into the plea of "come back next year."

From "this bed" to flower beds, from a tangle of bodies to a tangle of roots, "I Walk in This Garden" uses metaphor and metonymy to create a confusion of knowledges in a manner similar to "The Rose," with its hard past tense sidling up to its melancholy might-have-been. The fragility of form in the midst of calamity is expressed by doubt cast on something that should be indubitable: the seasonal, cyclical return of flowers from the frozen ground. The erotically charged myths of Hyacinth and Adonis (clearly in the poem's ether) suggest that people, like flowers, live on in one form or another, but amid the environmental peril of Jarman's moment he can't count on metempsychosis. Disease should be the poem's weft and nature its warp; people cannot come back from death, but gardens can. These assumptions, the postulates of long and varied traditions, are suddenly, startlingly tentative.

This state of unknowing crossed with statistical near-surety creates a deadlock in which the blighted present is held right against the indiscoverable future. To occupy that present is to face down the leap for which Pindar prepares himself, toward an action and endpoint on the other side of some elongated abyss. If we wanted to discover an ethics here, it would quickly focalize around the nature of the obligation existing persons bear to future ones. As the late Derek Parfit argued in his 1984 opus *Reasons and Persons*, existence cannot be what matters when it comes to determining the scope of ethical behavior, because our actions today constrain the actions and identities of people yet unborn. Tasked, for example, with making good environmental policy, we need to understand the necessity of that action as underwritten neither by the assumption of who future persons will be nor by our present self-interest. Ethics, in other words, requires a negative epistemology. It should address itself to the hypothetical being over and above the actual one, to the form of a life and not to a reference point tethered to some specific living thing. What we call ethics is just an exaltation aimed at preserving the future as a *there* for someone else.

This last formulation holds special interest in the context of this chapter and this book. Jarman's dead friends are available to him only through a poetic superscription, a springing upward in an attempt to cross the ultimate distance. The same is true of his garden, exhorted apostrophically to return next year. These gestures create closeness between the speaker and his absent intimates, as kinds of beings rather than concrete ones. Names—Matthew, Mark, Luke, John; gilly flowers, roses, violets blue—become types, and types become a lifeline to a future held open by generality or abstraction. More wish than command, Jarman's attempt to communicate with what we might call de dicto beings models an ethics grounded in rhetorical desire. It takes the customary, sad reflection on the might-have-been and distills from it an unexpected optimism about our collective prospects, even if they exist in words alone. "Tragen muß er, zuvor; nun aber nennt er sein Liebstes,/Nun, nun, müssen dafür Worte, wie Blumen, entstehn," writes Hölderlin. "First he has to bear it, now name his most beloved,/Now, now he must find words for it that, like flowers, can grow."[60]

* * *

In the post-Fordist allegory of Plato's cave tucked into his *Traité de savoir-vivre à l'usage des jeunes générations* (translated into English as *The Revolution of Everyday Life*), Raoul Vaneigem begins not with a handful of men chained to a rock wall but with "a few million people liv[ing] in a huge building with neither doors nor windows," where "the feeble light of countless oil lamps vies with the shadows" that permanently hold sway. The lamps are tended by the poor until a rebellion breaks out. A dispute arises: perhaps the lamps should be considered a public utility; perhaps the building itself, "unhealthy and unfit for communal living," should be torn down. The conflict turns violent, and a stray projectile—"un boulet mal dirigé"—hits the building, making a hole into which light from outside streams:

> After an initial moment of stupefaction, this flood of light was hailed with cries of victory. The solution had been found: it would be enough simply to make more holes. The lamps were tossed aside or tucked away in museums, and all power fell to the window-makers [*perceurs de fenêtre*]. Those who had been on the side of [the building's] total destruction were forgotten and so was their discreet liquidation, which went almost, or so it seemed, unnoticed. (Everyone was too busy arguing about the number and placement of the windows.) Their names were remembered a century or two later, when, having grown accustomed to seeing large bay windows, the people, that perpetual malcontent, took to asking extravagant questions: "Dragging out your days in an air-conditioned greenhouse," they said, "what kind of life is that?"[61]

Philosophy, on Plato's account, only goes one way: forward. It can never stall out, or miss its exit; nor is it duped even when power opens a safety valve to lower the pressure ("Dès que le pouvoir risque d'éclater, il fait jouer la soupape de sûreté, il diminue la pression interne"). It forges ahead, magnificently undeluded. Not so revolutionary consciousness, which, insofar as it is collective, is vulnerable to the schisms and obstructions, the failures of nerve and the misdirected energies that always beset people in groups. Still, there's hope. The greenhouse—air-conditioned and bright but no less a remand—teaches its inhabitants to want what is outside of it. "Who loves a garden," writes Cowper, in the third book of *The Task*, "loves a green-house too," but in Vaneigem's parable Cowper's pathway of reciprocal desire is bent beautifully out of shape (*T* 3.566). Love for the greenhouse must mutate into an appetite for its destruction, gratitude for stopgap comforts be expunged in the undoing of any structure of obligation to what is not enough. This is a Pindaric leap too.

"Unconscious of a less propitious clime,/There blooms exotic beauty, warm and snug" (*T* 3.567–68). And now we're treated to another performance of Cowper's leitmotif, in a roll call of Portuguese and Indian fruit trees, Italian and Levantine flowers, Azorean and South African jasmine; "foreigners from many lands/they form one social shade, as if conven'd" by Orpheus's lyre (*T* 585–87). True to form, Cowper comments on his parataxis and notes its fitness as a statement of poetic intent, praising the "just arrangement, rarely brought to pass/But by a master's hand, disposing well/The gay diversities of leaf and flow'r" (*T* 3.588–90). At this point in the poem, lines like these are supercharged with more ominous meaning, and it's hard not to hear echoes of the first two books in these pointed recurrences to their central theme: the perversion of social relations by lordship ("a master's hand") and bondage as well as poetry's compulsory involvement therein.

That this greenhouse too should or will fall is signaled with arresting bluntness, as Cowper caps off a litany of plants set in its "regular yet various scene" by comparing them to "the sons of ancient Rome," "once rang'd" in similar fashion (*T* 3.592, 3.596). The poem elaborates no further; nor does it need to, since in the eighteenth century there was no readier shorthand for civilizational decline than Rome, whose name is coincident with its fall. The suggestion, here as throughout *The Task*, is that the intimate entanglement of ordinariness—of hobbies, letters, books, and walks—in vast economic networks is at once the only subject for modern poetry and the one subject modern poetry cannot rationalize or redeem. In these conditions, the poem is at best the breaker of glass for those it can reach, which isn't many. Its language is one of hints and propositions, most effective when it appears least engaged in conventional practices of expository reasoning. Isolated and indirect, it is ultimately no more than a badly aimed bullet someone, on one side of the barricade or the other, let fly: going the wrong way fast, askance, a small thing with sudden consequences.

2

Wordsworth's Obscurity

If I am asked "Whether the clouded mind and moral dispositions I am alluding to are not frequently to be regarded as consequences, rather than causes of the impediments with which they are associated?"—I shall answer at once, that these are not the only circumstances in which physical and moral phaenomena run a circle, and become alternately cause and effect.

JOHN THELWALL, *Letter to Henry Cline, Esq., on Imperfect Developments of the Faculties, Mental and Moral, as well as Constitutional and Organic; and on the Treatment of Impediments of Speech* (1810)

Mind and body, hearing and tongue, eyes and skin . . . She seems to have lost them all, and to be looking for them as though they were external to her.

LONGINUS, *Peri Hypsous* (first century CE), trans. D. A. Russell

A man sits on a rock. He looks at a painting. He climbs a mountain. There is a poem he cannot write. He sees things differently than most people. He lives his life like everyone else. His world is small. He gets older. There is a poem he cannot write. His house is large. He thinks a lot about houses. He stops thinking. He has no intention of writing that poem; anyone can see that. He takes walks. He takes people for granted. The world is there for him and then it isn't. Every poem he wrote was a poem he could not write. The world is too close. The world is out of reach. There is a draft. He shuts the window. The world is small. He opens it. There is a draft.

* * *

Let me put it bluntly: I don't like Wordsworth. I almost said I don't care for him, but that's not quite true. A day spent writing about Wordsworth is a good day; when he comes into the classroom with me, things inevitably go well. And yet the eye I cast on his section of my bookshelf is doubtful, disgruntled. Never could I imagine reading Wordsworth for pleasure, though it is with pleasure that I recall someone's startled love for that cataract in the seventy-seventh line of "Tintern Abbey." It is with pleasure, too, that I've been taught about Wordsworth by professors and colleagues, by lectures and book chapters, and by the poems of others, especially those that share or repeat the "traumatological structure" of *The Prelude*, playing back some jackknife dive into "a chasm that is like a chiasmus in the way it both narrows and opens up."[1] But Wordsworth himself leaves me cold.

By cold I mean unmoved and unmoving, for it has long been my view that there is something insurmountable about Wordsworth, that the poetry is structured by a subterranean series of blockages that keep me from being involved in it, cajoled by any combination of affective, aesthetic, and intellectual prompts. The poet Nan Shepherd wrote of "a traffic of love" between herself and Scotland's Cairngorms mountain range; in his own immixture of nature-writing and *amour propre*, Wordsworth taps the fullness of that same thought to turn congestion into a form of intimacy, obstacles into channels of care.[2] I see that and yet, for me, these each feel uniquely impassive.

It's not like Wordsworth is a rebarbative poet; it's not like he pleads for a sympathy I might be compelled to withhold. So many of his experiences are familiar: disappointment and self-rebuke, the passion and fear of wildness—these are common enough, and I've known them too. Nor can I say, as others have, that my alienation from Wordsworth is political: I don't mind the sexism or the glacial sexuality, the turn against revolution and even reform. I don't mind the narcissism or the way it occasionally unfurled into full-blown nastiness ("A very pretty piece of paganism"), and like Hazlitt I'm unfazed by "the hebetude of [Wordsworth's] intellect and the meanness of his subject," happy to accept both as the calling cards of avant-garde innovation.[3]

In short, this isn't about critique; it's about a numbness that jump-starts irritation, an estrangement that cuts both ways. Why should Wordsworth fail me, and I him?

Recently it was suggested to me that I don't understand Wordsworth because I'm not English. This can't be true: I often think the only thing I understand is English poetry. Besides, why attribute to an accident of biography what might well be a matter of poetics? I'd rather not believe my resistance is meaningless or flatly identitarian, so this chapter is an effort to follow detachment into some better insight. Of course, whether I like Wordsworth or not is not anything to keep anyone up at night. What could, though, is how the poetic mode he develops—sober, a bit sodden, and yet tremoring with the concentrated force of momentum bound by meter—might produce a certain unintelligibility or intransigence, a poem facing us from behind a wall. Facing or, perhaps, fronting, as in the opening lines of "Michael":

> If from the public way you turn your steps
> Up the tumultuous brook of Green-head Gill,
> You will suppose that with an upright path
> Your feet must struggle; in such bold ascent
> The pastoral mountains front you, face to face.
> But, courage! for beside that boisterous Brook
> The mountains have all open'd out themselves,
> And made a hidden valley of their own.[4]

"Front" names the appearance of candor as concealment, for behind the prosopopoeia of the mountains' hard face lies a secret from which our attention is about to be redirected. The poem, after all, concerns neither the hidden valley nor any of the trail markers Wordsworth clusters around it but the shepherd Michael's unfinished sheepfold. It is to this ruin that Wordsworth's "story appertains," a curious verb that suggests a doubled or extraemphatic relevance, the story molded against its object like wax or gum ("M," 18).

The mountains turn out to be, in the colloquial sense, a front, a pretense, introducing the main line of "Michael" while continuing to keep their own counsel. They draw attention to deflect it and this might be said, too, of Wordsworth's poems: that they give off light without heat, face us without feeling, are opened out on a secret they're never going to divulge. As this passage suggests, it may well be that what the mountains hide is, simply, themselves, as if secrecy were their substance and to betray it would be killing.

"He has written to disclose a buried life," says David Bromwich, but "he does not pretend to know the meaning of those days."[5] If this chapter is about incomprehension, it is also a chapter about secrets, the ones we keep even from ourselves. These are taken or, more properly, *used* as a structure that solicits nescience in various guises—as attention, as annoyance, as paralysis, as compliance or willingness but never, pointedly, as the response to a seduction, because it is never the aim of Wordsworth's poetry to charm or entrap. My word for both this reticence and this bewilderment is *obscurity*, a poetic trope that has played a decisive role in the development of hermeneutics and, by extension, literary criticism.

Obscurity is the condition of being hard to understand, though not in the way William Empson means when he says that the long poems of modernism have acquired a greater dependence on notes and other critical apparatus as they have become more esoteric in their references ("Mr Eliot on *Shantih*").[6] This obscurity responds to a number of historical factors, among them an extension into ordinary consciousness of vocabularies on loan from specialized disciplines, like psychoanalysis and theoretical physics. Wordsworth's obscurity is historical in a very different domain. It is historical because it is involved in the reception of historical events, most obviously the metastasis of industrial capitalism and, more punctually, the unraveling of the French Revolution. It is historical, too, because it is the mode of figuration Wordsworth adopts to show the hiatus—the gap, break, lull, stutter—in life as it has hitherto been known, and as it cannot be known again.

As Geoffrey Hartman makes clear, this hiatus, or rather its poetic representation, is a form of traumatic knowledge, the barely tolerable wage of an experience that "bypasse[s] perception and consciousness" and is recollected only though its "perpetual troping."[7] Trauma may be universal, but Hartman notes the originary context of trauma *theory*, whose rise in the twentieth century intimates "our sense that violence is coming ever nearer, like a storm that may have already moved into the core of our being. The reality of violence," he continues, "not simply as external fate, but intrinsic to the psychological development of the human species, . . . is 'the fateful question' posed by Freud in the closing pages of *Civilization and its Discontents*."[8] That question, which asks what kinds of cultural forms might compensate for modernity's destruction of communal life, is also the "incumbent mystery" of Wordsworth's poetry.[9] How does the poetry of capital's storm look, and sound, and speak? How can it be written, and how can its writing be survived?

These riddles put the squeeze on Wordsworth, for this is what it means to be incumbent: to create pressure. They're also behind the burden Keats will convert into the ecstatic blankness of an unconditional sensitivity, welcoming the strain of the world until it cracks wide as freedom. But Keats is happy to risk his own dissolution (in truth he can hardly wait). Not so Wordsworth. For all its slight anachronism, the framework of trauma captures something essential about Wordsworth's lyric personality, namely the way it seems at once impinged upon and scaffolded by current events, by a violence called *now*. His poems need their obscurity, need secrets, need the storm but need its concealment even more. This is where their form begins.

I've begun by claiming my dislike of Wordsworth as a meaningful intuition, but I'm well aware that not everyone responds to him that way. For many people Wordsworth is a therapist or semisecular priest; others treat him daintily, as Mother Goose for grown-ups. Still, I hope that even the fans will agree that a lot of the poetry is obscure: mysterious, perplexing, hard to parse. They might also agree with the claim that the poetry is all these things without actually being hard to understand. Syntactically speaking, these are straightforward poems, easily rewritten as prose if the drift gets lost in lineation. They don't play bookish games or nod at secret intertexts. If they're metrically experimental, they are much less so than, say, these lines from *Don Juan*:

> "*Sodae sulphat. 3vj. 3fs. Mannae optim.*
> *Aq. fervent. f. 3ifs. 3ij. tinct. Sennae*
> *Haustus*" (And here the surgeon came and cupp'd him)
> "*Rx Pulv Com gr. iij. Ipecacuanhae*"
> (With more beside if Juan had not stopp'd 'em).[10]

By what species of courtesy (as Wordsworth might say) do we call this ottava rima? And yet, is there any question that Wordsworth is more challenging than Byron, and his poetry that much closer to the vanguard of modernity?

The business of this chapter is to consider how the frontedness of Wordsworth's poems—their austere articulation of themselves as manifest, or simply there—is built on their obscurity. How does writing so clear conceal so much? To begin, I'll look at obscurity as a poetic idiom, one moored to a well-known tradition linking figuration to prophecy. Mainstream antiquity and its Enlightenment revival saw obscurity as a consequence of bad writing or a lack of oratorical skill. At the same time, a competing strain within aesthetic theory takes it to be central to the historiographic work of literature, and to its potential for embedding intimations of the future in stories about the past. We should think, too, about the long shadow cast by Edmund Burke's *Enquiry* on any discussion of obscure representation in the Romantic period. All of these ideas work their way into Wordsworth's poetry, where they help sound the depths of its main concern: in brief, crisis and how we live it.

Another way to phrase this concern would be to say it's a problem of recognizing or registering historical causality. In the various prefaces, in his essays, and in his letters, Wordsworth is forever making bids to account for what Dorothy Wordsworth calls "the alteration in the times."[11] Still, his confidence in that effort is by no means robust. More often than not Wordsworth frets over poetry's inability to explain things, and this in a defensive crouch from which an apparent shortcoming is cast as a virtue, part of the set of features that distinguishes the poet from the man of science. And yet he remains fixated on the elementary subject of how life happens in time, specifically the strangely remembered, penumbral space of the recent and upsetting past. It is here that Wordsworth limns a hidden spectacle of cause and effect, one that *The Prelude* will at last displace, and personalize, into the providential question "Was it for this?"

With its famously veiled antecedent paired with a cleft construction, the question—which opens the two-part *Prelude* of 1799—is a neat example of the obscurity that identifies Wordsworth's meaning with an irremediable deficiency. *This* is typically characterized as having an absent or negative referent, but that's not quite true. For one thing, *this* is plainly the poem; for another, *this* is plainly the present-tense situation of the poet who is writing it, in all his itchy lassitude and self-postponement. *This* also moves further afield, its attenuated deictic aimed at a cloud of literary precedents, like the interrogative mood that launches Vergil's *Aeneid* and gets picked up by Pope, Thomson, Shenstone, and various other eighteenth-century lodestars.

The designatum of *this* is not empty. It is at once overstuffed and flamboyantly vague, and the yield of that unlikely alliance is a bundle of referents that are present and germane but can't be pinned down. These peel away from the demonstrative summoning them, not unlike the membranes cast off by more solid bodies in the fourth book of *De rerum natura*: "some more diffus'd, and broke," as "Fire, [and] heated Wood still breathe forth Smoke."[12] The more neglected *it*—"was *it* for this"—is what linguists call an existential proposition, the assertion of the subsistence of something that cannot necessarily be named. In this instance, *it* means everything that has gone before, from babydom to the poet's timorous now; it means, too, the steady cadence of iambs that unfurl a thinly intelligible past to discover in it a thinly intelligible present, a this that is hardly there.

And so if we think this opening passage is asking how Wordsworth's childhood might have prepared him for the unfinished task of his poetic maturity, we arrive at that conclusion with no hard evidence to show for it. We can guess what Wordsworth means; we can basically grasp it. Nonetheless, everything in *The Prelude* confirms that our guesses are provisional, even crude, that we squeeze sense from sound and pretend we don't feel it slipping through our fingers. In earlier work, most obviously in the first edition of *Lyrical Ballads*, the reader in search of an aphoristic payload is shrugged off as someone who likes books too much and the great outdoors too little. In *The Prelude* and, I'll argue, in "Michael," the stakes change, becoming intensively formal and historiographic. In these poems, we see the development of a way of writing that stands words at a distance from whatever they might convey. Arguments spin into bluster, confessions into digressions, and the overall effect is that of a poem looking up from under glass—up, and often away.

It is this impression of an actively deteriorating intimacy between a claim and its gist, of smoke floating up between what is said and what is meant, that the phrase "Wordsworth's obscurity" means to describe. Plenty of poststructuralists have found Wordsworth on similar terrain, entranced by the purity of things in themselves from which human history is ostensibly estranged. I am indebted to them, especially to Hartman's mistrust of exegesis, and to Paul Fry's elegant spin on a Wordsworthian ontology that makes itself known in the eruption of mute life into language. I more or less agree with them too, and yet I want to know why Wordsworth, whose work is so evidently unable to make claims about where we are and how we got here, still seems to believe that he is writing poetry about "the historical milieu"—about "the violence in France," "the slower trauma of industrialization," and an "apocalyptic rate of change and nature-loss."[13]

In a letter sent to Charles Fox along with a copy of the second edition of *Lyrical Ballads*, Wordsworth suggests Fox have a look at "Michael" and "The Brothers" to see "the most calamitous effect[s] which [have] followed the measures which have lately been pursued in this country," among them "the spreading of manufactures," "heavy taxes," "workhouses [and] houses of industry," all "superadded to the increasing disproportion between the price of labour and that of the necessaries of life." The most telling moment in the letter comes at its close, when Wordsworth submits that his art "might co-operate, however feebly," with Fox's efforts "to stem [these] and other evils with which the country is labouring."[14] Obscurity is the figure of this feeble cooperation, of the frayed relationship between the poem and the circumstances it is trying to report and correct. It is the husk or exhalation of a difficulty that goes deeper than syntax, that comes with being in the midst of a quickening that can't be clocked.

The calamity form, as I have defined it, is the reception and circulation of disaster as no one's fault or, alternatively, as the fault of an ideology rather than an agent, entity, or process. Like commodities, calamities make their social appearance as self-contained quantities endowed with life, where *life* signifies a fantastic principle of free movement and groundless independence. I don't want to push this analogy too far. Still, with Wordsworth we find that, lacking a theory of the commodity and any interest in producing one, the poet spends his time chronicling the obsolescence of diagnostic or otherwise informative histories in a world gone strangely fluid and flat. The reasons for that transformation are for Wordsworth poetically inarticulable; when they do not come, obscurity must.

Obscurity, on my account, is the aesthetic token of a cognitive impasse, the look and feel of not knowing how we got from point A to point B. This might seem like an odd way to characterize the work of a writer whose experiments in both lyric and epic registers have been so meaningful to historicist criticism. All the same, my feelings might be summed up by this line from the third book of the longer *Prelude*: "We see but darkly/ Even when we look behind us."[15] Obscurity is proper to this dark seeing, a style of apprehension quite unlike the blindness that poem so often uses to signal the turmoil of childhood, of being a person among other people, of nature and its indifference to us. No vehicle of the sublime or the transcendence it teases, and yet unmistakably present in the poetry itself, obscurity becomes an empirical anchor to a present that defies empirical evaluation, at least of the kind Wordsworth himself can imagine or bear.

After surveying obscurity from Quintilian to George Campbell, I'll turn to "Michael" and its elaboration of history as a vagueness problem, a query into the ontological status of indeterminacy itself. The last section confronts *The Prelude*. Looking closely at the structure of the poem's zigzagging lines, I find what might be called a prosody of damage, a nervous rhythm that can never catch up to the desire for tranquility Wordsworth insists he is ready to fulfill. Here there is no one secret, no single event cloaked in the nearly forgotten or almost unspeakable. There is, rather, an atmosphere of general nondisclosure, chaperoned by Wordsworth's astonishingly prescient, proto-psychoanalytic account of how people forget their own lives. You could say it's the lures of this account—its precocity, its lenity, its sheer charisma—that maneuver a more public political history out of the picture. And maybe it is.

* * *

The obscure is hidden, or unheard of. An obscure person is someone with no public profile or social cachet. Wordsworth's Lucy is obscure in this sense and another: half hidden from the eye, she is nearly invisible but decisively present. To be obscure also means to be hard to understand. Heraclitus was called *ho skoteinos*, the obscure, because his philosophy was so abstruse, and so was the third-century BCE poem the *Alexandra* (*to skoteinon poiêma*). In his review of *The Excursion*, Francis Jeffrey gives us a Wordsworth who is "more obscure than a Pindaric poet of the seventeenth century." "The doctrine which [*The Excursion*] is intended to enforce," Jeffrey continues, is "by no means certain" and, at the same time, trite and overrehearsed. The final verdict is damning: the poem is "a puerile ambition of singularity engrafted on an unlucky predilection for truisms, and an affected passion for simplicity and humble life, most awkwardly combined with a taste for mystical refinements and all the gorgeousness of obscure phraseology."[16]

Like *catachresis*, *obscurity* could be an umbrella term for poetic language. Catachresis is the abuse of words, obscurity their confounding. Insofar as the entire project of figuration depends on the unsettlement of signs from restricted referents, you could say that using a word fraudulently (to mean something it doesn't) or indistinctly (to mean something cryptic or imprecise) is simply what a poet does. This, as we've partly seen, is John Hamilton's hypothesis in *Soliciting Darkness*, his study of Pindar that begins with the ending of the Second Olympian and ends with the beginning of *Hyperion*, Hölderlin's novel of the late 1790s. For Hamilton, it is essential to "resist reading obscurity—or any one of its discursive varieties—ambiguity, difficulty, incoherence—merely as a *moment* toward some elucidation or ultimate clarification."[17] Obscurity is not an error but an assertion, and it proclaims darkness as an object worthy of study and appreciation. To treat it with respect, instead of viperous contempt à la Jeffrey, is to uncover a poetic tradition keyed to the existential drama of unintelligible life. It is also, and crucially, to toil in the long durée of literary-critical labor: "Insofar as it has consistently propagated issues of failed understanding," the "*traditio obscura* . . . is of the utmost importance for understanding all tradition," for "it has solicited an entire range of techniques, poetic and hermeneutic, that work in and through [its own] impossibility."[18]

You may not notice it right away, but both Jeffrey and Hamilton imply that obscurity is for smart people—or else the well educated. Wordsworth's obscure phraseology is out of step with his downhome parsons and peddlers, who break into their "magnificent orations with two or three awkward notices" about "selling winter raiment in the country," or about how "the changes in the state of society" have affected the rural economy; to understand the obscure tradition, you need to know your Greek and German, your Nietzsche and Cowley, your mythology and your aesthetic theory.[19] It's an assumption backed by the history of Western literary criticism, in which obscure language is almost always associated with pedantry, and with a highbrow discourse that revels in being hard to follow. Take Quintilian's swipe at those writers who, "in their horror of commonplace forms of expression," opt for roundabout phrasings that vex the limits of understanding, not to mention breath (*spiritus*). It's a fault he lays principally at the door of the Greeks:

As I find in Livy, there was once some teacher who would command his students to obscure whatever they were saying, using the Greek word *skotison,* "darken it!" From whence we get the extraordinary compliment, "So much the better: I couldn't understand it myself."[20]

The imperative will resurface in Diderot's *Salon* of 1767 as "soyez ténébreux," a good-natured crack at the expense of midcentury pictorial trends.[21] Meanwhile, a few decades later George Campbell will echo Quintilian's lampoon of obscurity as the rhetorical hangover of "school-metaphysics," an "address . . . to the patroness of sophistry as well as dullness" expressive of absolutely nothing except "an insatiable appetite . . . for absurdity and contradiction."[22]

Skotos comes from the Indo-European verb *skeutō*, meaning to cover or shut; hence its connection to the Greek σκίρον, or canopy. The etymological innuendo is that to be obscure is to appear both present and featureless, and that the effects of obscurity pertain to contours rather than mass, to the surface area of objects rather than objects themselves. In early Christian theology, especially in the writings of Augustine, it is this view of obscurity as a silhouette, scaffold, or screen that licenses its use for prophecy, or what will come to be known as figural interpretation. For Augustine as for his inheritors, everything in the world is obscure; what we take to be real is just a shadow of what is true, but these shadows are also real, which is to say they have a historical existence. The job of the biblical scholar is to pore over shadows to see both what they are and what they hide. Thus the Christian spin on obscurity doubles down on its classical alignment with occult authority while directing it, in Hamilton's words, *toward* some exegetical purpose. No longer just a rhetorical trope, obscurity now carries multiple interlocking burdens: hermeneutic, ecclesiastical, literary, and historical.

The origin of Augustine's thinking about obscurity is the passage from First Corinthians climaxing in "blepomen gar arti di esoptrou en ainigmati, tote de prosopon pros prosopon"—per the King James Bible, "for now we see through a glass, darkly; but then face to face."[23] It's the same passage Wordsworth rewrites as "We see but darkly/Even when we look behind us," in a characteristic deflation of Pauline metaphysics. Paul's argument is, of course, future oriented. It looks to a postapocalyptic moment when both God and God's truth will be known at last to us, and when the boundary between the world's aspect and its numinous foundations will dissolve. In Augustine's hands, this progress is also a movement from vehicles to tenors. Today we experience the world figuratively, tweaked and curved; one day we'll see it naked, at the end of the world as we know it. This is where modern hermeneutics begins: what you see is not at all what you ought to get if you think hard enough about it.

Since no one knows what the world will look like on the other side

of its negation, Augustine trains his energies on the nature and function of figures themselves, and on what it would mean to treat material
reality as an adumbration, a shadow outline of some more true thing.
From here he evolves his idea of figural interpretation, or the analysis of
figures—persons or events—from Scripture as both historically real and
prophecies of things to come. An erstwhile teacher of rhetoric, Augustine
turns reading into a devotional practice, and his writings on figural interpretation capture early Christianity's blend of committed historicism
and insurrectionary metaphysics. On Augustine's account, Old Testament patriarchs like Adam or Moses are *both* actually existing individu-
als and prefigurations of Jesus, who, as *both* a living human being and as
the Messiah, will fulfill in *both* sublunary and atemporal dimensions the
promise they incarnate. It's a take on Scripture that, in Erich Auerbach's
pithy summation, "creates a connection between two events or persons
in which one signifies not only itself but also the other . . . [so] that one is
also encompassed or fulfilled by the other."[24]

So far, so good. We should add, though, that Augustine's figures do
not exhaust their meaning by distributing it over two referents. Christian
thought always has the end of the world as its interpretive horizon, and
so Adam and Moses, as figurae of Jesus, not only signify Jesus but also
signify the Christ who will redeem that world (our world) after or as it
is destroyed. Figures are thus threefold, intimating the future from the
perspective of a past that looks forward to the abolition of time itself, its
dispersal into the static Kingdom. This event is as historical as any other,
which is to say that it will happen in due course, at the end of a linear
progression of ages. It is the last event that will ever be called one.

All this is to begin to show how Augustine's ideas about obscurity are
tied to his ideas about history, to the possibility of knowing what is to
come and of imagining the suspension, even the annihilation, of time
as a cosmic sequential order. *Pace* Auerbach, Augustine is much more
interested in obscurity than in figuration all by its lonesome, even going
so far as to pronounce obscurity a necessary element of Scripture. It is
obscuritas, and not *figura*, that inspires his most detailed thinking about
the theological purchase of occlusive speech or writing. This is nowhere
more obvious than in his obsessive scrutiny of Paul and in particular
1 Corinthians 13:12, in Latin: "videmus nunc per speculum in aenigmate,
tunc autem facie ad faciem" (for now we see through a glass in an enigma,
but then face to face). And what more is an enigma, Augustine writes,
but "an obscure allegory" ("aenigma est autem . . . obscura allegoria")?[25]

It may seem that the King James translation, which swaps out "in an
enigma" for the humble "darkly," has taken a wrong turn, but the choice
is appropriate, even inspired. Augustine took *aenigma* to be the Greek

version of *obscuritas*, a "trope"—to use his word—introducing an "obscure allegory" or else an "image [that is] obscure, or difficult to see through."[26] Elsewhere, enigma is nothing but an "obscure parable" that's especially hard to understand ("aenigma est autem obscura parabola, quae difficile intelligitur") or an "obscure and . . . problematic type of allegory" ("obscura et . . . problematica allegoriae species"). All this will be apparent to those familiar "with the books that contain the doctrine of those modes of speech the Greeks call tropes," and who are accustomed to teasing out manifest from implied or, better, prognosticated content ("doctrina quaedem de locutionem modies quos graeci tropos vocant"). What is obscure is dark; what is dark is an enigma; what is enigmatic is allegorical; and allegories are tropes. All these are hidden in shadows ("abscondita tenebrarum"), and all will be revealed in time.[27]

It's crucial to remember that, for Augustine, the nature of revelation and the apocalyptic event perched on its outer edge remains occult; the endpoint of figural interpretation is always behind a fog. We apprehend reality in a daze, as a watered-down projection of God's likeness; with the passing of historical time we come closer to the ultimate fulfillment of God's will in time's end, but our progress happens in the dark, in a state of perpetual doubt and partial confusion. In this model, obscurity is a master trope for our incompetence to history, and for our impassioned falter after the long-term significance of what we barely know now. This less confident way of thinking about theology and, more to the point, about its figurative vocabularies allows the latter to serve as instances of and conduits to the rational confusion whose own tropic exemplum is the obscure, the shadow at least partially divested of its capacity to foreshadow. For Augustine, *obscuritas* is both a figure and the impact of figuration, open to being interpreted but never to being made plain. It is also the signature of a half-sighted presentism: as the elliptical image of the glass in Paul suggests, when we look at the present we see only ourselves, and not very well.

Wordsworth is interested in two versions of the *traditio obscura*: the one that treats obscurity as a property of objects requiring no further explanation or analysis, and the one that treats obscurity as an allurement, an *X* marking the spot where more thinking needs to be done. The first belongs to rhetoric and is purely secular; the second belongs to theology, and more significantly to a worldview committed to the coincidence of literary representation and historical knowledge. I should say, rather, that the second belongs *initially* to theology; by the time Wordsworth gets his hands on it, the Enlightenment has recast history as a secular discipline, one more or less off the hook for treating all worldly events as portents of some apocalyptic apogee to come. Still, the allegorical disposition of obscurity is hard to shake, even when its associations become nominally or explicitly profane. Whether in the "queer baroque" of the early modern poet Luis de Góngora, whom Salvador Oropesa finds using *obscuritas* to define the proverbial closet, or in Alexander Baumgarten's Leibnizian pronouncement that poetic representations are "obscure and clear" ("obscurae et clarae sunt repraesentationes poeticae"), there remains an instinct that there is something beneath, behind, or beyond the shadow image.[28]

Allegory gets a bad rap among the English Romantics, who have long been said to prefer the many-fathomed instantaneity of the symbol. But the threadbare symbol-allegory debate muscles out the far more interesting and almost certainly more influential contributions of bread-and-butter rhetorical theory to the poetry of the late eighteenth century. For one thing, it is the sometimes mind-numbing, sometimes hilariously acerbic treatises on good and bad writing that the Romantics were exposed to in school, as part of a general emergence of literature as an instrument of class mobility, and so it is to these treatises that they frequently if not exclusively react.[29] For another, Enlightenment rhetoric is heavily indebted to contemporary developments in the philosophy of mind, and to the same slightly offbeat empiricism we find in Wordsworth's poetry and prose. From the unflinchingly corporeal language of the Preface, which ties and times verse to the fickle metronome of sensation, to the ubiquitous claim that "deep feelings" push objects "[u]pon [the] mind like substances," the fingerprints of this pedagogy are everywhere.[30]

The ambition of writers like Campbell, Hugh Blair, Adam Smith, and dozens of other less illustrious scholars and teachers was to apply insights gleaned from Locke, Hume, and Reid to a new version of literary criticism, one that began to elaborate the pragmatic intuition that words are deeds. Language, writes Campbell, is "the instrument of conveying [the] sentiments" of the writer or speaker "into [the] minds" of his audience, and successful communication is no less than a compounding of "language and thought" as if they were "body and soul" (*PR* 2.2). Statements like these rest on the conviction that ideas have to be felt to be believed, that they have to be funneled through the body and monographed on the mind. Campbell's theory of rhetoric holds that speech and writing can and should be constructed as appercipient objects, which the mind processes no differently than it processes rocks and buildings and cats and road signs. Its helpmeet in this effort is perspicuity, which, as Campbell says, "originally and properly implies transparency, such as may be ascribed to air, glass, water, or any other medium, through which material objects are viewed" (*PR* 2.16). The untroubled transmission of words as though they were things, the easy conversion of content into impact, is put at risk whenever the words in question get in their own way:

> Now, in corporeal things, if the medium through which we look at any object be perfectly transparent, our whole attention is fixed on the object; we are scarcely sensible that there is a medium which intervenes, and can hardly be said to perceive it. But if there be any flaw in the medium, if we see through it but dimly, if the object be imperfectly represented, or if we know it to be misrepresented, our attention is immediately taken off the object, to the medium. We are then desirous to discover the cause, either of the dim and confused representation, or of the misrepresentation of things which it exhibits, [so] that the defect in vision may be supplied by judgement. (*PR* 2.17)

"The case of language," Campbell concludes, "is precisely similar": "the least obscurity, ambiguity, or confusion in the style instantly removes the attention from the sentiment to the expression," and language loses the chance to disappear behind its curtain (*PR* 2.17).

The allusion to Paul, and to Augustine's reception of him, is unmistakable. Obscure language is that which we see through but dimly, although, in this case, what we're trying to get a look at is not impossible to view; it's just being presented badly. Campbell is so miffed by the harm done by the dim and confused that he gives almost the entirety of his chapter "Of Perspicuity" over to the delineation of its opposite. Obscurity, we learn, can come from poorly considered syntax, or arrangement; from using the same word in different senses; from missing or uncertain referents; from technical terms; from long sentences; from confusion of thought; from affectation of excellence; from want of meaning; from exuberance of metaphor; from "empty show[s] of science"; and from other such blunders and indiscretions (*PR* 2.126). In all cases, "the direct tendency of obscurity" acts "to confound our ideas, or rather to blot them altogether" in a mutual deformation of boundary and breadth (*PR* 2.133).

Campbell's obscurity is a bad thing, but it is more of an irritant than a catastrophe, ink dribbled on a clean page or a bug smashed against a windshield. In this it has a certain rapport with the quality of drag or strain calibrating J. H. Prynne's use of *resistance* in his 1961 essay "Resistance and Difficulty," a word Prynne tellingly associates with "the reserve or disagreement of [his] neighbor" and with "primary evidence for his really being there." The core of this short essay is Destutt de Tracy's description of inertial force in the first part of *Éléments d'idéologie*. "Sans elle, nous n'aurions pas connu les corps étrangers à nous, ni même ne nôtre" ("without it, we wouldn't know bodies foreign to us, nor even our own"). From this Prynne derives a notion of resistance as a sensuous encounter with what is "outside" us, whether it's the cold or cantankerous neighbor or "the stone's hard palpable weight."[31] Here, poetry comes to be tested against a physical world by whose laws it is also governed, and whose enrollment in variously trying forms of life it must share.

As for difficulty, it serves as the internal measure of the external impression of resistance—a model of affective response that turns a solidly eighteenth-century account of sentiments as impressions of reflection craftily inside out. Everything in this model is ontologically motivated and can never be got past; there is no veil on the other side of which resistance gives way and difficulty's burden is lifted—this is just how things are in a world of things. It seems fair to say that Prynne's resistance and what I've been calling obscurity are closely related if not identical. Each pills the fabric of the world to remind us that the world has substance, in which language participates. As a late-breaking entry in or else strategic revival of Romanticism's serial inquiries into the experience of mass, "Resistance and Difficulty" counts poetry among a relation of forces that accost one another, that are part of the world and obliged to it. To ask after the meaning of figuration in this context is to insist that the parameters of the question and of its answer remain material, too, that they never impose an eschatological frame on purpose or consider making as an appraisal of spirit. It is also to insist that any materialist conception of history, any sustained inquiry into real life, attend to physical laws as much as economic ones, to the forces and relations of natural production among others that might be named.

You may not need Marx to arrive at this way of looking at things, nor even Wordsworth's paratactical half-claim that metrical language has or simply is "the sense of difficulty overcome."[32] You do, however, need an empiricist philosophy of rhetoric. You also need to abandon any fixed association between obscurity, difficulty, and the wild and wooly character called the sublime. Burke, of course, uses both obscurity and difficulty as synonyms as well as exemplars of sublimity, but for him these qualities are anything but material. It is instead axiomatic for Burke that the emotional power or percussiveness of any phenomenon lies in inverse proportion to its intelligibility: that's why a verbal description that "raises a very obscure and imperfect idea of . . . objects" elicits "a stronger emotion than . . . the best painting," why poetry has "a more powerful dominion over the passions" than visual art.[33] In Campbell's *Philosophy of Rhetoric* the opposite is true. Things we don't understand are at worst an annoyance, at best a bore, and all the more of a headache for being vaporous or out of sight.

Certainly Wordsworth often yearns for the Miltonic achievement of being "dark, uncertain, confused, terrible, and sublime to the last de-gree."[34] And yet I wonder if we haven't been too quick to draw the line from Burke's hectic genius to, say, *The Prelude*, leaving out the deflation-ary contributions of a more vernacular Enlightenment. At the very least, the record shows that obscurity in the eighteenth century was not always a name for the fearsome and inspiring. It was, just as significantly, a name for infelicitous communication and missed signals.

No: "the Burkean trombone" is not Wordsworth's instrument, and it will not do for the still sad music of humanity.[35] His obscure is a darkness in the sinews of an object, a property consubstantial with whatever it tucks away. It doesn't exploit feeling but rebuffs it, resists it, like those grim vertical surfaces that slice through *The Prelude* (solitary cliffs, drowned man, discharged solider), or like Lucy, whose life and death pass little or lightly detected. In the simplest terms, obscurity stops Wordsworth's poetry from making comprehensive sense of things that happen and exist in the world. Less simply, this state of affairs has special consequences for thinking about history as an aggregate of causes and their effects, or for using it as a road map of what's to come. It is to these consequences that the next section turns.

* * *

We are going back, now, to the mountains of "Michael." From that poem's first word we find ourselves in the open ends of the conditional, whose promise becomes more vivid as the next several lines spool forth:

> If from the public way you turn your steps
> Up the tumultuous brook of Green-head Gill,
> You will suppose that with an upright path
> Your feet must struggle; in such bold ascent
> The pastoral Mountains front you, face to face.
> But, courage! for beside that boisterous Brook
> The mountains have all open'd out themselves,
> And made a hidden valley of their own. ("M," 1–8).

The climax to this loitering preamble introduces the "one object" to which the poem's story appertains, the "straggling heap of unhewn stones" that, over three hundred lines later, is finally given the name "Sheep-fold" ("M," 15–17, 334). I'll return to that name in a moment, but for now I'd like to note how quickly these lines revise the pastoral tableau from idyllic to uncompromising, and how deeply this revision embeds itself in the poem's time, at once metrical and historical. Prosodically speaking, the fifth line lops *pastoral* from three syllables to two, with an amplified emphasis on the first beat: if the green meadows of pastoral have been traded for rocks and crags, so has its mythic time been wrenched into the more proximate and historically particular frame of the *past*. Thus "Michael" sticks to what will prove its exemplary rhetorical logic of the "unhewn," already surfacing through the word (*pastoral*) into which Wordsworth's verse cuts without cleaving.

The accent, in these several introductory lines, is on edges: where words end and begin, where stones become heaps and heaps sheepfolds, where time past abuts time possible and *if* propels itself into *then*. Another way to put this would be to say that "Michael" greets us with a question about cause and effect and how one kind of thing turns into another kind of thing, as well as how this sort of change, like the word unhewn itself, suggests all at once an action, its absence, and its undoing.

"We may define a cause," writes Hume, "to be an object, followed by another, and where all the objects similar to the first are followed by objects similar to the second."[36] In "Michael," the unfinished sheepfold provides Wordsworth with a fit emblem of uncertain or occluded causation that, in turn, seems to bar the poem from offering a richly diagnostic account of contemporary history, in particular the history of industrial development. If the letter to Fox pitches "Michael" as a piece of social activism, its tale of a breakdown in the filial bond of the shepherd Michael and his prodigal son Luke—sent to London to earn the money that could discharge his uncle's debt, which it has fallen on his father to repay—never works up into the promised excoriation of political economy circa 1800.

When it comes to Luke and Michael's downfall it is hard to say that "if the first object had not been, the second never had existed."[37] The poem seems rather to eclipse historical detail in order to figure the present as it figures the sheepfold: at once unfinished and already destroyed. What we have in "Michael" is not a story about the shift from an agricultural past to a modernity of manufactures but writing that disputes "aboutness" as a means of inducing a testimonial relationship between poetry and history. Here, time becomes mere tense, as the disruption of the patrimonial order puts new and unlivable weight on the actions of the subject—on the lyric protagonist who discovers, little by little, the magnitude of his own inconsequence.

Little by little is how Michael builds his sheepfold, or rather how he builds what never gets built. If the poem's opening lines cast the sheepfold in terms that are maximally abstract ("one object"), its middle and final sections render it minimally present, on the far side of a series of syntactical obstructions. The first explicit reference to the structure comes couched behind an infinitive—"In that deep valley, Michael had de-signed/To build a Sheep-fold"—and the same structure and vocabulary are retained in the lines that wind the poem toward its devastating finale: "And to that hollow Dell from time to time/Did he repair, to build the Fold of which/His flock had need" ("M," 334–35, 469–71). Ten lines later, the verb *to build* migrates into the ambiguous phrase "He at the build-ing of this Sheep-fold wrought," which might mean either that Michael continues to work at the task of building or that he works on the kind of building called a sheepfold ("M," 480). Nothing of outsize significance hangs on whether *building* in this instance is the gerund form of *to build* or just an unassuming common noun. The point is the small, telling inter-val these essentially extraneous words place between agent and action, so that what Michael does is strangely uncoupled from what he achieves. Similarly suggestive is the repetition of *wrought* across the close quarters of the last two verse paragraphs, from that cliffhanging phrase "He at the building of this Sheep-fold wrought" (and then he died) to the cluster of enjambed lines that finish off the poem:

> The Cottage which was nam'd The Evening Star
> Is gone, the ploughshare has been through the ground
> On which it stood; great changes have been wrought
> In all the neighbourhood, yet the Oak is left
> That grew beside their Door; and the remains
> Of the unfinished Sheep-fold may be seen
> Beside the boisterous brook of Green-head Gill. ("M," 485–91)

Wrought is, of course, the past tense of *work*, a word that appears in "Mi-chael" no fewer than fifteen times: "The Housewife plied her own pe-culiar work"; "The Shepherd went about his daily work/With confident and cheerful thoughts"; "'This was a work for us, and now, my Son,/It is a work for me,'" and so on ("M," 128–29, 447–48, 395). When it comes to the working of those great changes, this final, metaphoric applica-tion of *wrought* sorts the concreteness of Michael's effort out from the anonymous and impersonal advancement of historical change, which is diffuse, uncentered, and at best obliquely conveyed. We might note too the difference between saying *wrought at* and simply *wrought*, a differ-ence that means a shift from transitive to intransitive forms of labor and thus arraigns at the level of the poetic sentence the extinction of real or objective labor from a rural scene subject to a double ghosting of the national landscape and the national economy.

As the mainspring of the poem's *obscuritas*, the sheepfold takes the measure of this extinction, its unfinished ambit "falling away," as Dorothy

Wordsworth puts it in her journal, from its final cause. For neither the first nor the last time, William seems to have sponged both the broad outline and the punctum of his poem from Dorothy's locodescriptive diary, which records a walk "up Greenhead Gill in search of a sheepfold" and the discovery of one "built nearly in the form of a heart unequally divided."[38] Like her brother's poem, Dorothy's prose is winding and equivocal, the sheepfold it surrounds ducking in and out of view between a suite of elegiac approximations: built nearly, in the form, unequally, divided. The Wordsworths reach a consensus on what is most suggestive about this humble object, namely how the sheepfold's uncertain status *as* an object of a particular kind helps set "Michael" against a view of poetry as a forensic or exegetical genre that approaches history in terms of a predestined doom, or whose orientation toward the future is confidently oracular: "When thou return'st," Michael promises Luke, "thou in this place will see/A work which is not here" ("M," 423–24).

Left shuddering in space, this future indicative anticipates the marriage of aesthetic presence and referential absence that (as I say in my introduction) distinguishes the conceptual art of the 1960s and 1970s. My argument there is that conceptualism inherits and adapts an eighteenth-century poetics committed to prying language apart from denotation. What we have in "Michael," or more specifically in the sheepfold, is a site-specific entity ("in this place") that becomes a placeholder for an object that is never produced and for an event that never comes to pass: when Luke returns, which he won't, he will see something that is not there, except it is. This piecemeal play of appearance and retreat is, again, a routine scripted into the syntactical feints and gridlock of Wordsworth's poetry, through which the sheepfold always arises on the far side of an intention—poised behind an infinitive—or half hidden by metonymy, as in the nearly duplicate descriptions "a straggling heap of unhewn stones" and "a heap of stones . . . thrown together, ready for the work" ("M," 337–38). It is also, I'd like to suggest, encoded in the use of *heap*, a word shimmering between the plural form of its own composition and the singular form of its perception: "one object," "a work."

Neither one nor many, the sheepfold, as heap, foregrounds its own ontological indeterminacy or, to use a technical term, its vagueness, which Daniel Wright—in an essay on George Eliot—skillfully interprets as "a dialectical model of the manifold ways in which difference and sameness interact in the genesis of form."[39] A vague concept is one whose formal extension lacks easily locatable boundaries, as when it's not clear what kinds of things that concept includes in its purview or when the concept does or does not apply. On a sign prohibiting vehicles in the park, the concept vehicle is vague: Certainly it includes cars, but what about skates or scooters? The concept of baldness is vague insofar as we can tell when a person is definitely bald and when a person is definitely not bald but remain at a loss when it comes to cases in between these two well-defined limits; in other words, it is impossible to specify just how much hair a person would have to lose before she became bald, but not at all impossible to tell when a person *is* bald. Thus, in Eliot's own words, "as knowledge continues to grow by its alternating processes of distinction & combination . . . it arrives at the conception of wholes composed of parts more & more multiplied and highly differenced, yet more & more absolutely bound together by various conditions of common likeness or mutual dependence."[40]

Historically, this genre of knowledge is associated with the sorites paradox, otherwise known as the paradox of the heap—*soros* meaning heap in Ancient Greek. While one grain of sand is clearly not a heap, and two grains of sand are clearly not a heap, if we continue adding grains to our pile, at some point we will have to say it is a heap—but when? We're sure when the vague term definitely applies, we're sure when it definitely does not apply, and we're definitely unsure about where the line between "applies" and "does not apply" stops and starts. In "Michael," the sheep-fold likewise appears in and is obscured by its constitutive forms, forms that are contiguous and interdependent but nonidentical. Those include everything from "the first stone of the Sheep-fold" laid down by Luke to the straggling heap of unhewn stones to the one and simple object those stones make up to the stones that never make it off the ground:

> And to that hollow Dell from time to time
> Did he repair, to build the Fold of which
> His flock had need. 'Tis not forgotten yet
> The pity which was then in every heart
> For the Old Man—and 'tis believed by all
> That many and many a day he thither went,
> And never lifted up a single stone. ("M," 469–75)

Wordsworth's counting begets a sequence of retractions: in these lines, "single" means "zero," a zero that invisibly and inaudibly concludes the reductive pattern running from "all" to "many" to "single," a "single" whose negation by "never" winnows its already slender claim on the world of human action and purpose. Not for nothing does "repair," with its double valence of "go" and "fix," sit alongside "to build," the comma that separates them a hinge in the eccentric chronology that has Michael coming back to mend what has never been made. Thrice in its final seventeen lines the poem invokes the sheepfold and twice calls it "unfinished," the sug-

gestion being, I suspect, that the sheepfold is less a sheepfold than an idea
lending its name to the parts that could make it matter ("M," 481, 490).

This is pretty simple: the sheepfold is a sorites series, a whole that
demonstrates the difficulty of assessing wholeness, a quality that cannot
be quantified but that is also subordinate to the mutual dependence of
its cases. It is obscure, for we might see it without noticing it, and it is
also an emblem of obscurity as a trope of what I've called dark seeing,
of the disarrangement that comes with trying to track the before and
after of a process whose effect is to annul easy identifications of "before"
and "after." That process is the full set of historical developments that
conceive Michael's undoing, that spoil the way of life—"ancient uncouth
[and] country"—for which he and the sheepfold both very shakily stand
("M," 113).

As usual, Wordsworth sets those developments at a distance from the
action of the poem, leaving them unnamed and underdescribed. On the
one hand, this would seem to be the very opposite of the lyric activism
of a near-contemporary like John Clare, whose poems work in adverbial
overtime to yoke world-historical causes to their local effects ("*Thus* came
enclosure . . . freedom's cottage *soon* was thrust aside"; "Who worked me
till I couldnt stand/And crush me *now* Im down"; "I've *often* thought,
the day appeared so fine,/How beautiful if such a place were mine;/
But, having naught, I *never* feel alone"; etc.).[41] On the other, it might anticipate Georgi Plekhanov's appeal to the sorites series to repudiate the
"naïve" formula "'Yes is yes, and no is no,'" the catchphrase of a positivist
historicism that idealizes verifiability in its account of the world.[42] Such
straightforward diagnoses of what is and is not, or what does and does
not exist, are appropriate "when we are asked a question as to the reality
of an object which already exists." However,

> when an object is as yet only in course of becoming, we may often have
> a good reason for hesitating as to our reply. When we see a man who has
> lost most of the hair from his cranium, we say that he is bald. But how
> are we to determine at what precise moment the loss of the hair of the
> head makes a man bald?
>
> To every definite question as to whether an object has this charac-
> teristic or that, we must respond with a yes or a no. As to that there
> can be no doubt whatever. But how are we to answer when an object is
> undergoing a change, when it is in the act of losing a given characteristic
> or is only in course of acquiring it? A definite answer should, of course,
> be the rule in these cases likewise. But the answer will not be a definite
> one unless it is couched in accordance with the formula "Yes is no, and
> no is yes." ("DL," 114)

Plekhanov's argument turns first on an analogy between philosophical logic and the philosophy of history, and secondly on an application of the former to the latter. To reason poorly about baldness is to assume that there is some "precise moment" at which the presence of hair becomes its absence; likewise, to reason poorly about the progressive mutation of class struggle is to assume that the contents of history are always "distinguished by . . . [the] marked solidity" of "indestructible substance" ("DL," 113). The dialectical materialism that is Plekhanov's stated quarry does not, however, simply posit two epistemic poles (the "yes" and the "no") and refer those contents to one or the other. Rather, it borrows from the paradox of the heap and the logic of contradiction the sorites supplies to situate and to describe change within a realm of ontological equivocality—to describe it, that is, as vague. The heap gives Plekhanov, as it gives Wordsworth, a concrete vocabulary for parsing that which is not concrete at all, namely "objects"—including composite objects, like historical situations—"permanently in a state of more or less rapid change" ("DL," 115).

Even that phrase—*permanently in a state of more or less rapid change*— reproduces the boldness of Plekhanov's formula, which strives to make materially present and positive that which would otherwise register as simple absence or negation. It's possible to be divided on the philosophical question of whether there actually is a clear-cut boundary between heap and nonheap; perhaps there is, but we will never determine where it lies, or perhaps there is not, and borderline cases of this sort just don't have truth values. Plekhanov swivels between these postures and thus keeps both in play, pooling stability together with variation and variation with terms of unfixed degree ("more or less") to affirm that some kinds of objects might be at once real, unknowable, and beyond adjudications like true or false. "Motion," he writes, "is a contradiction in action" ("DL," 117). From the degenerative progress of the sheepfold that is uncertainly a sheepfold to the boomerang of the logical sentence that defies the testament of the senses, vagueness becomes a principle of historical movement that gives simultaneously doubtful and incontrovertible evidence of historical rupture.

I don't have nor am I likely to find confirmation that Wordsworth was thinking about the paradox of the heap when he wrote a sorites series into "Michael." That said, it seems worth bearing in mind that Coleridge, in his *Biographia Literaria*, explains the project that would become *Lyrical Ballads* by presenting his own objections to the sort of poetry where "a point [is] looked for at the end of each second line, and the whole [is] as it were a sorites, or, if I may exchange a logical metaphor for a grammatical one, a conjunctive disjunctive, of epigrams." Pope and his translation of the *Iliad* are the targets here, as is Pope's habit of "translat[ing]" thought "into the language of poetry"—a habit, Coleridge admits, he only noticed when Wordsworth pointed it out to him.[43]

Ostensibly, Coleridge's claim is that Pope, by requiring each of his couplets to deliver a parcel of lay-philosophic wisdom, is driven by what Coleridge elsewhere calls "the Sophism a gradibus continuis" (Sophism of successive degrees) into writing poems whose pedagogy fails by laying out too many options—too many conjunctive disjunctives or either/ors.[44] However, we should also understand Coleridge to be making an argument not simply against didacticism in poetry but against poetry as a means of pointing, where to point at something means to draft it into the service of "consecutive narration" or historical explanation (*BL* 1.18). A sorites of epigrams unwittingly produces a windfall of narrative waste, as each couplet becomes a didactic event that collapses upon itself before it can lead to whatever ought logically to follow it. The result is a kind of freak-accidental poetry, a broken model of the mechanic form to which Coleridge opposes his own organic ideal.

As Coleridge generously puts it, "the same thought" was "started in conversation . . . far more ably, and developed more fully, by Mr. Wordsworth" (*BL* 1.20–21). What we find in "Michael," or rather in Michael's sheepfold, is an attempt to convert the immoderate accumulation of capital that drives the poem's proximate action into a figure of cognitive decadence, a falling away or lapse. Here, obscurity is a trope of invisible recession that, as Plekhanov suggests, offers an alternative to representing historical processes in the guileless terms for which matter and material life are everlasting, shatterproof. In failing to pass into the perspicuous, unified idea of a form that gives it its name, Michael's sheepfold issues a version of the challenge set by that which is real but without a fixed or specific referent. A literary peculiarity becomes a philosophical problem, and together they afford an obscure vision that makes history present as destitution, the evanescence of a world.

As a literary paraphrase of vagueness, obscurity makes a bid to count figurative representation as a materialism of the indeterminate, of those borderline cases where, concerning the reality of what a thing is or what is happening, there simply is no fact of the matter. Not surprisingly, this is not an especially useful or compelling way of thinking about what happens to political economy at the end of the eighteenth century. It is not a theory, and it is barely a critique; it is simply something that has happened and that is true, floating all but free of its causes. The poverty of reference brandished by tropes is also a poverty of function. Like Michael's stones, they call to mind a work that is not here, a labor of thought and action they cannot support but to which they might give some thinly intelligible shape or impulse. They might also give it nothing at all.

Wordsworth was writing "Michael" at the same time he was writing *The Prelude*, a poem that throws any activist ambitions completely overboard. In this wildly uncandid confessional, obscurity no longer bothers with the representation of particular things. The spectral forms creeping around Wordsworth's epic are mostly stagecraft, backdrops against which the poem's real achievement is tested and refined. This achievement is the conversion of obscurity into a principle of composition doubling as a principle of self-composure: a way of ordering lines that suggests without ever revealing how a person like Wordsworth manages the world.

By "like Wordsworth" I mean like the voice he puts on the page, a voice for which *personality* is too collected a term. Keats famously assigned it to an "egotistical sublime," the infernal engine that sucks the air out of every room and puts it back as bombast. It's easy to experience Wordsworth this way; the opening paragraphs of this chapter suggest as much. In the last section, however, I want to offer a focused, almost entirely formal treatment of *The Prelude* as a study in the savage effort of finding a way to record, repress, and transmute traumatic experience into a morality that is insistently apolitical. Plenty of ink has been spilled over the question of Wordsworth's lurch to the right. My own interest lies not with the ideological consequences of setting survival against even the thin sociality Wordsworth promised from *Lyrical Ballads* but with how that opposition takes shape *as* the poem. To find in *The Prelude* a desire to endure hurt in private, to sideline its historical conditions while staying mum on its intimate ones, is to see its obscurity as the imprint of a specific pain—most specific in its vague predication of whatever has caused it to be.

* * *

Predication is a big deal for Wordsworth, and it is a very big deal in *The Prelude*. Whether in logic, philosophy, mathematics, computer science, or just plain grammar, predicates speak the language of affirmative relation: they tell you what things are and what they are not; they assign values to terms and attribute properties to objects; in short, they engender the world. It is a curious though now hopefully explicable feature of "Michael" that the poem never pleats that sheepfold into any reliably inferential construction. The sheepfold never *is* or *was*, and the closest it comes to being named a thing that exists happens only behind the slack word *work*, as in "'This was a work for us; and now, my Son,/It is a work for me.'" Much like the lines that open the two-part *Prelude*, the demonstrative bobbing like a lost question mark at the beginning of this statement has an uncertain antecedent; and, much like those same elliptical lines, the missing parameters of *this* waft their ambiguity over to an it-cleft that has no antecedent at all other than a loose hypothesis that something has happened. Probably the work was and is the sheepfold, just as probably *The Prelude* means itself and Wordsworth's life by *this* and Derwent's blending-its-murmurs by *it*, and yet none of these paraphrases quite fit. We shouldn't expect them to.

I wonder if Wordsworth punted those exemplary opening lines nearly halfway into the completed first book of the 1805 *Prelude* because they were just too on the nose. The formula they set out is basic to the entirety of the poem, not to mention the attenuated totality of its political imagination. Again, this isn't about settling scores with Wordsworth the apostate of the French Revolution; it's about trying to discover the formal techniques that give *The Prelude* its paradigmatic access to the kind of character or soul that is unable to relinquish, let alone radicalize, its injury.[45]

Early on we called "was it for this" an existential proposition, and that's a good way to describe *The Prelude* as a whole, or rather *The Prelude* as a pattern of lines that staggers such propositions among moments (metrical, rhetorical, figurative) that undercut them. A long riff on an unanswerable question, the poem asks what it can mean to say that something has happened, especially for a person who experiences life as a sort of ghost train, coming on at deadly speed only to gust right through him. Part of the reason poststructuralist treatments of Wordsworth are so reliably convincing is that they don't believe in and so don't look for happy endings, for the "complete/Composure" (a suggestive line break if there ever was one) of personal and poetic maturity (*P* 1.122–23). Still, you don't have to think *The Prelude* is a nihilistic act of self-effacement to believe that its peals of optimism ring hollow, or that its bursts of delirious brightness are less instances of abundant recompense than a display of the psychic cost—the expenditures—of compensation. When Hartman calls the poem's structure traumatological, he picks up on something these analyses don't: the damaged subjectivity Wordsworth is trying to convey is not the negation of anything, just one form taken by a life chronically mislaid.

How to represent damage this way, as a poetic fiber so necessary and sustaining it seems hardly there at all? Adorno, whose phrase "damaged life" I've been avoiding out of an instinct that it doesn't apply, sees in capital the corruption of harmless triviality, the end of the holiday mood toasted in the *Osterspaziergang* scene from *Faust*. Since he has no interest in either triviality or harmlessness, Wordsworth encounters capital's watershed industrial stage quite differently. In "Michael," history is hard to see; change happens, but no one knows how and it doesn't much matter. In *The Prelude*, Wordsworth has backed himself into a corner. His epic is first-person and its chronology hot, so all the highs and lows, the insurrections and the executions, Pitt and the power loom, his own orphaning and his own illegitimate child, all these are, or should be, up for discussion. The problem, though, is memory. Imagine if even your most vivid recollections looked like this:

> The scenes which were a witness of that joy
> Remained, in their substantial lineaments
> Depicted on the brain, and to the eye
> Were visible, a daily sight; and thus,
> By the impressive discipline of fear,
> By pleasure and repeated happiness,
> So frequently repeated, and by force
> Of obscure feelings representative
> Of joys that were forgotten, these same scenes
> So beauteous and majestic in themselves,
> Though yet the day was distant, did at length
> Become habitually dear. (*P* 1.628–39)

This is one of several passages running up to book 11's big reveal of the "spots of time" proposal, once earmarked for book 1 and, like "was it for this," shifted to avoid the suggestion that all the keys to the poem are available at the jump. Along with Keats's Negative Capability, Wordsworth's spots are a Romantic device forever invoked without being well understood—and devices is what they are, instruments of access to whatever gives Keats or Wordsworth the activation energy to write. At the risk of adding to the confusion, let's say a spot of time is not a topic or a tableau but a repository, a well of virtue Wordsworth first tried to call "vivifying" and then "fructifying" before settling on "renovating." The final revision concedes harm, admits that our imaginative powers can need to be "invisibly repaired," battered as they've been by age, custom, and political emergency, along with all those things Wordsworth is not going to tell you about (*P* 11.265.) As in "Michael," the word *repair* implies motion alongside correction, a going-back (mostly) to childhood to remember the pleasures of its mental grandiosity, "the deepest feeling that the mind/Is lord and master, and that outward sense/Is but the obedient servant of her will" (*P* 11.271–73).

That said, there's more to this backward orientation than meets the eye; if there weren't, the spots of time would make feeble conductors for the poetic energy that shakes this poem halfway to pieces a good half of the time. Turning back to the passage from book 1, we ought to ask why this account of renovation is so seriously redundant, why it should seem like the best way to keep on trucking is simply to spin one's wheels. *Redundancy* seems to me a better word than *tautology*, which Wordsworth—pulling nearly verbatim from Campbell's *Philosophy of Rhetoric*—tosses out in his Note to "The Thorn" to alibi the repetition of words as a simultaneous marker of the pleasure and the inadequacy of using verbal language to express interior states:

> There is a numerous class of readers who imagine that the same words cannot be repeated without tautology: this is a great error: virtual tautology is much oftener produced by using different words when the meaning is exactly the same. Words, a Poet's words more particularly, ought to be weighed in the balance of feeling and not measured by the space which they occupy upon paper. For the reader cannot be too often reminded that Poetry is passion: it is the history and science of feelings.[46]

Like the evolving Preface to *Lyrical Ballads*, Wordsworth's Note develops an idea of poetry as an experimental discipline, worrying over the specifics of language-meter agonism and how it conveys various kinds of emotional disturbance. Words may repeat, Wordsworth suggests, but the feeling behind them can shift and bend. Staying responsible to this affective and not merely syllabic rhythm is what skilled versification does.[47]

What's at issue in *The Prelude*, however, is passion's near-total dislocation, which is to say the nerve-racking awareness that our intensities live somewhere other than *right here*. If this poem is redundant where the shorter lyrics are tautological, that is because it is using words to unmask life as a long haul of disappearances, some large-scale, others more domestic. Tautology is the tic of the heated moment, redundancy the knowledge that it can't be recovered—the heat, that is. Just look at lines like "the force/Of obscure feelings representative/Of joys that were forgotten," each break, each adjective and attributive phrase cooling the love at their center.

To be properly redundant and not just repetitious, language must have a particular trajectory and a particular effect. It has to organize itself into waves (the *undae* in *redundant*), shapes that are the same without being identical, different without being glaringly so. These shapes will have to move in a sequence so hard upon one another that—as when we're counting the stones in a heap—we're not sure where one thing ends and the next one begins. We need also to feel dunked but at no risk of drowning, irritable at an encore that seems overmuch, as if this all might have been done better and to a greater purpose. Thus the chiasmus of "scenes" and "joy" and "joys" and "scenes," these second scenes clotted by the adjective "same" (lines 629 and 636); thus the laugh-aloud anaphora of "repeated" (lines 633–34), of "So" (lines 634 and 637), of "daily" and its abbreviation in "day" (lines 631 and 638). Thus, too, the volley of sound between "remained" and "brain," "witness" and "impressive" and "happiness" and "majestic" (lines 629–30, 628, 632–33, 637), all wrapped in the guarantee of "habitually," which reads less as an assessment of the past or a pledge of things to come than as the adverbial form of an echo chamber. If habit happens in time, time in this passage moves without going anywhere. It is an impulse that judders these lines, which, borrowing their physics from "[t]he surface of the universal earth,/ . . . Work like a sea" (*P* 1.500–502).

None of these maneuvers are unique to this passage. Wordsworth's liking for the *re-* prefix is old territory and unsurprising, given that his poetry—to borrow from Johnson's *Dictionary*—is all about "iteration or backward action," or rather what it's like to occupy the zone of mutual repulsion between these two competitively correlative movements. *The Prelude* has a plan, which is to take the epic's trick of going backward to go forward and cast it as a psychological journey that has its own psychological challenges: Even important memories are faint and perhaps even false, so how will they carry the lyric or its subject onward? Thrown into the mix is the dilemma of current events with a capital *E*. These are all too memorable, but their contours are uneasy, smudged by that same impressive discipline that rubs the detail out of recollection and thereby makes recollection bearable. As we've seen, Wordsworth "was capable of thinking the mind of man as concrete a thing as any human figure he encountered on a country road," and likewise of treating ideas themselves as substances lying on a load-bearing brain.[48] Suppressed experience is at once the weightiest and most ill defined of those substances, a figure as spectral as a wounded solider.

There is, in other words, a link between Wordsworth's obscurity and his redundancy, between a language that flaunts its lack of denotative capacity or commitment and a language that flaunts its refusal to move forward without immediately doubling back. Part of my purpose in turning from "Michael" to *The Prelude* has been to tell a story about what critics used to call stylistic development. To say that *The Prelude* has found a way to abstract and elongate obscure figures (like the sheepfold) into an obscure manner (like redundancy) is not to say that *The Prelude* is a better and more interesting poem; anyway, these two poems are so different in so many registers, it's not clear what the purpose of the comparison would be. That said, in this shift from *stuff* to *style*, from the poem's furniture to its special gait, there is plainly an attempt to realize the hope embedded in the 1802 version of the Preface, namely that meter might "divest language in a certain degree of its reality, and thus . . . throw a sort of half consciousness of unsubstantial existence over the whole composition."[49]

In the Preface, Wordsworth quickly swerves from this astonishing, almost offhand remark into his usual idiom of pleasure and pain and the healthful rationing thereof; that's unfortunate, since what he's ascribing to meter here turns out to be the collective function of every aspect of his mature style—which, no matter what he says, has little to do with the hedonic calculus of Enlightenment aesthetics. This style wants to make the insubstantiality of difficult experience and the compromised consciousness we have of it palpable. It would be hard to find a better definition of obscurity—whose root, remember, lies likewise in an idea of *throwing over*, or hiding something under a sheet—than this metaphor of exposure spun out into a semiaffirmation of a presence that is utterly phantom. Why doesn't Wordsworth say that meter *invests* language with *unreality*, or turns it strange? Why the strikethrough or stripping away? Why establish both language and reality off the bat as objects in costume, covered up? As a theory as well as a mode of representation, obscurity names exactly this drive to bringing what has been hidden, even voided, into view by wrapping it in darkness visible. It is the poetics of what has been taken from what was barely there to lose it, from Michael's tiny household to his pile of rocks-meant-for-bricks to the child engrossed by threats too big for him, "huge and mighty forms that do not live/Like living men" and are "the trouble of [his] dreams" (*P* 1.426–28).

The half-consciousness of unsubstantial existence herds us back to trauma, and to Hartman's description of traumatic knowledge as a form of nescience or unknowing. Nescience has come up in reference to Cowper's poem "The Rose" and its formalization of harm in the instant aftermath of a caesura: "I snapp'd it, it fell to the ground." Hartman never fully explains what he means by nescience other than to say that the mind's grasp on trauma is "more" nescient than it is knowledgeable, a definition that implies a thick near-absence. He compares it, too, to Wordsworth's spots of time, each an overfull emptiness or, better yet, a "blank desertion." This phrase, like the "dim and undetermined sense/Of unknown modes of being" that precedes it, is both about something obscure and working to dilate obscurity into "a darkness" that can "h[a]ng" over the poem as it hangs over the poet, reinforced by objectless agitation (*P* 1.420–23). Clock again the superfluity of a desertion being called blank, a state of abandonment doubly evacuated; of modes of being that are dim *and* undetermined *and* unknown, and are each of these things because they are so scarcely the others.

Such modes of being comprise the unsubstantial existence in which meter shrouds poetry. It is as if the poem on its own, as a mere ordering of parts, is a social whole—in disguise, yes, but also dressed to go out into the world, wearing a reality it is ready to join. Meter takes this competence away, belies it, and then conjures up a loopy, corroded, or incorporeal form of life to be the rightful object of investment and attention. Here, then, is yet another way to understand the idea that *The Prelude* is traumatological in its structure, designed to study wounds in an invisibly aggravated state. By definition trauma entails the inevitability of being organized by something that is outside your control and yet never not part of you. To treat meter *as* that organizing something—which is to say, as the pilot of bad decisions, abandoned hopes, permanent crisis, relational despotism, and rigid inconsistency—is to tag it as a skill learned under duress and used to detain the encounter with what is intolerable, which is everything. It isn't used, as Wordsworth suggests, to twiddle knobs of pleasure and pain. It is used to make pleasure and pain alike into empty threats, limping after a body long since determined to be dead to them.

If we have assumed that Wordsworth's heart is in his descriptions of nature and childhood while the French Revolution triggers all his aloofness, we have failed to grasp just how fundamental aloofness is to every aspect of his art. This is, again, a harrowed detachment, expressed as a compulsion toward unreality that governs the words on the page as much as it does the growth of the poet's mind. *All* events, not just "public News," are to him "loose and disjointed"; his affections are *in general* "left/Without a vital interest," where *vital* means sutured to life (*P* 9.100, 106–7). That said, it is also the case that the political interludes of *The Prelude* are the most frostily disposed. As spots of time in their own right, they blend "features bold and intelligible" with "an under-expression which [is] strange, dark, and mysterious" (which is how Wordsworth saw the Convention of Cintra).[50] And, as spots of time, they are reparative in that quintessentially Wordsworthian sense of being defined by repetitive action, a going-nowhere that takes the pose of self-defensive stillness:

> I cross'd (a blank and empty area then)
> The Square of the Carousel, few weeks back
> Heap'd up with dead and dying, upon these
> And other sights looking as doth a man
> Upon a volume whose contents he knows
> Are memorable, but from him lock'd up,

Being written in a tongue he cannot read;
So that he questions the mute leaves with pain
And half upbraids their silence. But that night
When on my bed I lay I was most mov'd
And felt most deeply in what world I was;
My room was high and lonely, near the roof
Of a large Mansion or Hotel, a spot
That would have pleas'd me in more quiet times
Nor was it wholly without pleasure then.
With unextinguish'd taper I kept watch,
Reading at intervals; the fear gone by
Press'd on me almost like a fear to come;
I thought of those September Massacres,
Divided from me by a little month,
And felt and touch'd them, a substantial dread;
The rest was conjured up from tragic fictions
And mournful Calendars of true history,
Remembrances and dim admonishments. (*P* 10.46–69)[51]

There's so much to say about these lines, so many echoes sounding in this space. They gather up some of the poem's favorite nouns (*sight, silence, pain, fear, dread, remembrance*), adjectives (*blank, empty, mute, substantial, dim*), verbs (*lay, moved, felt, pressed, touched*), and tense pair of almost-opposite adverbs (*half, most*), about which more in a moment.

I want to begin, though, with that parenthesis, the one cupping "a blank and empty area" in 1805 and "an empty area then!" in 1850, when this whole passage came in for frenetically bad revision.[52] If we ignore the lunulae, "I cross'd a blank and empty area then" is a solid line of blank verse, though some English speakers will have to fudge the *r* in "area" to rid themselves of a syllable. Alas, this makes the line fall completely apart. Undammed by any endstop or lull, "then" sloshes over into "The," and the only hope for grammatical purchase is to take Wordsworth's meaning to be something like "I crossed a blank and empty area *that was then*, at that time, the Square of the Carousel." But since the seventeenth century the Place du Carrousel has always been the Place du Carrousel; it was the Place du Carrousel in 1792, when Wordsworth had his residence in France, and so it remained. If you want to keep the sense of the line, which is simply that at the time of Wordsworth's crossing it one evening, the Place du Carrousel was blank and empty though it had recently been engorged with dead and dying guards and servants of the Tuileries, "the quick Succession of a few flowing syllables that constitutes the Harmony of . . . English blank verse" is not going to cut it.[53]

So how to read this floating aside, either out loud or in our heads? Brennan O'Donnell writes of some other parentheses—"(And the expressive powers perhaps no less/Of the whole species)," from *The Excursion*—that they are lent "the rhythm appropriate to a sotto voce insertion" by the idiosyncratic stresses of the line that follows them, but which rhythm would that be?[54] It's true that line 47 in the passage above ("The Square of the Carousel, few weeks back") is metrically bonkers; what effect could that have on the timbre of "a blank and empty area then"? We might say that line 47 is *so* bonkers that it forces the line preceding it to try for staidness, exaggerating the conflict between line 46's metrical responsibilities and the two curving cues that make them impossible to fulfill. If "the Passion of the sense" is, as Wordsworth opined to John Thelwall, the ultimate arbiter of any "dislocation of the verse," we have to wonder what exactly the affect behind "a blank and empty area then" is such that it might solve the puzzle of how to express it.[55]

The bad revision of 1850 gives everything away. "(An empty area then!)" makes it luridly clear that the passional motive of the line is the contrast Wordsworth is trying to establish with the all-too-full Square of "few weeks back": then an abattoir, now back a bit to normal. The 1805 version, by contrast, has the spirit of *1805*—it is anxiously inscrutable, a reaching out at arm's length. Here the parenthesis is opened and closed by a catch of air, its interior contents hurried along like Wordsworth himself en traversant la place. This is a light disruption and, as O'Donnell suggests, also something secret, to be spoken in a quiet voice. A peek at some contemporary elocution manuals confirms the instinct. In his 1781 *Rhetorical Grammar*, John Walker says parentheses should be inflected by "a moderate depression, and a pause greater than a comma," though presumably shorter than a period. "The tone of voice," Walker continues, "ought to be interrupted, as it were, by something unforeseen," while the voice itself should move "a degree swifter" than over the rest of the sentence, "as this still better preserves the broken sense" and "relieves [our auditors] as soon as possible from the suspense of an occasional and unexpected" disturbance.[56]

The unforeseen interruption is both a classic feature of trauma and the morphology of a spot of time. In this passage from book 10, the two come together not in the parenthesis but in its impact—in the awkward fermata swelling the space between content and comment, in the confusion of one line tilting into the next, in the effort it takes not to slur together "and" and "empty," "empty" and "area." It is the impact of a soft-pedaled declivity, and it is softness that the exclamation point in *1850* dissolves in an outburst entirely too forthright. For Walker, the depression of the voice marks a repression: an imperfect erasure and partial safeguarding. Wordsworth's great feat is to take this elocutionary standard and use it to reinvent prosody as a psychological form, one that can *enact* the complicity of temporal with emotional patterns well in advance of their scientific (or, if you prefer, pseudo-scientific) discovery. What is voiced in the pause of an uncertain interval, what we hear, is the sound of a thought so difficult the poem has to take its distance from it; it is the sound of remoteness bordering on apathy and apathy bordering on an anguish inadmissible to verse. That may sound like a contradiction in terms, but the ability to set great pain on ice is the linchpin of this poetics, whose unrelenting pressure on every single word, line, mark, and foot is simply the upshot of keeping both "the fear gone by" and "the fear to come" at bay, in unshakable anticipation of being "overwhelmed without forewarning—fearful like men who feel themselves to be helpless, and indignant and angry like men who are betrayed."[57]

This pressure never lets up, but it is far from uniform. The hitch or beat demanded by a digression, an interpolated confidence or a pointed aside, gives no relief; it simply varies the amplitude. What we have, in the moderately depressed trespass into an ideal of easy flow, is a stutter in the pulse of the poem and the embodied consciousness it wants to express—a shift, that is, in the felt reality of living. Here is one way that meter dismantles the appearance language gives of being firmly attached to the world, by reminding us that "the world" is not just that which is present and accounted for but also that which is intrusively absent or else held off, blocked out. The world is the fact of dead bodies disappeared and the blankness that still entombs them; it is the labor of remembering them and, more to the point, of making that memory tolerable. When we pause around that parenthetical, we feel what Wordsworth does, or did: the interruption of the unforeseen into what seemed a fixed quantity, an existence that was sure to be weathered. This was a myth and it wasn't. You can walk back through horror, and cross it, get through it, but you can't shake its shadow. It's there in the beat that doesn't quite skip, in the breath you can't quite catch, in the need to hurry on by.

"But that night," Wordsworth says, with a drumroll, "[w]hen on my bed I lay, I was most moved/And felt most deeply in what world I was." The curtain rises on nothing, an undercover aposiopesis. Wordsworth does not explain or describe the world he was in; nor, despite an audible parroting of the last stanza from "I Wandered Lonely as a Cloud," does he account for any workings of his inward eye. He simply tenders a comment on his flat, "a spot/that would have pleased . . . in more quiet times." Revisions in *1850* make it obvious that something is being withheld, as the passage there tips very nearly into the unintentional self-parody of "The Thorn," with the same gesture of aimless precision: "But that night/I felt most deeply in what world I was,/What ground I trod on, and what air I breathed."[58] In both versions of the poem, it's the superlative "most" that does the heavy-lifting, setting us up for a disclosure that will be important, even revelatory, and never comes.

It never comes because mostness—the quality of an extreme—is almost always a dodge for Wordsworth, an exit ramp along which we're hustled away from a far more difficult admission. The truth is that it's not mostness but *halfness* that best characterizes the emotional temper of this poem as it moves from a childhood that never seems personally safe to an adulthood boggled by violence on a global scale. It is by halves that Wordsworth "upbraids" the mass grave of the Place du Carrousel, whose secret is, he says, kept hidden even though the poem has it in plain sight: something terrible happened here, and Wordsworth even has a name for it ("those September Massacres"). It is as though the censure of the past must always be incomplete and the past itself partly fictitious, "tragic" in a generic register and, because generic, impersonal.

The past, in other words, is always a thing that's happened to other people; it is beyond Wordsworth's blame, its inaccessibility stressed by another brace of redundancies. "I felt and touched them," Wordsworth says; we want to reply, *But these are the same, feeling and touching.* The line makes us see how they're not, how you can take something into your hands without it getting into your heart, how you can be knocked sideways by a shock absolutely beyond your reach. Here, by the way, is the Wordsworthian angle on Prynne's concept of resistance: the thing in the world that hits you the hardest is your sensation of the absence of things, your conviction that all you'll ever know of objects is their negative form, their outline fastening on your brain. This is an emotional, not a philosophical, predicament: Wordsworth's not really an idealist, though he would do a good impersonation of one in later years; he was just unhappy.

We've now come to the point where Wordsworth's psychological poetics and the explicitly political dimension of his history collide. Political commitments, whether republican or reactionary, require identification, and revolutionary politics in particular require an identification with harm: sustaining it and causing it. Wordsworth is no more the dead bodies of the palace guards than he is the "hunger-bitten girl" against whose poverty and "heartless mood/Of solitude" the Revolution is fighting, and that's how he'd like to keep it (*P* 9.512, 517–18). Maybe he can't help but keep it this way; maybe the flip side of a lyric consciousness that encounters the whole world as a field of vacant but heavy obstacles is that it has no real talent either for solidarity or for conflict: all it wants is to survive. If we had to give one more name to Wordsworth's obscurity, we might call it a defense mechanism, a way of treading water in a fear gone by as though it's "almost like a fear to come." That bizarre construction is another half-measure, another retreat from what is inadmissible to the poem and the mind whose development it tracks. "Almost like" implies a fixed point of comparison: this known quantity (a fear gone by) is almost like this fixed quality (a fear to come). But what is still to come is not a fixed quantity; it is not even a quantity at all, because it hasn't happened yet. All that has happened is the idling of dread, the stagnant shadow thrown by the past on the present but offering it no object, no single thing to fear or fight or be.

Ambling up to the end of *The Prelude*, we're directed to look upon the charms of nature as a "genuine counterpart / And softening mirror of the moral world" (*P* 13.287–88). This is the same mirror of which we heard Paul tell; it holds the image of a world of pain and muddies it, making it more real but less true. For Wordsworth, predictably, the muddying can only happen through the subtraction of detail, a softening or smudge: with him, we are always looking in a mirror that shows us less than what we are. I think this is what I have meant all along when I've said that Wordsworth leaves me cold—that this poetry finds the fullness of life too much and that, as a certain kind of reader, I find myself in the unenviable position of representing that fullness every time I want more from Wordsworth's world picture, more humor or history, more lightness or desire, more political seriousness. I know that this poetry wants me gone, and this is a singular indignity, being a gatecrasher in your own dreams. The problem is, it forms a habit.

3

Keats and Catachresis

It is a *Greck* word, and signifies *Abuse*.

The Art of Rhetorick Laid Down in an Easy Entertaining Manner (1746)

I have an habitual feeling of my real life having past, and that I am leading a posthumous existence. God knows how it would have been—but
it appears to me—however, I will not speak of that subject.

JOHN KEATS, letter to Charles Brown dated 30 November 1820

The passage from Wordsworth to Keats can seem corrective, whether poetically, morally, or both. If this were a simple popularity contest, Keats
has all the advantages needed to win it. Wordsworth the man was by all
accounts arrogant and ungenerous (in particular to other poets) and
Keats is famously lovable, his charm thrown into excruciating relief by his
early death. As for the poetry, Wordsworth's can be downright repellant.
This is especially true, of course, of later, brazenly reactionary offerings
like *The Excursion*, but it is also true of the early work, strung up as it
is on the "strangeness and auwkwardness" of Wordsworth's versification
and suspended over a vision of human life that flickers between weakly
supportive and downright bleak.[1] The only thing bleak about Keats is that
he died young, poor, far away from the person he loved, and believing
the world thought his poetry was trash. But that is a matter of personal
circumstance. The poetry itself is life, cut loose.

   This does not mean, however, that Keats's poetry is all fun and games,
nor even that it is—as readers often have it—an exercise in unrestrained
sensuality. This chapter will argue the opposite: that what has been taken
for an over-the-top emphasis on the pageant of the physical body is in
truth a highly pressurized blankness, an attempt to evacuate that body
and thereby to protect it from expropriation. Blankness of this kind is a
poetic variant on what Keats, not three months away from death and in
the very last of his letters, called his posthumous existence. It is also an

aesthetic mode or device that yearns to repossess existence on its own terms, to recover a passion for vitality from the conscious and embodied experience of a death that seems to go on forever. On the one hand, existing posthumously—being manifestly alive and yet already dead—means getting stuck in a body that has become a burial ground. On the other, it points the way toward a state of freedom in which the body will no longer be used to prop up forms of life not worth living.

Understanding this aspect of Keats's poetics requires paying attention to his anxieties about the emerging social fact of industrial labor, which squeezes energy, power, and potential as well as actual blood and sweat from those on whose immiseration industry depends; capital, too, consigns the worker to a posthumous existence, to a life that is no life and so is sunk into a ghastly atmosphere of general unreality. It also, and more significantly for my purposes, requires being attentive to Keats's use of catachresis, the poetic figure of inelegant or just bad metaphor. And as everyone, even his most committed votaries, can admit, if there is one thing Keats is not short on it is bad metaphors.

The word *catachresis* combines the Greek prefix *kata-*, i.e., down, against, or wrongly, and the verb *chresthai*, which indicates use. Essentially it means an action against propriety or custom, a blunder or even a case of misconduct. We might also call it a degradation, a downward turning or—playing off the literal meaning of *posthumous* as "past or after the ground"—the consignment of something below where it should be. In the first epigraph to this chapter, from an eighteenth-century rhetorical manual, there is what will turn out to be a fairly common pairing of catachresis with abuse or injury, particularly as it is directed toward the body. Like Wordsworth's obscurity, Keats's catachresis is indebted to these early modern and Enlightenment-era tweakings of classical definitions, which are straightforward in theory but, in practice, lend themselves to the offbeat and extravagant, to the point where catachresis may serve as a multipronged instrument for treating the lavish contradictions of the historical moment.

To produce a catachresis in antiquity, you have to refer to something that has no specific name by the name of something physically or figuratively close to it. Quintilian gives the examples of calling any bottle a vinegar bottle (*acetabula*), any casket a box-wood (*pyxides*), or any murder of a family member a parricide; a thousand years later, Joseph Priestly hews to the spirit of this broadly spatial or approximal gloss, spotting catachresis "when trees are called the *hair of mountains*, or the walls of cities their *cheeks*." The difference, as is apparent, lies in the degree of "gradation" the vehicle takes from the tenor, for in Priestley's words, while there are some metaphors "in which the analogy between two objects is so great, that the figure is evanescent," in catachresis "the analogy is scarce perceptible, and consequently the metaphor is harsh and unnatural."[2] Quintilian's catachreses come from analogies that seem lazy or forgetful and so reach for the association nearest to hand. Priestley's are, in our modern vernacular, a reach.

The reach is Keats's signature gesture. His poetry owes both its highs and its lows to catachresis, from the astonishing cranial metaphor that crowns his "Ode to Psyche" with "the wreath'd trellis of a working brain" to the slush of *Endymion,* whose dramatis personae say things like "Then, like a new fledg'd bird that first doth shew/His spreaded feathers to the morrow chill,/I tried in fear the pinions of my will."[3] Because these misuses, whether successful or unsuccessful, almost inevitably concern the body, its parts, or its appetites, they have come to seem like secondary indices of Keats's obsession with feeling, which might be and often is boiled down to that celebrated whoop "O for a Life of Sensations rather than of Thoughts!"[4] However, in Priestley's description of catachresis as founded on the "scarce perceptible" and *therefore* coarse, unsettling, jagged, or perverse lies a more accurate way to understand this poetics, along with its place in the critique of political economy. It is, I'll argue, through a series of immoderate experiments with bodies and the things closest to them that Keats tropes capital's theft of life, as well as the possibility of life's survival in some genuinely emancipated form.

George Bernard Shaw, to whom I'll return below, once said that if Keats had lived he would have become a revolutionary, and that if Marx had written a poem instead of *Capital* it would have been *Isabella; or, The Pot of Basil.* Neither of these hypotheses needs to be believed for their force to register. As Shaw knows very well, Keats's poetry (if not his letters) is almost entirely devoid of politically prescriptive content, and the indictment of industry that comes through loud and clear in *Isabella* isn't especially novel or illuminating. We are talking, after all, about a person who wrote his most watertight poem, "To Autumn," just weeks after the Peterloo Massacre; the ode could not be less topical if it tried, even as the entire country and certainly Keats's own circle talked of nothing else. What Shaw understands is not that Keats was a radical, which he more or less was, but that the springy, spongy, tensile build of his poetry is very good at mimicking the arrogation of "human brain, nerves, muscles, and sense organs" by the social form of industrial labor and at imagining how it might be undone.[5]

Now, Keats's catachreses are inescapably poetic, and no one would recommend them to any kind of far-reaching anticapitalist analysis. As Keats himself so often insists, he begins from the assumption that art is a palliative and not a diagnostic tool. The questions he wants to ask of

the world—about pain, about death, about grief and cruelty and distress
and waste on an unimaginable scale—are not questions he deems soluble
by poems. His purpose seems rather to acclaim life's capacity to defy its
forcible metamorphosis, and to do so by pitting rhetorical misuse against
economic abuse. If, as Marx says, the commodity, in order to "operate
effectively as exchange-value, . . . must divest itself of its natural physical
body" and undergo an "act of transubstantiation" more rigorous, perhaps, then "the casting of his shell for a lobster," Keats contemplates what
it would be like to run this process not in reverse but through and past its
worst variant, all the way up to history's end (*C*, 1.197).

* * *

Catachresis cuts at least three ways. It is a positive dereliction, a win-
ning effort at going against the grain; it is a mistake; and in any case it is
a disturbance, even, as some commentators suggest, an act of violence
or an offering of injury. In the early modern context, this third sense of
catachresis as harm lies not far afield from its association with sexual
impropriety. Dudley Fenner, in his *The Arte of Rhetorike*, observes that
if all metaphor is language "driven by force unto" a "change of significa-
tion," catachresis is an instance of that change unwilling to act appropri-
ately "shamefaste, and as it were maidenly" about it; meanwhile, John
Hoskyns, laying the ground for my own association between Keats and
the risky reach, notes that it is "somewhat more desperate then [*sic*] a
Metaphore."[6] By the eighteenth century, the charge of licentiousness
will have dissipated, but catachresis will remain a sign of "impropriety,"
"harsh and shocking" and skirting the bounds of what is acceptable, not
just stylistically but also socially.[7] Hence Pope's canny intimation that, as
a figure of mismatch, catachresis might breach the decorum of the division of labor. Grouping catachresis under the first of three kinds of figures
that produce bathos—namely, those that are "variegating, confusing, or
reversing"—he offers:

A master of this will say,

> *Mow* the beard,
> *Shave* the grass,
> *Pin* the plank,
> *Nail* my sleeve.

From whence results the same kind of pleasure to the mind, as doth to
the eye when we behold Harlequin trimming himself with a hatchet,

hewing down a tree with a razor, making his tea in a cauldron, and brewing his ale in a teapot.[8]

To those familiar with the high-stakes definitions of catachresis leveraged in poststructuralism—Jacques Derrida deemed philosophy itself to be catachrestic, while Gayatri Chakravorty Spivak argues that all "*political uses of words*" are necessarily instances of it—this must all seem rather deflated.[9] However, what these earlier commentaries underscore is the uncommonly corporeal nature of this particular figure, which is rough-grained, overeager, and brought home by scenes of incongruous work: mowing, shaving, pinning, nailing, trimming, hewing, brewing the wrong thing the wrong way.

This is exertion on a small scale; the tasks are those of a servant or artisan or else the kind of thing one does for oneself. And yet they are also examples of those "concrete forms of labour" that vanish into the commodity as "human labour in the abstract," when the commodity ceases to be "the product of the labour of the joiner, the mason or the spinner, or of any other particular kind of productive labor" (*C*, 128). It is a curious feature of Keats's poems that they include almost no work of any kind but are nonetheless freighted with the exhaustion of having been working; compare a text like Blake's *Jerusalem*, which is organized entirely around the spectacle and the rhythm of Los at his anvil as he forges Golgonooza, the city that contains everything that has ever existed or been felt or thought, or Wordsworth's "Michael" with its unfinished sheepfold. By contrast, labor in Keats is generally something that has already happened, leaving behind what Marx will call "the residue of [its] products" and Keats, in "To Autumn," its "last oozings" (*C*, 1.128; "A," 22).

In "To Autumn," the mystery of labor's disappearance sticks to its products, like those oozings that go on, improbably, for hours even though they are the last, or the honey that "has o'er-brimmed" the cells of bees, that well-worn emblem of the social character of both work and value ("A," 11).[10] Even the "full-grown lambs [that] bleat" at the ode's end belong in this group, for they too suggest a distension—in the poem's own terms, a "swell"—that pulls the object outward and nearly past its physical envelope, like a balloon pumped full of too much air, ready to pop ("A," 30, 7). To another poet, a full-grown lamb is just a sheep, and liquids brim over their containers rather than (as "o'er-brimmed" implies) thickening their containers' brims, but we are in the domain of catachresis, of variegating, confusing, or reversing uses of language in proximity to human effort. Here, effort is in its aftermath, and its effects are lightly grotesque, "budding more,/And still more" toward the phantom limits of an embodiment that is also a "winnowing," a ripening that thins out

("A," 8–9, 15). Above and around all this the dematerialization of human activity sounds in the poem's tightly orchestrated static, the uprush of aspirated *-oft*s (oft, soft, croft, aloft) and somnolent /z/s (hazel, drows'd, oozing, dies, skies) that are "the wailful choir" of Keats's "small gnats" ("A," 27).

The peculiar difficulty with Keats's poetry is that it often fools us into thinking it makes the sensible world hyperbolically available instead of hyperbolically tenuous, thin as in thin-skinned. Picture, again, the over-inflated balloon, which seems at once to press *into* its surround and back *onto* its own insides. This is how Keats's catachreses work, their distortions exposing a significant and occluded relationship between language and matter, between the poem, the body, and their joint situation. The poem, too, presses into and onto, its membrane losing thickness as it negotiates what, in physics, is called the stress-strain curve: the give and take between force and deformation, the progress of the balloon from limp and stiff to tight and nearly still until it reaches its point of fracture, and pops. When Matthew Arnold says that Keats had a "sensuous strain" but also "something more, and something better," he's got it halfway right and inside out.[11] Sensuousness, for Keats, is indeed a strain, a measure of the distance between some body and its capacity, or what it can bear. It is also a stress, the drama of a substance trying to hold itself together even as it is tugged and wrenched and spread apart, afraid to burst and wanting to, for the relief.

Keats afflicts his words this way for a reason: to assess the condition of human life cast in terms of value, with its extenuating promise of "more,/ And still more." His poetics is thus not unlike Marx's, which charges the account of the fetish-character of commodities with an expository enargia. As Keston Sutherland writes, the figurative turns of *Capital* force "a materialist re-emphasis of the physical human experience at the origin of exchange value" while also satirizing capital's own liquidation of the human body, its conversion of the "living hands, brains, muscles and nerves of the wage labourer [into] mere 'animal substances.'"[12] Sutherland's example of such a turn is the word *Gallerte*, which Marx uses to describe labor in the abstract as "bloße Gallerte unterschiedsloser menschlicher Arbeit," the mere *Gallerte* of homogeneous human labor. *Gallerte* is also a catachresis, though when it is translated, as it usually is, as "congelation" that becomes hard to see; but *Gallerte* is really a name for "the undifferentiated mess of glue-yielding . . . animal substances industrially boiled down into condiments," "the product not of reversible freezing but of irreversible boiling followed by cooling."[13] It thus conforms to the classical definition of catachresis as a word nearest to hand, most near to the worker who is reduced to *Gallerte* by wage labor, and who suffers the evacuation of subjectivity that comes with socially necessary abstract labor time. *Gallerte* is the box-wood of the worker's sarcophagus, the parricide of his and every life.

To test this argument about the catachresis derived from "menschlicher Arbeit" in a different medium, I want to look briefly at some drawings by the German humorist Wilhelm Busch, whose most well-known work, *Max und Moritz: Eine Bubengeschichte in sieben Streichen* (*Max and Moritz: A Knavish Tale in Seven Pranks*), was first published in 1865, when Marx was hammering out the final draft of the first volume of his critique of political economy. Figures 1 and 2 show eight images, four each from *Max und Moritz* and 1864's *Der Eispeter* (*Ice-Peter*), which, like *Max und Moritz*, is a tale told in rhymed couplets and accompanied by illustrations.[14]

Max und Moritz is organized into a series of seven "pranks," all of which involve nontrivial acts of violence: killing the Widow Bolte's chickens, filling a teacher's pipe with gunpowder, luring the tailor onto a broken bridge, and so on. The boys get their comeuppance in the seventh and last prank, when Max and Moritz cut open a farmer's bags of grain only to be taken to the mill themselves and ground to chaff: "Rickeracke! Rickeracke!" reads Busch's caption, "Geht die Mühle mit Geknacke" ("Rickeracke! Rickeracke!/Goes the mill with a crack"). They are then eaten by a pair of geese and—as a final image of the birds turning their tails toward the reader suggests—eventually excreted. The fate of Ice-Peter is even more unsettling. Against the advice of grown-ups, he goes skating on a frozen pond, falls in, and turns into a block of ice that, brought before the stove to warm up, simply melts. His remains are scooped up by his parents and poured into a jar, which is set on a pantry shelf.

The parallels with *Gallerte*, likewise a product of the grinding up of bones and the liquefaction of their remnants, are striking; Ice-Peter even ends up a condiment or on a shelf with them, deliquesced and decanted between the pickles and the cheese. To borrow Shaw's formula, these might have been the sort of cartoons Marx would draw had he drawn cartoons, their images gleaned from the factory floor but transposed into an antiquated, even slightly fairy-tale world. In the image that shows the miller peering into the mill's funnel, the machine is working without anybody working it; Max and Moritz are no more than the grain being spat out through a shaft whose mouth is framed by a human face. Like the outline of their forms in chaff or the jar labeled "Peter," the face vomiting those dregs is a catachresis making brutally vivid the dispersal of the body in the production of even the most basic commodities: wheat and water. When the body survives, it survives either as a superfluity (a jar of water in the snowy winter) or as surplus routed right back into the

FIG. 1. Max and Moritz ground and eaten. From Wilhelm Busch, *Max und Moritz: Eine Bubengeschichte in sieben Streichen* (1865).

FIG. 2. Eispeter melting and in storage. From Wilhelm Busch, *Der Eispeter* (1864).

supply chain, as feed strewn upon the floor. Busch's mill, in other words, is a version of the *Zwickmühle*—literally "double mill" and figuratively "double bind"—Marx identifies with the process that hurls the worker "back into the market as a seller of his own labor-power and continually transforms his own product into the means by which another [that is, the capitalist] can purchase him."[15]

As naughty or careless as Busch's children may be, the extreme horror of being crushed to death or melted down clearly outstrips the offense of adolescent disobedience. The exorbitance of their punishment, and the impression of outsize harm it conveys, mime the scalar dysfunction on which capital depends—not just the economics of inequality but also the magnitude of all its structures can hold. The smallness of Busch's comic mode only enhances this effect, shoring up both the sheer grotesquerie of the *Zwickmühle* and the sense that comedy or satire, for all its critical energy, is implicated in its movements. With their thickly looped lines and their emphasis on circles or other curvilinear shapes, his drawings suggest boundaries that are infinitely expansive and yet secure, dynamic consolidations of space and life. To the theory of catachresis they introduce the idea of a harnessing together, so that catachresis appears not just as an awkward association of disparate things but also as their commixture and consolidation—in a word, their jelling.

In this same line of annihilated yet preserved existence is the severed head in Isabella's pot of basil, just one of the many disarticulated body parts strewn around Keats's poems, with their brains and hands and wombs and eyes and whole hearts. You will sometimes find this gorier aspect of his writing called sadomasochistic: statements like "You must be mine to die upon the rack if I want you" are certainly grist for *that* mill (*L* 2.291). But this is a phrase from a private language (it comes from a letter to Keats's next-door neighbor and fiancée, Fanny Brawne), and when we talk poetics we are talking about a vocabulary and a set of procedures that are resolutely public, held to a different standard of coherence and complexity. If anything, seeing Keats's work as an example of sadomasochism fails to capture the rigor of the violence it likes to do to all bodies, not just those that are plugged into the circuit of his desire. It fails, too, to pick apart or even to recognize the intricate knot of sinister and radically benevolent energies that allow these poems to vibrate right on the edge between excess and extinction, between a form of life that is basically death and a form of dissolution that opens onto freedom. Finally, it fails to appreciate the place this poetry holds in an intellectual tradition for which—as we'll see in detail below—"sexuality . . . is the most social of expressions" and, as such, a channel or at least a promissory note for "the dissolution of autonomy" itself.[16]

But first, the pot, or rather the pot and the head inside it, a pairing as macabre as Busch's human body in a glass jar. *Isabella; or, The Pot of Basil* was written in 1818 but not published until the edition of Keats's *Poems* that came out in 1820. That edition, which contains the Great Odes and *Hyperion*, announces a dramatic shift less in style than in program, for it is in this volume that something like a deliberate poetic intention—along with the means of serving it—begins to emerge from the messy trenches of *Endymion*. We've seen some of those means at work already in "To Autumn," but *Isabella*, which is likewise pledged to a sonic anti-boom of sibilation and quiet, puts them to work for a story that is explicitly cata-chrestic insofar as it concerns—and commits—misuse. I'm not thinking only of the head of poor Lorenzo, Isabella's dead lover. I am thinking, first, since they are introduced first to us in the poem, about the bodies scattered across the stanzas Shaw has in mind when he says that "if Karl Marx can be imagined as writing a poem instead of a treatise on Capital, he would have written *Isabella*."[17] Now, Marx did for a time write poetry, but not anything like this ottava rima romance, adapted from a tale in Boccaccio's medieval *Decameron*:

> With her two brothers this fair lady dwelt,
>   Enriched from ancestral merchandize,
> And for them many a weary hand did swelt
>   In torched mines and noisy factories,
> And many once proud-quiver'd loins did melt
>   In blood from stinging whip;—with hollow eyes
> Many all day in dazzling river stood,
> To take the rich-ored driftings of the flood
>
> For them the Ceylon diver held his breath,
>   And went all naked to the hungry shark;
> For them his ears gush'd blood; for them in death
>   The seal on the cold ice with piteous bark
> Lay full of darts; for them alone did seethe
>   A thousand men in troubles wide and dark:
> Half-ignorant, they turn'd an easy wheel,
> That set sharp racks at work, to pinch and peel. (*I*, 105–20)

In this straightforward indictment of Isabella's brothers as "profiteers and exploiters," Shaw finds "everything that the Bolshevik means and feels when he uses the fatal epithet 'bourgeois.'" Keats, meanwhile, would seem to feel Bolshevism before he can mean it: his attack on the broth-ers "contains all the Factory Commission reports Marx read, and that

Keats did not read because they were not written in his time," securing
Keats, with Shelley, his place "among the prophets," able to apprehend
with a visionary sensual intelligence the wrack and ruin of "capitalistic
civilization." "Had he lived," Shaw concludes, Keats "would no doubt
have come down from *Hyperion* and *Endymion* to tin tacks as a very full
blooded modern revolutionist." In other words, and not unlike Marx, he
would have turned away from a poetry of juvenile gimmicks and stopped
being "the sort of youth who calls a window a casement," finding refuge
in tinsel and not those tin—some would say brass—tacks to which Shaw
commends them both.[18]

Aside from the fact that Keats *had* likely been reading Leigh Hunt's
article "On the Employment of Children in Manufactories" when he
was writing *Isabella*, Shaw's account is persuasive.[19] Isabella's merchant
brothers, who are running some kind of multinational corporation, are
the villains of the piece—"ledger-men" and "money-bags"—long before
they murder Lorenzo and hide his body in the woods (*I*, 137, 142). They
traffic in precious metals, gold, manufactured goods, pearls, and the fur
and oil of seals slaughtered on faraway ice; they own mines, factories,
and plantations where people are whipped until they bleed. Keats isn't
pulling punches, and contemporary reviewers took notice. Stanzas like
the ones quoted above, bristled John Scott, "are no better than extravagant school-boy vituperation of trade and traders," and when "contrasted
with the larger philosophy of Boccaccio, and his more genial spirit . . .
are additionally offensive"; to rail against "the profitable side of things"
is a sign of immaturity and excess, all at once "florid," "flippant[,] and
false" in its insistence on attacking "classes of men" rather than "crawling
minds" per se. "Let him write," Scott advises, "in the bold indignant style
of Wordsworth's glorious Sonnet[,] 'The world is too much with us!'"[20]

Notice that Shaw and Keats's critics agree about an aspect of Keats's
anticapitalism: it is indivisible from his youth, which is in turn indivisible
from his tendency toward overkill. When Shaw teases him as the sort of
youth who calls a window a casement, he joins a long line of Romantic-
era readers whose attacks on Keats gathered his age, his class, his friends,
and his politics into a kneecapping scrutiny of his style. As Marjorie
Levinson indelibly argues, these negative judgments can be revelatory—
can uncover, that is, how what Byron called Keats's "Onanism of Poetry"
expresses the social relation as it stands in the Regency period, near the
top of the ninth inning of the Industrial Revolution. If, "time and again,"
Keats's "poetry is labelled 'profligate,' 'puerile,' 'unclean,' 'disgusting,'
'recklessly luxuriant and wasteful,' 'unhealthy,' 'abstracted,' and 'insane,'"
not to mention "prolix, repetitive, metrically and lexically licentious,
overwrought," that is because it is keyed to the erotic and fiduciary

drama of the petty bourgeoisie, and to a modern negotiation of what Scott calls classes of men. His is "a discourse," Levinson writes, "which 'feeds upon' but does not assimilate its sources," "rehears[ing] the protocol whereby the middle class of his day produced itself as a kind of collective, throbbing oxymoron: achieved by its ambitiousness, hardworking in its hedonism, a 'being' that defined itself strictly by its properties, or ways of having." The onanism of poetry acts out a bourgeois desire to be "vitally, *capably* incomplete," getting everything it wants by making nothing that it has.[21]

Applying both Marx and Freud, Levinson goes on to locate the place where fantasies of aesthetic autonomy and a style on loan from self-abuse might coincide: in the idealization of some fetish object that takes effort to produce but that must nonetheless seem to come as naturally as leaves to a tree, lest it risk liquidating the pleasure it ought to provide. If "the triumph of [Keats's] great poetry," in contrast to "the awfulness of the early work," lies in its achievement of this fetishistic wholeness under the ascendant rubric of organic form, it does so at the expense of the social facts embedded in those earlier, earthier representations and in their reception.[22] Although Levinson does not quite say so, these social facts are also sensuous facts, which is to say that sensuous human activity is the condition of their emergence as part of the structure of the world. To take masturbation as a figure for that activity is like taking tin tacks as a figure for revolutionary commitment. Both catachreses do what Quintilian says catachresis must: "adapt the next available [in proximo] term to describe something for which no actual term exists."[23]

Keats isn't waiting on Marx to make him intelligible. My point is that the "oddly abstract materialism of [this] poetry" reliably proliferates yet more abstractions on its way to being understood.[24] It's interesting that Shaw, in his effort to imagine an impossible future Keats more in touch with real life, relies on a figurative and idiomatic expression ("down to tin tacks") that ultimately occludes whatever being a full-blooded modern revolutionist might entail: the point at which Keats might abjure romance and meet the problem of capital directly is also the point where Shaw cedes his own capacity to refer to anything concrete. The masturbatory trope that got so much traction among Keats's enemies in the press (and with Byron) works, perhaps, in a similar way, for it too relies on the phantom promise of its own explicitness only to terminate in euphemism, hiding what is most electric and impertinent about the poetry by literalizing its metaphors and holding them to voyeuristic account.

In short, there is something that Keats does with his style, and it has something to do with capital, but when we try to give it a particular name—to turn its querying of a relation into the representation of an object—we find ourselves locked into an "irritable reaching after fact & reason" that reduces the poem to testimony or exegesis (*L* 1.193). This is at least part of what Keats meant when he complained that *Isabella* was "too smokeable," that readers would see through it because its moral was so pat and its bouncy, limber form such a good delivery system for it (*L* 2.174). Smokeability, in other words, invites an overeager hermeneutics that tiptoes perilously close to an "idealism . . . [of] altered specification," by which all art is taken to reflect "real and verifiable social and historical processes" easily visible once we finally see through all the "distortion, falsification, and superficiality" of its manifest content.[25] To smoke a poem is to get past it, get over it, and to tell it what it means in a way that forces it to be responsible to its conditions. To write a poem that is able to be smoked is to play into the desire for this sort of specification, in a way that risks reducing poetry to commentary, a loose cluster of opinions we "see through and . . . find nothing in" (*L* 2.19).

In defense of *Isabella*, not all of it is smokeable. The parts of the poem that ask for difficult thinking about the status of appropriated life are anything but, and that is because (unlike the stanzas attacking Isabella's brothers) they are about evacuation instead of explicitation. These are moments where catachresis, the figure of matter out of place, works to confuse one body with one another or else to model the body's emptying into sound. As an example of the first we have, of course, Lorenzo's head, hacked off his dead body by Isabella and concealed beneath—and eventually growing part of—a bed of mulch and a flowering basil plant. But we also have Isabella, whom grief coaxes into a literally vegetal state, "wither[ing] like a palm/Cut by an Indian for its juicy balm" (*I*, 447–48). Later her brothers see her "drooping by the basil green," a line whose syntax leaves tantalizingly ambiguous whether "green" describes the plant or its lovesick mistress; incidentally, when the head is disinterred it too is "green," as if corpse, vegetable life, and living lady might be united in a genus whose name is a color (*I*, 458). The poem's last stanza ends on a similar note: "And so she pined, and so she died forlon,/Imploring for her Basil to the last" (*I*, 497–98). To pine, of course, is to long for something, but after such a rush of botanical double entendres it's hard not to hear in "so she pined" "so she turned into a tree," just as she once stood rooted at Lorenzo's gravesite "like to a native lily of the dell" (*I*, 366).

It is under "the dark pine roof" of the forest that Lorenzo dies, and pining bends Isabella down toward her own end, when she will join Lorenzo beneath a "sodden tur[f]" (*I*, 294–95). Always an enthusiastic maker of puns, Keats puts his facility to ontologizing use, so that by the poem's end its disjunctive title—its claim to concern either Isabella *or* her pot of basil—is a simple statement of identification. We leave Isabella both pot and basil, a vessel of sprouting and decaying life and sprouting and decaying life itself. The poem may not have that bold indignant style Scott was hoping for, but it is absolutely Wordsworthian in another, deeper respect: in this circuit of figuration and literalism that makes people both like and into plants, dead to the world but alive in their regenerative cellular decay.

Despite its whimsical mode, *Isabella* does have Wordsworth on the brain, and signals as much in Keats's reference to Isabella "nurtur[ing]" her basil with her "human fears" (*I*, 429). It's not an unusual phrase, exactly, but it does appear in a poem with a pronounced thematic resemblance to this one, namely "A Slumber Did My Spirit Seal," one of the four so-called Lucy poems published in the 1800 edition of *Lyrical Ballads*. "A slumber did my spirit seal," goes that poem; "I had no human fears." As several readers have noted, this numbness or apathy likens the speaker to his dead beloved, "Roll'd round in earth's diurnal course/With rocks, and stones, and trees."[26] This is Lorenzo's situation too, and the one in which Isabella joins him—a unification that might be called cosmic were that word not so unfittingly extraterrestrial. Both Keats and Wordsworth also use redundancy to conjure the feeling of things, like words and their senses, vanishing irretrievably into one another. Why rocks *and* stones? Aren't rocks stones, and stones rocks? Compare Keats's statement that the basil siphons "Nurture . . . and life" from Isabella's tears and Lorenzo's head: Certainly nurture and life are, in this instance, synonymous (*I*, 429)? The effect is the same as with Keats's pun on *pine*, the rhetoric of duplication churning up a centripetal force that draws incongruent elements (life and death, plant and person, dirge and trance) toward a subatomic consensus.

We may seem to have come far from *Isabella*'s anticapitalist stanzas, but moments like these intercede in their anxieties from an oblique angle. Both the versatility of the pun and the needless addition of "stones" or "life" to "rocks" and "nurture" oppose the unidirectional, acquisitive economy those earlier lines condemn. If the pun repurposes itself, stretching beyond its apparent capacities, the line that folds under the weight of its own circular reasoning is also emblematic of a linguistic generosity, a gift that keeps on giving in a manner unique to poetry and hostile to "merchandize" and "red-lin'd accounts" (*I*, 106, 125). As Félix Guattari puts it, the "eco-logic" (*écologique*) of a poetic text comes the fact that "it may transmit a message or denote a referent while functioning at the same time through redundancies of expression and content."[27] Like Lorenzo's head, delivered not simply from death to life but from human waste to horticultural use, Keats's poetry tries to defy capitalism's metabolic incursions, which consist "not only of robbing the worker, but also of robbing the soil," and to offer a multivalent germination in its place (*C* 1.638). At the level of political economy, we might call this a movement from capitalism to permaculture, or from gold to green; at the level of genre, it might be a movement from tragedy to georgic, from a poetry of unprofitable loss to that of prodigal generation.

In *Isabella*, the aggregation and proliferation of meanings made possible by poetic language improvise an ecocritical ethos that might otherwise be historically inscrutable, and that is not exhausted by Keats's tableau of dead seals and noisy factories. This ethos is tightly keyed to the fantasy of low-impact productivity hanging around Keats's mature verse, and to the pursuit of blankness as a figure for harmlessly creative decay or degradation. Before treating this later work in detail, I'd like to point out one last catachresis in *Isabella*, this time the kind that subtilizes the physical body into the sounds it can make, wasting matter—in the shape of a particular word—so completely that it up and vanishes. Below is the poem's ninth stanza. It concerns, as so much of Keats's poetry does, an act of touch apprehended through the ear, with a clever assist from typography and the white space of the page:

> Love! thou art leading me from wintry cold,
> Lady! thou leadest me to summer clime,
> And I must taste the blossoms that unfold
> In its ripe warmth this gracious morning time
> So said, his erewhile timid lips grew bold,
> And poesied with hers in dewy rhyme:
> Great bliss was with them, and great happiness
> Grew, like a lusty flower in June's caress. (*I*, 65–72)

So Lorenzo and Isabella kiss—but when, or where? The best we have is that highly artificial metaphor catching lips in the swing of mutual versification, poesy-ing in rhyme. Thereafter tumbles forth a quartet of words that do, in fact, either rhyme or chime with the word that says what Keats will not: "bliss," "happiness," "lusty," "caress," these last two pointing us upward even to "leadest," "gracious," "lips," "taste," and "blossom." "Blossom" is especially striking because it is to a blossom that Lorenzo compares Isabella's lips, so that "taste the blossoms" makes a statement nearly identical to "poes[y] . . . in dewy rhyme." It is even more striking because the first syllable of "blossom" is so close to "bliss," the only word here that rhymes faithfully with the occluded "kiss." In sum, this emphatically catachrestic stanza, with its jarring, even mawkish comparisons of lips to flowers and kissing to rhyming, has also hidden the kiss—put it out of place—somewhere between "blossom" and "bliss." It's an ambush, a sonic displacement that realizes Keats's famous maxim that heard melodies are sweet but those unheard are sweeter, if by "unheard" we understand caught in the act of their withdrawal, accessible only through attention to the same dampened sounds that make those melodies almost inaudible.

This is far from the only poem in which Keats gets some of his words to stand shushingly in place for others. Not two years later, the temple of the mind erected at the end of "Ode to Psyche" all but evaporates "in the *midst* of *this* wide quiet*ness*," "*dress*[ed]/With the wreath'd trell*is* of a working brain" ("P," 58–60). This more supple application of the same technique doesn't take a conspicuous word like *fane* or *sanctuary* and melt it into rhyme's surround but instead conjures the object—Psyche's temple—only to expose it to a series of gentle abrasions. "Psyche" is a progress poem, but the prosodic movement of *Isabella* is declerative, using the hum of words lazily or sluggishly heard to bind its horticultural economy to its erotic one, its blossoms and basil to its blisses and kisses. Given the economic context Keats insists on assigning to the poem, this studied slowness and faintness implies or at least aspires to a circumvention of industrial time, while the retreat of single words into shared phonemes ducks away from the onomatopoetic shrieks of those lines on the brothers' enterprise. Gone silent are the swelting and torching and stinging, the barking, seething, pinching, and peeling, muzzled by a louder peace, or the dream of one.

The body that loses itself through catachresis, that becomes unfixed from its ontological parameters, is the historical body, belonging to an age and hurting in it. In the next section, I build a tentative link between the Keatsian catachresis and more contemporary paradigms of erasure or emptying, less for the sake of positing an experimental genealogy that runs from Romanticism to the art practices of the twentieth and twenty-first centuries than for the sake of understanding Keats, better. We've seen how "To Autumn" and *Isabella* traffic in the ecstatic paradox he calls "the feel of not to feel it" by localizing its effects in figures of debasement and mortification, of physical forms and units of language.[28] What remains to be seen is how these programs of misuse become positive and not just subtractive, how they turn the volume down on private bereavement in order to amplify the demand for other ways of passing through history. If existence is to be more than posthumous, it will have to learn to make that demand for itself.

* * *

"The feel of not to feel it" is a useful phrase, but it's also an oversimplification. As we've seen, Keats's negations are only ever partial: you may never read about Isabella and Lorenzo's kiss, but you hear it, which is another way of saying that it touches you. I've filed these negations under the category of catachresis, both because they involve processes of displacement, or putting things where they don't belong, and because they are, in their way, harsh, nagging, uncomfortable. The hiss of that kiss and the buzz of a mosquito—or of the gnats at the end of "To Autumn"—are not very far apart.

That disruptions of this sort might be quiet, might be felt in the muffling of sound or the tensed hush of arrested motion, is a hypothesis tested again and again in Craig Dworkin's 2013 book *No Medium*. *No Medium* attends principally to works of visual and poetic art that record what Dworkin beautifully names "the aftermath of a deletion" and that elaborate blankness as an aesthetic and sometimes an ethical choice.[29] These works, like Keats's poems, often feign total disembodiment only to show that disembodiment too is a medium, a material and a milieu that takes up a surprising amount of space. More to the point, their self-repealing gestures—expulsion, cancellation, blotting or smudging—are almost always aggressive. More desperate (as John Hoskyns might say) than metaphors, they insist on being recognized even as they throw all known standards of recognition into deliberate disarray.

It's important to ask how these sorts of gestures square with the well-trodden theme of Negative Capability, which Keats very, very hastily defines as shedding one's own psychic specificity and passing into the consciousness of other things—from fictional characters to household objects to people and pets—without expectation or judgment. The "poetical Character," he muses to his brothers, in a letter from December 1817, "is not itself—it has no self—it is everything and nothing—it has no character" but is "camelion," "continually . . . filling some other Body":

The Sun, the Moon, the Sea and Men and Women who are creatures of impulse are poetical and have about them an unchangeable attribute—the poet has none; no identity—he is certainly the most unpoetical of all God's Creatures. If then he has no self, and if I am a Poet, where is the Wonder that I should say I would write no more? Might I not at that very instant have been cogitating on the Characters of Saturn and Ops? It is a wretched thing to confess; but is a very fact that not one word I ever utter can be taken for granted as an opinion growing out of my identical nature—how can it, when I have no nature? When I am in a room with People if I ever am free from speculating on creations of my own brain, then not myself goes home to myself: but the identity of every one in the room begins so to press upon me that I am in a very little time annihilated—not only among Men; it would be the same in a Nursery of children. (*L* 1.191–4; 193–94)

This is a well-known ars poetica, and Keats is probably quite serious about it, even if it also comes to us from the early days of his career. Still—to speak personally—my own experience of reading Keats has never quite aligned with the expectations that others seem to have concerning Negative Capability. As Coleridge might say, "I object, in the very first instance, to an equivocation in the use of the word" *negative*.[30]

What makes Dworkin's discussion so useful is its insistence on viewing white pages, empty spaces, and wordless poems as affirmations: pointed and purposive, sculptural and substantial, as invested in content as in form. If we assume that Negative Capability is the elimination of personality rather than its muting, we miss the experimental intricacies of Keats's poetry, especially as it lopes into the second decade of English Romanticism. We also miss a chance to learn something about the formal strategies whereby lyric, so often tarred with the brush of "the egotistical sublime[,] which is a thing per se and stands alone," cultivates the charisma of the impersonal (*L* 1.387). If there's such a thing as the Keatsian sublime, it lies in the poet's engagement with the per quod rather than the per se—with those demonstrative forms of relation that anchor him to things in the world. To render this relation as thickness, presence, haecceity, gravity, or ballast, to treat it as a strange or abstract incidence, is the work of Keats's poetics; it is the work, too, of some versions of the avant-garde that just happen to postdate it.

The relation of catachresis to blankness knits cleanly into Dworkin's treatment of a scene from Jean Cocteau's *Orphic Trilogy*. The second film, *Orphée*, introduces us to the celebrated but slightly uncool poet Orpheus, who, in the first scene, is handed a journal containing some poems by his rival, the up-and-comer Cégeste. The journal is called *Nudisme*, and its pages are blank. Orpheus is unimpressed, then defensive, "the typical response of an establishment put upon by the avant-garde and unwilling to assimilate a gesture (*ce geste*) of radical reduction." Worst is the "quick double punch" that elicits "the shock of the prudish bourgeois reader by announcing a salacious subject" only to deny "the prurient (and equally bourgeois) expectation of any titillating material within." And yet the "pornographic and exhibitionist associations of *nudisme*" must also contend with the fact that "*nudisme* implies an unveiling more than a negation," a "throwing off of metaphorical sheets to reveal" the embarrassment of a poem's substrate, which is to say paper. "Erasures obliterate," Dworkin writes, "but they also reveal."[31] One of the things they disclose is the overlooked bedrock of the poem; another is the commodity form of the body behind it, the residue of natural (or, to put a finer point on it, au naturel) existence pulped into stationery and glued, sheet by sheet, into a volume.

Keats's poems enlist similar themes, and they can be similarly coy, especially when they're on a mission to thicken metaphors into somatic events "proved upon our pulses" (*L* 1.279). Like *Nudisme*, they pose as though about to unfurl one type of obscenity—sex—then suddenly pivot toward the far more embarrassing exhibitionism of a winking prudery, sex in the rubber mask of tact. Anyone who reads Keats can feel this happening, the flirtatious two-step that suddenly pitches backward into reserve. It's exactly this constellation of phony bashfulness and open appetite that prompts Byron to come up with the shrewd (if not entirely satisfying) insight that Keats's is a poetry of "mental masturbation," and Kenneth Burke, much later, to burst the serene bubble of "Ode on a Grecian Urn" by insisting that the enigmatic penultimate line means nothing more than "body is turd, turd body."[32] Orpheus feels personally beset by Cégeste's *nudisme*, and Keats translates his own experience of being "press[ed] upon" by other people's identities into an experiment in alternating pressure with slackness or enervation, at the level of the line and as a technique of engaging—and often disaffecting—his audience. It's a gambit that twiddles in turn the aesthetic nodes Dworkin dubs "hard core" and "soft focus," the pornographic and its partial alleviation or gentling. Like a pixelated close-up of an X-rated image, Keats's poetry mines alienation from extreme, overbearing proximity, the recondite from what no one wants to admit is actually familiar.

To talk about Keats and catachresis, then, is to talk about an effacement that is somehow brazen and crude, an evanescence in your face. Following up on Byron's quip that Keats was "always frigging his imagination," we could describe this with comparable indelicacy as a poetics of rubbing one out, indulgence as excision.[33] Keats's poetry, so often tagged as unduly sensual, is in fact making its exorbitant demands on carnality in an effort to surprise us with stillness. If, in Anne-Lise François's words, that poetry's "complex gender politics" helps establish "form . . . not as that which endures, inured to the effects of time, but as that which requires 'enduring,'" its more general troping of sex and desire similarly springboards into a Romantic variant on *nudisme* for which "aestheticism and asceticism become nearly indistinguishable."[34]

Whatever we think of Burke's cheeky coarsening of "Grecian Urn," it does have the advantage of obeying the summons issued by all of Keats's great poems and most of his bad ones: it turns the senses into theoreticians. Here too lies the work of catachresis, which might be helpfully recovered from those occasions when the senses are called upon to do a thinking so serious it can only appear awkward, obtuse, cloying, and improper. Having been first asked to parse some gawky or otherwise objectionable passage, they are then forced to break themselves upon it, to suffer the abolition of their nice intelligence. The vaunted synesthesia of Keats's writing really comes down to this: an attempt to put into words the response of a body under emancipatory duress. Pushing vulgarity until it opens up into vacancy, the poetry expresses both the longing to be delivered from the isolation of being a single body and the discomfort of that release. If there is political allegory here, it has to do with the pain of realizing who we are in the coarse yet exquisitely various encounter with other lives, when they are briefly stripped bare of their social abstraction and restored to the indiscreet predicament of being merely nakedly human.

This notion of the senses as theoreticians comes from the section on private property and communism in Marx's Paris Manuscripts, early writing that, not unlike Keats's poetry before 1819, is regularly dismissed as immature. I won't get into any defense of the humanist Marx in these pages. I simply want to note the compelling kinship between his emphasis, in these documents, on the "complete *emancipation* of all human senses and attributes" and Keats's tackling of the same project on a smaller scale but in reciprocal terms.[35] Needless to say, for Marx the prerequisite of such an emancipation is "the transcendence of private property," by which the human becomes indissociable from the social; with property out of the picture, "the eye has become a *human* eye, just as its *object* has become a social, *human* object—an object emanating from man for man." In this way, "the *senses* have . . . become directly in their practice *theoreticians*," while "need or enjoyment have . . . lost their egotistical nature, and nature lost its mere *utility* by use becoming *human* use" (*EPM*, 107). That these ways of being happily bereaved unshackle the social relation from capital's catachresis—a catachresis Marx elsewhere terms *abgeschmackt*, fatuous or corny—is essential to this argument, as is its volubly Romantic emphasis on sensation.[36] Or rather, not just sensation but the sensuous dispersal of the self into a world whose custody we share:

> Man appropriates his total essence in a total manner, that is to say, as a whole man. Each of his *human* relations to the world—seeing, hearing, smelling, tasting, feeling, thinking, being aware, sensing, wanting, acting, loving—in short, all the organs of his individual being, like those organs which are directly social in their form, are in their *objective* orientation or in their *orientation to the object*, the appropriation of that object, the appropriation of the *human* world; their orientation to the

object is the *manifestation of the human world*; it is human *efficaciousness* and human *suffering*, for suffering, apprehended humanly, is an enjoyment of self in man. (*EPM*, 106)

In sum, "man is not lost in his object only when the object becomes for him a *human* object" but "when the object becomes for him a *social* object . . . just as society becomes a being for him in this object" (*EPM*, 107). To be lost, on this account, is to retrieve sociality as the historical and quite possibly the genetic destiny of the species; it also to enrich the depleted metaphor of the social body. For all it has weathered, corporeal experience remains a trail of breadcrumbs that might lead to this state of self-abàndonment, when being human will mean getting folded into a sumptuous, deeply moral, and not at all painless continuity with the lives of others.

I have suggested that Keats's poetry—both mature and immature, major and minor, virtuosic and baldly imitative—aspires to emancipate the senses via a strategic mishandling of linguistic and semantic entities, often in scenes of the body's degradation. This is perhaps a fanciful spin on Marx, not to everyone's liking. I undertake it all the same to keep faith with Raymond Williams's generous account of "the aesthetic" as an "affirmation . . . of certain human meanings and values which a dominant social system reduce[s] and even trie[s] to exclude."[37] My treatment of catachresis in Keats's poetry is an attempt to elaborate such meanings in a writer who is not Marx but who bears with him the weight of a unique historical situation. Rather than insist (as others have done) upon Keats's sublimation of his own petit-bourgeois identity into the syntax of his poetry, I claim catachresis as a device that limns the fissuring of life into something that can be bought and sold. It is also, and by the same token, the device Keats uses to begin to imagine how life might be mended, or what it might feel like if it were.

If we wanted to use another idiom, we might swap out catachresis with defamiliarization, the technique by which works of art lengthen the time it takes to perceive them. And yet what is genuinely disarming about Keats is his quirk of presenting in verse things that are not there, not things that are simply strange or off-color; their sensuousness is absolute but present only *in an aftermath*, as the pulse of something almost gone. It is through these local figurations of the substance of blankness, vacancy, elision, or deletion that Keats hones a poetics capable of registering the human essence of nature and the natural essence of man as an abandonment or emptying-out, not just of the ego, self, or lyric subject but of the body itself as a target for expropriative activity.

The body targeted, by capital, for this purpose remains so through its compulsory stamina, its posthumous persistence as a resource of value. When Keats cinches that persistence to representations of ongoing states of being and feeling, it is with an eye toward recapturing the senses for blissfully impersonal purposes, of the sort laid out in his account of Negative Capability. Those states, unsurprisingly, often look a lot like death, and not the smug libertine *petit mort*. What we learn from Dworkin, however, is to hold off identifying complex aesthetic phenomena with the most extreme verge of their intimations. A posthumous existence is, brutally, a different matter than the cessation of life. To take blankness seriously is to believe that it signifies something other than a null set; to take catachresis seriously is to believe that it signifies something other than an impossibility or dead end. As a down-turning, catachresis is a figure of inclination: How do the senses learn to stomach the midpoint or even the edge of their emancipation when it does not come, and does not come, and does not come again?

* * *

This final section turns first to the "Ode to Psyche" and then briefly to the *Hyperion* poems, both of which deal in fantasies of what James Chandler calls "the end of a public history" of social stratification.[38] As Chandler notes, that history is tied in Keats's mind to "the present struggle in England of the people" against despotism, and against those who have seized upon the "unlucky termination" of the French Revolution "in every way" (Keats says) "to undermine our freedom." The current state of things is disheartening, and yet, Keats offers, "perhaps the present distresses of this nation are a fortunate thing though so horrid in their experience"(*L* 2.193). Or, as he puts it in a different letter while at work on the ode, "Do you not see how necessary a World of Pains and troubles is to school an Intelligence and make it a soul?" (*L* 2.102)

Because the Greek word *psyche* means "soul," the poem is often taken as an allegory for this schooling, a process that necessarily includes mortification of various kinds. It has the same basic conceit as Keats's sonnet "On First Looking into Chapman's Homer": the poet is the intrepid latecomer to classical learning, and this time he has a friend in Psyche, the Greek goddess who doesn't feature in any of the old myths but is immortalized in Apuleius's second-century novel *The Golden Ass*. Unable to find a husband despite her great beauty, Psyche is directed by an oracle of Apollo to turn herself over to a supernatural creature, "a dire mischief, viperous and fierce," who will be her mate.[39] The marriage is more pleasant than expected, and yet Psyche isn't allowed to see her husband's face. When she risks a peek by candlelight, a drop of wax falls from her taper onto his shoulder—the shoulder of none other than Cupid, god of love. Cupid awakes and, betrayed, deserts her. The rest of the tale concerns Psyche's trials at the hands of Cupid's mother, Venus, her reunion with her husband, and her own apotheosis; it ends with the birth of Cupid and Psyche's daughter, Pleasure.

There is not much in Apuleius's story that lends itself to a critique of despotism, even if "Psyche" does issue a challenge to religious authority: since the goddess has come into culture "too late for antique vows," the poet decides that he "will be [her] priest," and build her "fane/In some untrodden region of [his] mind" ("P," 36, 50–51). I've written elsewhere about how this temple of the "working brain" functions as a drastically innocuous structure, one that commits both poet and poem to an ethics of voluntary deterioration ("P," 60). Like Lorenzo's head, the image of the poet's mind, "Where branched thoughts, new grown with pleasant pain,/Instead of pines shall murmur in the wind," sketches an alternative economy, opposed to the excesses of antiquity and their analogues in the present ("P," 52–53).[40] If the pot of basil represents an impulse toward reuse or recycling, the imaginary shrine to Psyche offers to exit the world altogether, to die with the poet and be lost with his poem. This understanding of the ode still seems right to me, but images of benign growth and happy obsolescence aren't the only parallel between *Isabella* and "Psyche." Ordering the second poem, too, is a lush fidelity to the hard parts of embodiment, to those pains and troubles that must be felt *through* before they can (nearly) disappear.

It's not necessary to say that "Psyche" improves upon *Isabella*, even if Keats did think of his work in gradient terms, with each poem scrubbing the mistakes of a previous one and inching the bar ever higher. Interestingly, when the ode sets its sights on abstruse philosophical questions, it pursues their answers in similar fashion to the earlier romance. In *Isabella*, the undercover and yet unmistakable kiss between the two lovers tests a poetics designed to implode, sighing for an economic form that might do more or less the same. "Psyche" has no capitalist stanzas to call its own, and yet it too sees kissing, or not kissing, or having kissed as an opportunity to gauge the capacity of words to convey the historical condition of flesh. The ode begins "to-day," with the poet's vision of Psyche lying with Cupid on a forest floor:

Mid hush'd, cool-rooted flowers, fragrant-eyed,
  Blue, silver-white, and budded Tyrian,
They lay calm-breathing, on the bedded grass;
  Their arms embraced, and their pinions too;
  Their lips touch'd not, but had not bade adieu,

As if disjoined by soft-handed slumber,
And ready still past kisses to outnumber
    At tender eye-dawn of aurorean love. ("P," 13–20)

Unlike its sibling passage in *Isabella*, this one highlights space over sound, nestling the lovers in a pose of erogenous alertness that makes this a scene of suspense as well as suspension. The lovers are tense, *ready still*, taut from a longing that can be tranquil but never stationary. This phrase— "ready still"—joins those catachrestic pairings that mold "To Autumn" along the contours of a dimension located somewhere behind or beyond its lines. Like "full-grown lambs," "ready still" belongs to a rhetoric of bodies pushed up against their limits, for to be ready still is not to be still ready, nor even ready, still. It is to be primed, turned on, about to arrive at a life that is immortal but carnal and feeling that immortality and carnality all at once, as relative velocities. And, like the inversion of "o'er-brimmed" (as in "o'er brimmed their clammy cells"), "ready still" forces us to trip over our syntactic expectations and thereby to undergo some measure of what Cupid and Psyche do: joy etched with discomfort, an itch for the grammar that was forecast but denied. We are pressed inside the little room between these gods and between Keats's words. It's a tight, taxing fit.

    This reading can go further, further in the line. Cupid and Psyche are "ready still past kisses to outnumber," a condition Hermione de Almeida describes casually as one the lovers "endure" (that word again).[41] For de Almeida, the word *past* functions prepositionally: it is on the far side of their kisses that Cupid and Psyche are found to persist. The interpretation is vexed but not implausible. A simpler read would be that Cupid and Psyche are prepared, getting ready, to give each other still more kisses than they have already given, as Catullus exhorts Lesbia to do for him in his fifth ode ("deinde centum,/dein mīlle altera, dein secunda centum,/ deinde ūsque altera mīlle, deinde centum").[42] If we hear de Almeida's suggestion that they *endure past* their kisses, we could preserve the elementary reading while also finding hints of its transcendence. What Cupid and Psyche must get beyond is the very idea of "kisses to outnumber," which is to say kisses that might be counted, jealously tallied ("ne sciāmus,/aut nē quis malus invidēre possit,/cum tantum sciat esse bāsiōrum"). Getting past that idea means shrugging off the logic of enumeration. To outnumber is to strike number out; to say that this is something that would have to be put up with or braved is to begin to mark the difficulty of being a free body among others, neither singular nor aggregate but part of a cascading *more*—more kisses, more pleasure, more life.

    Thomas Taylor, whose translation of Apuleius's tale is the one Keats knew, glossed Psyche's story as "the descent of the soul from the intelligible world into a mundane condition of being, but yet without abandoning its establishment in the Heavens."[43] In a more secular vein, we might recast this tension in the point of contact between the individual body—the thing with lips and pinions and arms, that sleeps and kisses and breathes—and the form of existence it has in common with other bodies. It is the form of existence called duration, or history, and as history it too must be endured. Rather than see the lovers on the grass as a tripartite allegory of the earth, the heavens, and the soul somewhere intervening, we might look on the space *between* Cupid and Psyche—the space importuned by their ready stillness—as a figure for being historical, living through time as a more than biological but no more than corporeal creature.

Compare this figure to Giorgio Agamben's definition of the gesture, a movement in which "nothing is being produced or acted, but rather something is being endured or supported." Agamben claims that "the Western bourgeoisie" loses its capacity for gesture—which is to say, for carrying the weight of the flesh as flesh and not as a repository of value— "by the end of the nineteenth century," but Keats seems to anticipate some version of that fate here, and to campaign against it.[44] This thought returns us to *Isabella*, as it should since, as I've said, "Psyche" ends with things growing in the poet's head as they likewise grow in Lorenzo's, with a vision of a culture happy to give itself over to decline. In "Psyche," however, we are left with a hope *Isabella* has no room for: that there *is* life after numeration, calculation, valuation, and crass utility. The hardwon, hard-pressed union of Cupid and Psyche rehearses or (to use Keats's word) readies that life by bearing up under a version of the unalienated sensuousness it promises. "Sweet enforcement" is the name of this game, as sex rings out what it has "wrung" from the body, namely the promise of its own deliverance ("P," 1–2).

Keats's arrangement of Cupid and Psyche is often compared to the scene painted on the urn of "Ode on a Grecian Urn"—namely, the image of the "bold lover" chasing down some likely unwilling "she"—but this is a mistake, and a telling one ("GU," 17). For one thing, Cupid and Psyche's embrace is consensual where that "struggle to escape" is not: Keats is a poet who finds mutuality erotic, and in "Grecian Urn" he takes care to present his male and female figures locked in an asymmetrical relation, in which he will forever "love, and she be fair!" ("GU," 9, 20). "Psyche," by contrast, refers to its lovers as a "they," one unit of barely distinguished parts (feathers, lips, arms, in- and exhalations). But "Psyche" is also eager to undo fantasies of capture and coercion at every level. It borrows from its governing trope of reciprocal conjunction or couching side by side a key to guessing what happens, or what might ideally happen, *after* the trial of which sex is both example and emblem. As the ode moves from the postcoital couple to the poet's brain, it follows satisfaction with impoverishment, as the world of the poem gets washed out by Keats's hush:

> Far, far around shall those dark-cluster'd trees
>   Fledge the wild-ridged mountains steep by steep;
> And there by zephyrs, streams, and birds, and bees,
>   The moss-lain Dryads shall be lull'd to sleep;
> And in the midst of this wide quietness
> A rosy sanctuary will I dress
>   With the wreath'd trellis of a working brain,
>   With buds, and bells, and stars without a name,
> With all the gardener Fancy e'er could feign,
>   Who breeding flowers, will never breed the same:
> And there shall be for thee all soft delight
>   That shadowy thought can win,
> A bright torch, and a casement ope at night,
>   To let the warm Love in! ("P," 54–67)

Mucilaginous is the word we need. Read these lines out loud: a phrase like "far, far around shall" pulls your mouth open as though it's wrestling with a ladleful of peanut butter, while the same hissing that surges around the ninth stanza of *Isabella* returns to much the same effect, scoring silence and making it "soft," a thing with texture and the suggestion of weight. These are the kinds of tricks that prevent what I've just called a movement from consummation to dispossession from terminating in a just-numb or just-vacant loss: this calm is *loud*. And sticky.

"Psyche" begins with intense corporeal delight, and it ends in intense corporeality. The first is a gift exchanged between two people, the second cannot be gifted because it can never belong to anyone restrictedly: it is always all of ours. So much is made abundantly if by no means crystal clear by the suggestion of some kind of proprioceptive intelligence mapping the shape of Keats's brain, feeling into the wide quietness to learn that it is wide and quiet. These ("wide" and "quiet") are relative judgments, but they are not privileged or confidential ones: some arms are reaching out to take the measure of this serenity; some ear is tapping out its limits. Experience of this sort is beyond appropriation. As Keats implies in his remarks on the gardener Fancy—"who breeding flowers, will never breed the same"—everything in this place is at once fully felt and ephemeral, incapable of being reproduced or even named ("P," 63).

If this is the dream of one poet, it's also a dream about the removal of the constraints of being singular, about being propelled out of integers by the vigor of a collective, coordinated existence.

"Let us suppose," writes Marx, in his comments on James Mill's *Elements of Political Economy*, "that we had carried out production as human beings." Let us suppose that we were not enjoined to consider one another as wells of impounded value, or as ambits of exchange, or as hurdles to overcome on the way to an individual freedom directly proportional to our earning power. In that joyous case, "our products would be so many mirrors in which we saw reflected our essential nature," and "this relationship would moreover be reciprocal, [for] what occurs on my side has also to occur on yours." It's stretching things a bit too far to see the loving correspondence of Cupid and Psyche as a dream-image of this sort of relation. Nonetheless, at its utterly Romantic core, Marx's ambition is the same as Keats's: to confirm and realize "human nature" as "communal nature." What else could Negative Capability mean than this, the competence to recognize beneath the "*sensuously perceptible covering, the hidden shape*" of the person understood as what Keats calls a fact— a manufactured thing—the shared condition of living in time?[45]

It can't be said enough that Keats's Capability is active, or even that it is an action. The word implies a state of latency, and yet to be negatively capable is already to be undertaking the semideliberate self-compression and self-dissolution that deletes character, crosses it out. Neither the wise passiveness of Wordsworth nor Kant's *Gemeinsinn*, Negative Capability is effortful and it is indiscriminate, being entirely unconcerned with verdicts on merit or taste. This is why its signature gesture is a sexual one. Sex subjects the elite category of aesthetic judgment to a gentle burlesque, turning taste from a cognitive property of person or a community to a voluptuous relation between whomever. In the perpetual unfolding of Cupid and Psyche's embrace, there is a match for the condition of being "blind bodies . . . in the same room," stealing interminably closer in an arc of privation and presence (*L* 2.5). These blind bodies deliver a lesson about how to live generously together, because what sex means, for Keats, is the gravity of other people. It tests the unlikely hypothesis that gravity might be the sensation of freedom—from oneself, certainly, but also from the built environment of an unhappy human history, visible to the present only in its most catastrophic form.

The standard line on Keats's writing—that it is undercooked and overwrought—misdiagnoses exactly this cluster of humanist intuitions. What looks like a poetry of surfeit and sloppy address takes from erotic insinuation a way of imagining loss, forfeiture, or removal as a true enjoyment of life: remember, "suffering, apprehended humanly, is an enjoyment of self in man." This is what is at stake in the subtle but persistent representation of sex as a type of hard work, an activity that is physically and psychologically stressful. Sex, for Keats, is an affliction, a clear example of what it means to bear the mark of others. Never a game and always an ordeal that goes on into its aftermath, it hallucinates a communist form of work that is also a free manifestation of sensuous existence, which we might now understand as just another word (or pair of words) for Matthew Arnold's "sensuous strain." As part of life it is never free from pain, but it manages to boil pain down to a simply somatic phenomenon, on such a complete continuum with pleasure that both may be expressed in the broad perpendicular terms of impress or force.

Because "Psyche" structures itself around a scene of intimate discovery, even spying, it's easy to forget that its context is bluntly historiographic: that was then, and this will be now, past old-time religion, past Christianity, past the swaggering skepticism of the Enlightenment. Past, too, any social or institutional framework for art and poetry: the anatomical temple in which Keats's endlessly new, endlessly irrecoverable fancies bed down is not just postsecular; it is postcultural, glancing perhaps at the kind of empty-world scenario Mary Shelley will develop, in a more somber key, in her *Last Man.* And yet, whatever dystopian energies may haunt its farewell to civilization, the poem is determined to get beyond them, to commit to a full-throated endorsement of the end of culture and the reclamation of humanity as a locus of passionate existence. "Psyche" is made possible by a series of historical deletions the poem archives modestly in its syntax ("no altar . . . nor choir . . . no voice, no lute" and so on), but behind this playful adieu it is taking the winner's perspective on the ruin of other times and places. To the "faint Olympians," good riddance.

What does the emancipation of the senses look like outside the victory lap of divine love? In his long poem *Laon and Cythna,* Shelley offers a vision of utopian society tagged with a surprising footnote. "[M]an and woman," he writes, "[t]heir common bondage burst, may freely borrow/ From lawless love a solace for their sorrow," for even in utopia "oft we still must weep, for we are human."[46] This is a curious fantasy, by which I mean not that it is unreasonable but rather that its speculative mode is hungering, even lustful, since here as throughout *Laon and Cythna* Shelley yokes love to injury and makes from them the crucible in which the revolutionary subject is formed. More than that: put love together with sorrow, and a refinement on conventional pictures of utopia as a perfect world emerges. A good life is not one in which people are no longer in pain. A good life is one in which all our distress is purely human, none of it caused by what Shelley would call slavery and Marx the social relation of capital. What Shelley imagines is the emancipation of suffering itself. He also implies that to suffer is more fundamental to the human experience than to love, and so the consequences of its bondage are all the more severe.

The *Hyperion* poems, too, have absorbed a fascination with the political meaning of pain, and with the strange intuition that it is our difficulties "the ever-watchful spirit of fraud and tyranny" is most cruel to take away from us.[47] In them, we see the aftermath of the overthrow of the ancestors of those pale Olympians who are long gone by the time Keats's Psyche comes on the scene. Surprisingly, it is their anguish with which these poems are chiefly concerned. As this protracted genealogy implies—the Titans precede the Olympians Psyche is too late to join, and long after her comes Keats's religion of the heart's affections and the brain's tabernacle—*Hyperion* and *The Fall of Hyperion* are poems about the descent not of man but of humanity, and about an evolutionary movement that pulls even primordial beings toward their best end. As in "Psyche," that end is effacement, for how can the human world thrive when it remains in the thrall of hierarchy of any sort, whether supernatural or secular? The difference between the poems is that the later ones embrace the context of political struggle over and against the more fantastical narrative "Psyche" uses to kick-start its vision. Not unrelatedly, the *Hyperion* poems are less about poetry and poetics than they are about a general disposition toward monumentality, and the necessity of destroying or letting die what remains of power once its time is up.

Monumentality or, in simpler terms, buildings. The big idea of the *Hyperion* fragments, both of which kill time in the fallout of the Titans' overthrow by the Olympians, and both of which contemplate the poet's role in interpreting revolutionary events, is that the Titans' bodies are giant architectural forms, and that they are both ample and animate. In *Hyperion*, the goddess Thea has a face as "large as that of Memphian sphinx,/ Pedestal'd haply in palace court," and all the Titans sit around, in mourning and frustration, "like a dismal cirque/Of Druid stones" (*H* 1.31–32, 2.34–35). This last may be a nod to Burke's invocation of Stonehenge in his *Enquiry* chapter on "Difficulty," which follows hard upon the chapter on "Magnitude in BUILDING" and seems to have precipitated out of it. "Those huge rude masses" of stone, Burke writes, "exclude ... the idea of art, and contrivance," just as the physical body for Keats seems likewise to represent a blunt if not brute materiality with which his own aesthetic practice is dialectically engaged.[48] Writing, for Keats, condenses the truth of life as an obligation to be made of stuff. It is also inevitably a deviation from the human and historical agony it can broach only in general and into which it cannot intervene, as the Grecian urn says coolly of its own mythic scenes of harm always about to happen.

Where do the Titans' own rude masses come from? Keats's debt to Spenser and Milton is, as always, emphatic: figuring embodiment at mammoth proportions is a skill he cribs from blue-ribbon epithets like Spenser's "sea-shouldering whales" and the epic guarantee of scale.[49] As Keats said of *Paradise Lost*, it's the work of a poet "stationing" and being "*statuary*," who shows us "not only . . . how the Birds '*with clang despised the ground*'" but these same birds "'*under a cloud in prospect.*'" "So we see Adam," Keats continues, "'*Fair indeed and tall—under a plantane*'—and so we see Satan '*disfigured—on the Assyrian Mount.*'"[50] And so we find Keats, a century and a half later, lodging Saturn in a lair where "Forest on forest hung above his head/Like cloud on cloud," or Hyperion, who is after all the sun, "leaving twilight in the rear" while he "slope[s] upon the threshold of the west" (*H* 1.6–7, 203–4).

In an uncanny turn of sympathetic imagination, Nicholas Roe conjures another hypothesis. Keats's parents owned a stable on the edge of Moorfields, from which their son "could see regiments of volunteer soldiers, loyal to King and Country, on parade"; "directly opposite, Bedlam," England's infamous first hospital for the mentally ill, "was a colossal, unavoidable presence." It was also in a state of obvious disrepair. When Keats was a child, plans for a new building were already under way, and in 1815 Bedlam would move across town to St. George's Fields. Today, the Moorfields building is an eye hospital and has been relieved of its eighteenth-century gate, which, by Roe's account, must have been a sight. "Presiding over [the] comings and goings" of patients, their families, and curious visitors were Caius Cibber's enormous statues of "raving" and "melancholy" madness, one on each gatepost; "fashioned from Portland stone," Melancholy Madness was "a naked wretch propped on his forearm, mouth slack and eyes vacant," with Raving Madness "manacled in torment, a terrifying embodiment of what lay behind Bedlam's elegant façade."[51]

These "gigantic embodiments of anguish," Roe offers, would "reappear as the fallen titans in *Hyperion*." This seems a stretch of Roe's own until you actually look at Cibber's statues, now on display in the museum of the Bethlem Royal Hospital (figure 3). They are indeed gigantic, but what is most striking about them is the way their form seems to press upward and outward into the surrounding air, as though what is being represented is not madness in any of its variants but rather madness as a consequence of having dimension.

Lying on his side, leaning on his elbow, Melancholy looks like an Atlas who quit, his shoulders still lifted as though the weight of the world

FIG. 3. Charles Grignion (1784), statues of "raving" and "melancholy" madness, each reclining on one half of a pediment, formerly crowning the gates at Bethlem [Bedlam] Hospital. Engraving, after Samuel Wale, after Caius Gabriel Cibber (1680). Photograph: Wellcome Collection (CC BY).

remained upon them; in a clear nod to the male figure at the center of the ancient Laocoön group, Raving tilts his head, opens his mouth, and pushes his chest forward. Interestingly, although he is bound with a single chain cuffing wrist to wrist, and although his torso, face, neck, and clenched fists give the impression of a body thrashing against imprisonment, the chain is lax, not taut as it would be if he were truly trying to pull away. Upper and lower body contrast torment and repose, with the chain that bisects the space between them drawing extra attention to this mutual composition of kinetic and inertial force. In Cibber's allegorical figure rests a partial and perverse illustration of the laws of physics: action and reaction become visible when their rule is suspended, when a chain that should snap tight flops upon the floor.

Roe's hunch is a good one, and it captures the ways in which the *Hyperion* poems are organized around slow-moving, gear-grinding encounters of bodies in space and bodies and space. What this has to do with revolution is an open question. The revolutionaries—the Olympians—are missing, and so are the events leading up to their coup. In the middle of a long concessionary speech, Oceanus appeals to "the eternal law / That first in beauty should be first in might," though this is altogether too neat; it also sounds a lot like the equally sophistical conclusion to "Grecian Urn" (*H* 2.228–29). Again and again the Titans' bodies are described as repositories of narrative, but narrative is nowhere to be found. In the first poem Apollo and in the second poem the poet are looking for the truth of what's happened, and every time they are denied its sight. Getting in their way is Titanic form itself, as though it were at once the only archive of historical existence and yet a persistent obstacle to reading it. I say "as though" but, of course, this is simply true. Apollo's plea to Mnemosyne sums up the problem:

> Mnemosyne!
> Thy name is on my tongue, I know not how;
> Why should I tell thee what thou so well seest?
> Why should I strive to show what from thy lips
> Would come no mystery? For me, dark, dark,
> And painful vile oblivion seals my eyes. (*H* 3.82–87)

Walter Jackson Bate makes the luminous observation that as Keats's work matures, it loses its aspirant Latinity and leans on monosyllabic Germanic words, which slow down the poetic line. Mnemosyne may be Greek—in *The Fall of Hyperion*, she is the Latin Moneta—but as a polysyllabic name of classical origin, it stands in stark prosodic contrast with almost every other word in this passage. The exceptions are the "mystery" with which "Mnemosyne" rhymes and the "painful vile oblivion" (three Romance words in a row) she shows Apollo. The rest of Apollo's speech plugs away one compact syllable at a time, growing "stronger in consonantal and phonetic body" so that the speech partakes in the same sturdy ubiquitous mass that gives the Titans their heft.[52]

Set alongside the very different music of Mnemosyne and those other lithe Latin sounds, Apollo literally voices the conflict between a view of civilization as things remembered—"Names, deeds, gray legends, dire events, rebellions,/Majesties, sovran voices, agonies,/Creations and destroyings"—and some doubly dark, emergent means of apprehending historical process that goes beyond what can be merely seen, heard, or recollected (*H* 3.114–16). The first view belongs to the Titans: it is grand, but old and outmoded, and can only trip backward into "oblivion." The second will involve a "fierce convulse" like the one that shakes Apollo's limbs, which at the poem's end stand ready to "die into life" but remain forever on the threshold of what happens next (*H* 3.129–30).

The Fall of Hyperion is littered with similar scenes, where the Titans' big, blocky selves hold out only to thwart insight into the recent event of their undoing. Saturn's "broad marble knees" work like this, as does "the view of sad Moneta's brow" that sets the poet—our protagonist here—"ach[ing] to see what things the hollow brain/Behind enwombed" (*FH* 1.214, 1.275–77). Notice that any direct line to Moneta's face is off the table: instead the poet gets her brow, and instead of being able to see it, he merely confronts the view, the catachrestic nearer-to-hand. For a split second, the poet is ready to drive his eye into these "sullen entrails," through that brow and into that brain as "rich with ore" as a mountain flecked with gold (*FH* 1.272–74). But he doesn't; with everything set inside this exceedingly strange nesting doll of metaphors he wouldn't know where to aim.

A basic question about syntax: Is Moneta's brain the womb inside of which shelter the things the poet wants to see? Then the brain isn't hollow at all; anyway, brains (as Keats the medical student knew) aren't hollow but dense and heavy. And the prepositional *behind*? Ostensibly it places Moneta's brain *under* her brow, where it should be, but "things the hollow brain/Behind enwombed" is so hard to parse you might reasonably think the brain is enwombing something behind its own walls, as a uterus enwombs an embryo or a tumor. The image is grotesque, especially when we recall that all the Titans are titanic and Moneta, the mountain to be mined, is no exception: this is a huge brain, a huge womb, planetary in scope. The image is not, however, smug; nor does it hint at an assault, despite the uncomfortable setup that has the male poet getting ready to peer into Moneta's head as though it were or contained her reproductive organs. But this *is* a setup, a bait and switch that risks activating various cultural frameworks—sexual, surgical, misogynist—in order to dismantle them. Fumbling away from a naïve conflation of materiality with surface, and of form with gender, the passage begins to unfurl a representational ethics that treats living beings as a collection of carnal tissue: organs cradled by bones surrounded by skin and nothing else besides.

The poet's moment of historical discernment, when it finally comes, is ingressive without being puncturing, spirited away from humdrum tropes of penetration and impregnation, wombs and wounds. In Keats's words, it is a seeing that "take[s] the depth/Of things as nimbly as the outward eye/Can size and shape pervade" (*FH* 1.304–6). *Pervade*: move through, suffuse, fill up. It is, finally, an internalized subjective version of the embrace between Cupid and Psyche, for whom the transit of shared breath is one small movement of a comprehensive process of mutual and expansive saturation. In "Psyche" too, that movement is part of history, nearly its terminus, except that belongs to someone whose wish is to dissolve into the earth and take commerce, culture, social difference and sexual orthodoxy—in brief, hitherto existing society—with him. If this return to the poet's exemplarity and its moral-political endowment is unsatisfying, remember that it too will be ruined, overwritten, put to other purposes. That was always and remains its gamble and its gift.

* * *

This chapter has been guided by the idea of the posthumous existence, the burden of being alive in the wake of a conviction that we are already dead. What has been lost, under these circumstances, is not just "real life" but, as Keats says, "how it would have been." In the same letter Keats will make clear that by this agonizing counterfactual he means how his relationship with Fanny Brawne would have been, how he might have persisted in being "well, healthy, alert &c, walking with her" instead of laid up on his sickbed, waiting (even if no one would say so) to die. "The knowledge of [this] contrast [and the] feeling for light and shade" may be "necessary for a poem," he observes, but they are "also great enemies to the recovery of the stomach"—Keats's stomach being, or so his doctor believed, the seat of his illness (*L* 2.359–60). It was to avoid agitating his stomach with the pain of juxtaposition that Keats refused to read any of the letters Brawne sent to him from England; in the end they were buried with him, unopened.

Unlike real life, real death is a black box. There is no wondering about how it might have been; the dead don't send letters we can leave pointedly sealed, as if to say "that's all over now." And yet at the unfinished end of *Hyperion*, there is nonetheless an indication that some forms of existence, by virtue of being cut off from the world, are also forms of death that can be, have to be, perished out of. This is what happens when Apollo's fierce convulse and his dying into life remove him from the sub rosa emergency of "feel[ing] curs'd and thwarted," compelled to "spurn the green turf as hateful" (*H* 3.92, 3.94). Buckling under the massive download of historical information Mnemosyne gifts to him, Apollo becomes "[like]one who should take leave/Of pale immortal death"—an enigmatic simile belying his own insistence that "knowledge enormous makes a god of me" (*H* 3.128 3.113).

Since Apollo is *already* a god, these closing lines of the poem's third book cannot be a traditional apotheosis. Rather, Keats is positing a fine difference between immortality and divinity or, minimally, between unripe and mature branches of godhead. The "fearless and yet . . . aching ignorance" that bedevils Apollo is not removed simply because he is forced to ingest the entire archive of civilization (*H* 3.107). It is removed, rather, by his half-willing withdrawal from death, where *death* means depressive duration more than any actual demise. A pale immortal death, like a posthumous existence, is a life of unnatural interminable suffering. What separates these two unfortunate states of being is that the first, unlike the second, really can be amended, died out of, changed for the kind of life that is immortal in a much better sense: on intimate terms with the world and everything that's ever happened in it.

"Is't not strange," Mnemosyne asks, leadingly, "[t]hat thou shouldst weep, so gifted?" To this question Apollo has no answer. "I strive to search wherefore I am so sad," he offers, "[u]ntil a melancholy numbs my limbs,/And there upon the grass I sit, and moan,/Like one who once had wings." (*H* 3.67-8; 88-91). The poem's answer to Mnemosyne seems to be that Apollo will remain sad, and beached, until he fits his skill to the great task of understanding human history and how it might be redeemed— how it too might take leave of death. It's a task at which the poem seems to fail, for just at the climax of Apollo's great seizure Keats abandons the project, rebooting it a few months later as *The Fall of Hyperion*. If poetry can make a joint effort with "knowledge enormous," it can't make it here, not in the presence of a melancholy dysfunction only partially overcome.

Catachresis is not, nor does it pretend to be, a reversal of that dysfunction. It's not even really a picture of it. Whatever its tone—elegiac, optimistic, satirical, abashed—it seizes on the trope of a hapless or impossible collaboration to demand a referendum on what might be considered *of value*. And yet by the time *Hyperion* splinters off after "Celestial," the first and only word of its last line, the poem has lost confidence that its dependably catachrestic poetics are up to the job of imagining an art that could undermine value and redefine it, or even—less ambitiously—an art that might take the measure of social crisis. This may be all for the better. The insights of catachresis are ethical and emotional, but they are by no means scientific, and by no means precise or explanatory. As I have been arguing, the Romantic preoccupation with poetry's uninformative or, better yet, negatively informative character might be said to limn the epistemological difficulties of capital rather than confront them. In the following, final chapter, the collision of affective and empirical idioms comes to define a new genre whose problems and parameters are likewise tied—as Keats is, as Romanticism is—to the emergence of industrial modernity.

That genre belongs to the cloud, to cloud poems and also cloud paintings. These too are marked by embarrassment, but of an ontological rather than sensuous kind. *Hyperion* will return here, as will "To Autumn," as examples of a poetics of frustrated address that is sometimes linguistic and other times visual or pictorial. In one way of framing things, we have just now been spending time on the ground, in the mill, around the gravesite, never far off from the factory. Next and last stop, the sky.

4

Apostrophe: Clouds

Die Fenster geben auf Nordwest Aussicht, so daß ich manchmal schöne Abendwolken sehe, und Sie wissen, daß mich eine solche rosige Wolke allein entzücken und für alles entschädigen kann.

[The window has a northwest view, so that I sometimes see beautiful evening clouds, and you know, one such rosy cloud can enchant and make up for everything.]

ROSA LUXEMBURG, letter to Sophie Liebknecht
from Breslau prison dated 2 August 1917

Dost thou O little Cloud? I fear that I am not like thee.

WILLIAM BLAKE, *The Book of Thel* (1789)

Clouds don't tell you a lot. Volatile and various, a cloud—cumulus, stratus, thunderhead, wind-dog—exists only in the present tense. What has brought it here, where it's going next, these are at best best guesses. Stretching every moment into some new and shivering form, a cloud appears not at all to know its own mind. As Goethe says, you look to a cloud the way you look at the face of your lover, and you get as much information back:

Du Schüler Howards, wunderlich	*You student of Howard's, wondering*
Siehst morgens um und über dich,	*Look round the morning, about yourself,*
Ob Nebel fallen, ob sie steigen,	*See whether the fog is falling, or rising,*
Und was sich für Gewölke zeigen.	*And what the clouds disclose.*
Auf Berges Ferne ballt sich auf	*Up distant mountains climbs*
Ein Alpenheer, beeist zu Hauf,	*An Alpine-army, thickening,*
Und oben drüber flüchtig schweifen	*And fleeing overhead*

Gefiedert weiße luftige Streifen;	*Feathered white dainty stripes;*
Doch unten senkt sich grau und grauer	*But below it is gray and a gray*
Aus Wolkenschicht ein Regenschauer.	*Layer of clouds lets a rain shower down.*

Und wenn bei stillem Dämmerlicht	*And if in the still twilight*
Ein allerliebstes Treugesicht	*One darlingest faithful face*
Auf holder Schwelle dir begegnet,	*Meets you on a tender threshold,*
Weißt du, ob's heitert? ob es regnet?	*Do you know, is it fine? is it raining?*[1]

Weißt du, ob's heitert? ob es regnet? The question angles in the air, metallic. The weather of love scarcely knows its own mind either.

Clouds make good metaphors. Everyone remembers thinking, as a child, that a cloud had to be solid, like a pillow or a cotton puff; it seemed unthinkable that your hand would go right through it. Metaphors, too, conjure soft places to fall, cushioning between definitely possible expressions the phantom of an impossible *is*. A similar longing for ontological concretion travels into the game of pareidolia known (if it even has a name) as finding animals in the clouds. *Pareidolia* means "little shapes besides"; we see a face in a circle with three straight lines, a flock of geese in a cirrus. My daughter likes a book that ends with a parent and child looking up at the sky, somewhere in a universal suburb of bright green grass and trees. In the car riding to school she points at the windshield: "Some fog coming down. That cloud says mee-ow!"

It's easy to think of clouds as vacant, and as signifying vacancy. But clouds aren't nothing. If you touched one, it wouldn't feel like a pillow or cotton puff. It would be damp, humid. It would feel, that is, less like an object than the residue of one, less like feeling than having felt. Alternatively, you might experience it as a preparation to feel, as the inkling, mood, or ambiance of an object coming to you in advance of the object itself, the way heat rises off a griddle.

Here's a paradox, or a problem. Clouds have a present-tense existence but a body whose density has been spread out over time and grown thin. This is quite different from saying that clouds "mysteriously combine visibility and volume without surface."[2] In Goethe's poem, I see another order of things: a visible and, if you could reach it, tactile surface of uncertain volume. These clouds thicken, but aren't thick. Their layers have color, but not number or bulk. They live in near-flatness, in the dispersal of depth across a shifting plane. Not nothing, but very little: a threshold expression, a tender subsistence.

The compound *Treugesicht* is apparently Goethe's coinage. It means something like, and I have translated it as, "faithful face," although "visage" is probably a better rendering of *Gesicht*, which flags a face as something that is seen. Planting *treu* (faithful, devoted) in front of *Gesicht* doubles down on the suggestion that the beloved face is a plane in very subtle forward motion, dedicated *to*, tilted *at*. It's a familiar gesture from Goethe, the alchemical nudge of feeling into a kinetic form, and in this poem it does something very important. It establishes that clouds—gray and gathering, rolling over the mountains—belong to an atmosphere of address, and that they are its figures.

This chapter will be about the kinds of address implied by the trope of apostrophe, and these, Goethe tells us, are also the kinds of address implied by love: speaking to and leaning toward. *Apostrophe* means "to turn aside," and to the orators of antiquity it meant to turn away from the judge in a court of law, directing one's speech instead to the audience, to one's enemies, to the dearly departed, or even to nature. In any case, the point is to call out to an entity who cannot respond, maybe because it is required to be silent, because it doesn't have access to language, because it is far away, or because it is dead: O Rose, o happy dagger, di coeptis adspirate meis.

Goethe's poem begins and ends with an apostrophe to a "you" who's read Luke Howard's influential 1804 *Essay on the Modification of Clouds*. That "you" could be Ulrike von Levetzow, for whom Goethe composed "Du Schüler Howards" and five other cloud poems; it could be the poet himself; it could be some nonspecific person. The crucial part is that whoever it is never talks back. Perhaps, the poem muses, this is a condition on love: it's not that I don't want to hear you speak, it's that I need to learn to bear your reserve. Jonathan Culler would add that apostrophes are always triangulated, that they summon a being incapable of speech in the implied presence of a being who is merely silent, i.e, the reader.[3] The reader is there too, clicking between stations like a radio dial: Is it raining, is it fine, what is the temper of your face today and what does it mean for me? The reader, obviously, doesn't talk either.

What does it mean to say that clouds are figures of address, given that the target of Goethe's apostrophe is not the clouds but the person who studies them? It means simply that they are an abstract and diffused image of the apostrophic trope, interpreting its effects in an alternate medium. Apostrophes bring to mind something that is there, but hardly. Like clouds, they invoke shapes of palpable insubstantiality, uncertainly anchored to the world and yet solicited to give some account of their place in it. In "Du Schüler Howards," the opening appeal to a second-person addressee comes back to confront the face of the beloved, a cloud in human form; "du" signals apostrophe in the poem's first line, and "du" signals it again in its last, in a loop leading from simple conviction ("you look around in the morning") to tremulous doubt ("Do you know?").

This is a variant on Culler's theme and an illustration of what Lorraine Daston terms "cloud physiognomy:" the poet looks to the student who looks to the clouds that are like a face to which the student also looks.[4] By the poem's end we are looking at it too, caught inside a question to which the face gives no answer except its own reticence and the unspoken prospect of its mutability.

Reticence is not blankness, not oblivion. We know that the beloved's face is active, leaning forward in a show of some kind of fidelity, perhaps attraction. This is a poem about states of being that are muted and unpredictable but vigorously so; and historically, apostrophe was associated with charged-up feeling, a kissing cousin to prosopopeia and other figures most likely "to be attempted . . . when the mind is considerably heated and agitated."[5] As Wordsworth puts it in *The Excursion*,

> The Poets in their elegies and songs
> Lamenting the departed, call the groves,
> They call upon the hill and streams to mourn,
> And senseless rocks; nor idly; for they speak,
> In these their invocations, with a voice
> Obedient to the strong creative power
> Of human passion.[6]

This is already the conventional wisdom around 1800, which is why it's especially striking that "Du Schüler Howards" uses apostrophe in such idiosyncratic circumstances. There, the trope steps in to flesh out a scene of earnest, even frantic desire whose way is nonetheless paved by lines that are uniformly cool and colorless, gray on top of gray. The chill of the air and the swelter of love don't seem like they ought to go together; the high-pressure idiom of apostrophe doesn't seem like it ought to be set bouncing off these foggy hills. And yet here we are.

If you like, you can call this the work of Romantic lyric: to make the nature of minimal modes of existence maximally present and intense, to find the threshold of what is hardly there and color it as vividly as possible. Apostrophe is one way of pulling that off. It calls the slenderest reality by some name, picks out horses and armies from wisps and stripes, asks a question about the weather and makes audible the response called silence. It talks to clouds to see what they're made of, and borrows their images as mascots for the prospect of being decisively almost gone. In slightly grander terms, we might add that lyric, in contrast to more plainly referential genres like epic or satire, is where figuration can really show its gift for making the phenomenology of attenuated life credible and conspicuous. If readers like Culler have been tempted to identify apostrophe with lyric itself, that may be because apostrophe so explicitly concerns the activity of things that seem hardly to exist at all, and because that is the kind of life lyric seems weakly to lead.

In an essay built around the phrase "it is raining," Anne-Lise François finds in the modest epistemology of weather reporting a template for exactly this lyric ideal: the expression of a distributed consciousness whose knowledge of the world is not centered in any one person's perspective. Romantic poetry talks so much about the weather, François suggests, because it wants to invest lyric utterance with a certain degree of detachment, and constative statements—it's fine, it's raining; the clouds are getting thick—put a quick distance between the subject of knowledge and what she says she knows. Anyone can see it's raining; there is nothing special about this judgment, and it is certainly not just mine.

I take François's characterization of Romantic lyric to heart, especially insofar as it opens onto the possibility of a collective ecological intelligence, a "non-appropriative relation to the natural world . . . as 'a no-man's land'": owned by nobody.[7] We don't see that possibility in Goethe. It is the nonalignment of impersonal habits of observation and personal objects of attention—and, relatedly, the nonalignment of the language of science and the language of love—that draws his eye. Nonetheless, his poems do have a talent for anchoring the point of view of no one in particular in the phantom preparation of a body. That dispersal of perspective, combined with or set alongside the ecological concerns François invokes, is a guiding principle of this chapter and of its own, mildly heretical analysis of lyric form or forms.

Generalizations about lyric will always be contested, but let's have one more. Lyric, or so we've been told, is an utterance that is overheard. In the second half of this chapter, I'll focus on an aesthetic genre that is preeminently overhead, namely cloud paintings. The discussion is organized around a thought experiment, one that asks what might be learned from locating distinctively poetic tropes, like apostrophe, in works of visual art. This exercise is inspired by apostrophe's connection to address, which Rosalind Krauss (riffing on Merleau-Ponty) defines as a "phenomenological vector."[8] Krauss is talking about video art, but there is nothing about the phrase itself that needs to be constrained to the postmodern moment, nor to video as a specific practice or media example. If anything, her language stirs comparisons with recent work on the lyric as a transhistorical mode, one especially good at combining descriptive austerity with sentimental abundance.

The figure of apostrophe, then, will serve in what follows as a bridge between the cloud poem and the cloud painting. To make this connection, we'll have to tweak the conventional link between lyric address and voice. Many critics lean hard on the assumption that apostrophe is incantatory, that it raises a vocal apparition of the poet from the page while harkening back to lyric's roots in song; it's another version of the thought that lyric is preeminently the utterance that is overheard, or even that it is preeminently an utterance, disclosed in and as speech. It's been suggested that the Romantics' particular version of this paradigm has a lot to do with a creeping ideology of private, personal expression gaining ground around 1800. That seems likely to be true, though a bit to the side of my purposes.

   As far as I'm concerned, a too-constrained view of the existential contours of "voice" keeps us from understanding what a painter like John Constable is doing in his cloud paintings, which do not speak nor cry out loud but are nonetheless beholden to a structure of declamatory address. Constable's skyings, as he called them, don't talk to clouds but ask something of them; the unanswerability of the question is precisely what these paintings transform into "a pictured prosody of weather," space stamped on time in fickle motion.[9]

   We began with doubts about clouds: about what they can tell us, and how reliable that information is. We began, too, with Goethe's passage from the climate to a human face, whose features become exponentially less trustworthy the more heat is on them to give an account of just what is going on. A lot of this chapter will be about doubt, just as a lot of this book has been about the doubtful—nonreferential, nonexplanatory—qualities of aesthetic representation. In my introduction, I suggested that poetry poses a challenge to anyone interested in using it to talk about climate change. Literature will never tell you just what is going on, and climate change demands clarity on that front: it demands that we recognize and name its causes, including the deep cause of those inequities a warming planet will only reinforce. This chapter circles back to that challenge, not least because clouds have become such a powerful symbol of climate change, especially of climate change in the near past. We have melting ice and mass extinction, but their preamble was "the modern plague-cloud" made, or so John Ruskin surmised, from fossil fuels and "dead men's souls."[10]

   I don't think we should look to Goethe's poetry or Howard's essays or Constable's paintings or Ruskin's lectures for the evidence to believe or the political will to combat climate disaster. My turn to clouds as both objects and figures of apostrophe is meant simply to continue building up the lexicon for what I've been calling nescience: a form of knowledge that provides neither true nor false information about the world but that is nonetheless real. That form of knowledge does not have to be an ally in the fight against climate change or capitalism; it might be, but it might not, and if it weren't, that would compromise neither the fight nor the epistemic power of aesthetic objects. What would it mean to stand by these objects in the face of their political inutility? What would it mean to continue to think about arcane topics like apostrophe or lyric address in the face of charges that this is a worthless and even a damaging pursuit?

I don't have answers to those questions, and the poems and paintings I talk about below won't either. What they will do is model a certain way of being in the world and with others that we might want to call commitment—not in Adorno's very specific sense but as another way of construing apostrophe's relational bearing. The bend of apostrophe, its intentness toward things it can't even see or can't expect to look back, is a sign of sustained attention. That attention is one-sided, and in certain circumstances devotional habits of this sort might be toxic; stalking, for example, is one genre of one-sided attention, surveillance another. But these are not the circumstances we're in here. The work I discuss in what follows always means a little bit less than the world does, no matter how it might be socially leveraged, misappropriated, or redeemed.

It is nonetheless to the world that apostrophe looks, as the thing it cannot explain and with which it can only partially communicate. When Goethe's poem affixes its final apostrophic summons decisively to a scene of uncertainly requited love, which can't promise to end well and may threaten to end badly, it's because he is trying to imagine the situation of poetry with respect to its material conditions: intent, desiring, projecting outward both the ardor and the detachment it knows are its own lot. People say poetry is indifferent to the world. Goethe knows it's the other way around, and that this is the real heartbreak.

* * *

Clouds and apostrophes are not the same; how could they be? But they are similar and inspire similar thoughts. This section gathers a handful of poetic performances that seem motivated by the overlap between tropological and meteorological phenomena—that are processing clouds and apostrophes as transcriptions or restatements of each other. Every case italicizes some of the most prominent concerns of Romantic art. These include the natural world and our relationship to it, the distance between human and nonhuman life, and, as I've said, experiences that are no less memorable for being slight or deficient, or for otherwise flying below the radar of comprehension or consciousness.

Since Howard published his *Essay*, there has been no shortage of cloud theory. Clouds are key notes in nearly all Ruskin's writings on art and culture, from the demand issued in *Modern Painters* to learn the truth of the open sky to the ominous drumbeating, thirty years later, of "The Storm-cloud of the Nineteenth Century," with its complaints of "dense manufacturing mist."[11] They are, in large part thanks to Ruskin, a favorite theme of art historians, perhaps most dazzlingly for Hubert Damisch in his *Théorie du /nuage/*, whose central notion of the pictorial cloud as "the thing that cannot be fitted into a system but which nevertheless the system needs into order to constitute itself as a system" Krauss borrows for an essay on Agnes Martin's grids ("Agnes Martin: The /Cloud/").[12] There has been a late windfall, too, of accounts of "the cloud," as in "I saved the file to the cloud." These include everything from Tung-Hui Hu's *Prehistory of the Cloud*, a concerned media history of the economics of data and its preservation, to the 2014 film comedy *Sex Tape*, in which a couple accidentally shares private footage with their friends, family, and mailman ("It went up! It went up to the cloud!" "You can't get it down from the cloud?" "It's a mystery!").

All these accounts, in one way or another, find that clouds synchronize the concrete with the immaterial. For Damisch, the shorthand /cloud/ alludes to the different "levels, or rather the registers" layered in the cloud's painted image, whether it lies in the background or foreground of a canvas. Keeping track of all these different registers requires "circumvent[ing] the flat surface upon which the image is depicted in order to target the image's texture and its depth as a painting," and thus to determine how "superposition (or intermeshing) and regulated interplay . . . define the pictorial process" as both representational and part of the physical world. Every cloud is every cloud, and this cloud, and that cloud, and all clouds have "textural effects" easily made to toy with "a negation of the solidity, permanence, and identity that define shape."[13] In short, the very form of a painted cloud—its paradoxical, overextended form of embodiment—is always threatening the cloud's own deformation.

It is this lamination of thin substance on thick significance that the theory of clouds has in common with the theory of apostrophe, which, as I've already said, is meant to bring things—absent others, an audience, and the poet's body—into the common ground of an artificial space. A less sophisticated truth is that both clouds and apostrophes are paradigmatically *up* from where we are, and that we are always under. Even the lateral summons Keats launches at his Grecian Urn seems aimed toward an object at some height, if only because the urn is so august; even Shelley's prosopopoeia in "The Cloud," whose speaker passes with ease between the pavilion of heaven and the ocean's pores, insists so much on the first person that the poem seems ultimately to divide the earthbound poet from his aerial persona.

Now for a confession: the germ of this chapter lies not in Romantic poetry, nor in rigorously imagined art-historical speculation, nor in dystopian media archaeologies. It lies in a Kate Bush song. That song is "The Big Sky," off that justly celebrated album of Petrarchan détournement, *Hounds of Love* (1985). "The Big Sky" is the third track on *Hounds*; when it was released as a 7-inch single, its B-side was "Not This Time," a Bush rarity that begins with a line that could easily be Goethe's: "Oh, with a mind that renders everything sensitive/What chance do I have here?"[14] It's a good pairing. "Not This Time" is about the tangle of self in other ("When you're near, I feel you/And I forget myself"), and "The Big Sky" is likewise trained on acts of projective identification, specifically those that cross human and meteorological lines. The song bounces between sky and clouds, at times appearing to confuse them entirely. These are its opening lines:

They look down
At the ground
Missing
But I never go in
Now

"They" is probably the clouds, which Bush goes on to invoke, but the word also seems to pluralize the sky. These aren't cherubs looking down on us; *they* is an elemental collective. But what is "missing"? And where would "I" go in? Before we have long to contemplate this spill of ambiguities, the refrain is dropkicked forward:

I'm looking at the big sky
I'm looking at the big sky now
I'm looking at the big sky
You never understood me
You never really tried

Notice how the sudden hostile turn of those last two lines sweeps into the billowing overstatement of an average ordinary breakup: you never understood me, you never really tried. Both songs, then, belong to the last minutes of things, but where "Not This Time" is primal and spare, a love song about trying to come to the end of love, "The Big Sky" is positively baroque, and it does in fact steer away from flatly interpersonal drama. That steering happens through Bush's tactical and varied use of prepositions, which chiefly concern me here. I won't quote all the lyrics, but suffice it to say the speaker or singer's position vis-à-vis the sky cycles through *at*, *in*, *with*, *over*, and *out*, while the clouds themselves, in that very first line, look *down*. One thing the clouds never are is *up*; and the singer is never *under*.

This is striking. As I've said, clouds are paradigmatically up, and skies are too; Bush's accusatory address to "you" might seem to point the finger high as well. These are the obvious coordinates: the heavens are up and we are underneath. Bush, however, has no time for them, opting for topsy-turvy constructions like the two lines that compose the outro, "Rolling over like a great big cloud/Walking out in the big sky," or the even less probable "We're leaving with the big sky." That second bit follows hard upon a conceit of the clouds as animals on Noah's ark, who call out, "[I]f you're coming, jump!"—a subtly apocalyptic twinge to which I'll return in a moment. First, though, let's pause over the strangeness of Bush using so many prepositions except the most obvious ones, turning a song that should be about two different places (up there and down below) into a song that actively and erratically reconfigures space. Nothing is where it should be, and yet everything is interlarded, differently scaled beings or objects dotted through a single plane.

What Bush manages in this track isn't far off from the closing lines of the first book of Keats's *Hyperion*. Hyperion is headed to earth in search of Saturn, having left the sun and, with it, the seasons in the care of his father, Coelus:

> Hyperion arose, and on the stars
> Lifted his curved lids, and kept them wide
> Until it [i.e., Coelus's voice] ceas'd; and still he kept them wide:
> And still they were the same bright, patient stars.
> Then with a slow incline of his broad breast,
> Like to a diver in the pearly seas,
> Forward he stoop'd over the airy shore,
> And plung'd all noiseless into the deep night.[15]

The effect, which goes full bore across both *Hyperion* poems, is to calibrate human to empyrean movement by leaning hard on alien depictions of space and speed. Milton gave himself the same challenge, and these lines wink sympathetically at Satan's flight in the third book of *Paradise Lost*. The Titans are huge, and they move slowly, and like Bush Keats wields grammar like a set of dance steps, sending Hyperion shifting, revolving, stretching over elemental landscapes of stars and seashores, mountain tops and ocean deeps. And, like Bush, at no time—not once in the poem's nearly 1,000 lines—does Keats use the word *under*. Nothing can contain what is older even than the gods, the brutally large bodies that, even "stoop'd," are indomitable within the vault of any heaven.

What we get, instead, is the entirely appropriate near-homogeneity of Hyperion, his fellow Titans, and the universe whose parts they literally are. To look at the stars is to look his father in the face; to leave the sun is to leave part of himself behind; to dive into the sea is to dive into Saturn, who waits for him there.

Bush is not talking about Titans, but her song is mythic, biblical, and, with that reference to Noah's ark, flirting with disaster of the planetary kind. And yet, if the song has one eye on catastrophe, its refusal to make explicit humanity's subordination to the clouds "changing in the big sky" sets it apart from the apocalyptic mood of other Bush tracks, like "Breathing" or "Experiment IV." With its preference for *at* and *in*, "The Big Sky" absorbs change, and perhaps catastrophe too, into the body of the person who is never under but rather always among; with its preference for *with*, the song cites a Wordsworthian belief in the consubstantiality of clouds and crowds, which is to say people; with its preference for *over* and *out*, it taps into that childhood fantasy of the solidity of clouds and thus the possibility of sensual contact with what seems out of meteorological and, for that matter, ontological bounds. It's a fantasy of whirling around in the clouds the way Wordsworth might have yearned to whirl around in his daffodils, a dream of being neither above nor below but collateral with the world.

I like the way Keats and Bush throw under over. I like it because it seems to reveal an impulse—variously Romantic and post-Romantic—to use the sky and more especially clouds to test novel ways of inhabiting an environment. This hypothesis might have additional purchase in a time, namely our own, so often described as "under climate change." "Under climate change" is a phrase ubiquitous in scholarly journals, popular media, and everyday conversation, and it packs a great deal of ideology into three small words. For one thing, it strongly implies that climate change is a political regime, that we might be under it the same way early modern England was under the Tudors. This in turn assigns a collective but still personalized, even vaguely human agency, not to climate change's causes, but to the phenomenon itself. It likewise implies that climate change might be usurped or unseated by forces too disorganized and vicissitudes too sudden to name in advance, just as certain obscurantist accounts of the French Revolution characterize it as having been at once unforeseeable and inevitable.

Most significantly, the politicization of climate change implied by our ordinary ways of talking about it tactfully conceals the fact that climate change on the scale and at the speed it's happening in the twenty-first century is first and foremost an economic problem. Climate change, as I have said before in this book and as plenty of others have said elsewhere, is indivisible from capitalism (which is not to say that if capitalism did not cause climate change we wouldn't have to abolish it). To claim, then, that we are under climate change is to shift the burden of the catastrophe from its causes to one strata of its consequences: we have the political systems that we do because they are amenable to capital, and those political systems sponsor capital even in the face of its cataclysmic upshots. It is also to suggest that the solution to the climate emergency is a shift merely in the political orders of society, when what is required is considerably more extreme and far-reaching, a transformation that would strike the root of the issue instead of taking occasional whacks at its fruits.

Meanwhile, and more pertinently for this chapter, describing ourselves as under climate change establishes a topographical edict concerning what lies above and what lies below. The phrase itself suggests capture: we are under climate change like bugs beneath an overturned bowl. It also suggests that climate change is somehow *in* the sky, that it is an object that can be located and that where it should be located is up. This may be why so many recent literary-critical takes on climate have focused on clouds, although, as Allison Carruth nicely points out, the rhetoric of the cloud—whether as atmospheric hieroglyph or part of contemporary information technology—punts the vast infrastructure that powers human energy systems skyward, into a disembodied and naturalized elsewhere.[16] Just as polar bears and other charismatic megafauna have become the face of the conservation movement, clouds have become the code words for climate and for its crisis. Always overhead, they suggest at once the pervasiveness of the crisis and "crisis" as something that looms without ever arriving: storms for others to weather, eventually.

Mundane and sinister, visible but beyond reach, objects of fantasy and signs of uncertain import, the clouds of climate change are oracles and overlords of slow-motion but ever-accelerating disaster. That, at least, is what our contemporary ways of talking about climate suggest. As it happens, this mode of representing our relationship to the weather and the earth is a habit learned from the eighteenth century, which first mastered the art of the locodescriptive *prospect*, as in prospect painting and prospect poetry.

The prospect is an especially fraught genre for thinking through the spatial relationship between human beings and the rest of the earth. On the one hand, prospects—as John Barrell has shown—are a quintessential expression of class society. They represent the view of someone looking down and out upon a landscape that often belongs to him or, if it doesn't, certainly belongs far less to the laboring figures conventionally sprinkled across the canvas or page: see, for example, Edward Haytley's painting of the Montagu family at Sandleford Priory, whose wide survey visualizes

FIG. 4. Edward Haytley, *Extensive View from the Terraces of Sandleford Priory, near Newbury, Looking towards the Village of Newtown and the Hampshire Downs,* popularly known as *The Montagus at Sandleford Priory* (ca. 1744).

a pecking order that is not merely social but ontological, as the workers tucked into the distance of the painting's middle ground seem almost one with the hedges they trim (figure 4).

On the other hand, the prospect is fraught with anxiety. As it faces down a nature human beings should, in theory, be able to control, it telegraphs a barely suppressed fear of nature's resistance and revenge, its potential to "threaten . . . the progress of civilization" by usurping both civil and ecosystemic order. If this anxiety is "common . . . among writers two or three generations after Newton," it is also, particularly by the end of the eighteenth century, a response to the exponential appropriation of earth, water, and space by new industrial technologies.[17] *Prospect*, then, names both a habit of looking and a habit of worrying: looking down at something that might rise up against you.

Contemporary idioms of climate change invert the prospect model. Instead of looking down, we are looking up, but the threat remains the same: nature is going to get us back. These idioms are highly fearful, and, in the main, they are also uncritical, for they seem to mourn the loss of cultural authority embedded in specific routines of perception and specific genres of representation. At their heart lies a sneaking and thoroughly disorienting suspicion that some great chain of being has been turned on its head, that the secular ascension of human beings to the top of the proverbial pole has been catastrophically undone. By clinging to a positional vocabulary—one more time, *under climate change*—we imply that a simple reversal of this topsy-turvy order will set things to rights. Thus, for example, the dream of geoengineering, which promises to put humanity back in charge of the weather it has rendered so unruly. The term *Anthropocene* has come under fire for sponsoring a similar idea, and for acting out a fetishistic denial of the existential vulnerability climate change represents. How convenient, to assert human dominance over the planet at the very moment where the planet looks like it might kill us.

It is certainly true that poems like Pope's "Windsor-Forest" or paintings like Haytley's are part of a significant aesthetic tendency to peddle an idea of civilizational excellence that depends on social stratification; the prospect is indelibly part of that tradition. Still, that is not all the prospect does, nor all it represents. And so, before turning back to Keats and moving on to Constable, I want to spend a moment with Jonathan Kramnick's compelling assessment of what might be called a counterphenomenology within the eighteenth-century prospect. The account is notable not just for its sensitivity but also for its treatment of locodescriptive modes of writing as proleptically ecological, storehouses of better ways to live with the earth that avoid both sentimentality and hubris. Working in the same vein as David Fairer, who identifies a subgenre of poetry he calls eighteenth-century "eco-georgic," Kramnick finds in locodescription a sense of place that opens incidentally onto a sense of planet.[18] This is a new way of reading prospect poetry; it is also a new way of situating labor at the heart of eighteenth-century literary culture, so long as poetry gets to be counted as work.

Like the heavy-handed prosodic routines against which the Romantic poets rebel—heroic couplets and heroic stanzas, end-stops and initial inversions—eighteenth-century nature poetry has a certain conspicuity about it. By that I mean it emphasizes presentness, the ridged quality of a real body in space, just as volubly as Pope's couplets flaunt their own nuts and bolts. For Kramnick, this amounts to a surprisingly benign mandate, according to which the task of the poet "is not to distinguish [the] poem from the rest of the world but to create something that is exactly like that world," only to find that "the rest of the world turns out to have exactly the same properties as the poem."[19] Formally, these effects are achieved by a dual-pronged technique of addition and contraction, a foreshortening that brings some natural object or nonhuman creature nearer within the poet's surround. Everything seems suddenly here, held close, set down with a detail easily misrecognized as artifice but ultimately more akin to care.

The best way to achieve such effects, according to Kramnick, is apostrophe. Apostrophe, he writes, is "a turn of speech that reaches out to something that is just here"—"just" because it is close at hand and "just" because it is quietly, unspectacularly so (*PM*, 92). The "great example" of the Thames in Denham's "Cooper's Hill" is great and an example because the river is so very calmly present, "Though deep yet clear, though gentle yet not dull,/Strong without rage, without oe'rflowing full." No sooner has Denham saluted the Thames with "O could I flow like thee" than his lines become the thing they love; the poet has walked up to the river and engaged it in a mirror exercise, mimicking its easy rhythm with his own (*PM*, 81). Meanwhile, the "one sheltered hare" Cowper's *Task* wrenches from some three dozen agitated lines denouncing the hunt is nigh to enough to lick the hand that feeds her, and the same hand that writes the poem:

> Yes—thou may'st eat thy bread, and lick the hand
> That feeds thee; thou may'st frolic on the floor
> At evening, and at night retire secure
> To thy straw-couch, and slumber unalarmed;
> For I have gained thy confidence, have pledged
> All that is human in me to protect
> Thine unsuspecting gratitude and love. (*T*, 3.342–48)

Apostrophe "is so tamped down in these lines that it easily goes unnoticed," "not 'O hare!' but something more like 'oh, hey, you here, hey hare.' This "subdued and tactile troping," in Kramnick's phrase, matches the hare's proximity; it serves "an intimate address to a creature who is just here," part of the world and the poem and giving its shape to both (*PM*, 95–96).

By "shape" I mean form, and by form orientation and impulse. Cowper's hare brings order and verisimilitude to his environment: his hand, his floor, the time of day are curving toward this animal companion, and so is *The Task*, which, in this apostrophic moment ("Yes—thou may'st eat") manages a faint illusion of mobility in three dimensions. The poem, in a word, turns. It turns casually to the side, not so much surprised by the hare as recollected to it, as Cowper collects himself from his extended diatribe. That the apostrophe opens with an affirmation ("Yes") before naming its object captures some of the therapeutic mandate of *The Task*: to oust Cowper's depression and bring him to "repose." Psychological wellness, perhaps, is a matter of getting outside of one's head—apostrophizing, turning away—to be intimate with other creatures. This is achieved less through the tonic effort of producing blank verse than by means of a rhetoric that obligates embodiment: turn, speak, see, be licked.[20]

I've said that apostrophe often seems to address something that is a little ways off and also slightly up. Cowper's turn moves to the side and down, and yet the impulse is the same: a desire to be lateral, on the same footing as something that has captured your interest or perhaps your love. To emphasize the specifically formal properties of apostrophe is to ask how it creates this shared plane as well as a propulsion toward it. This is form as flight path, nearly Aristotelian in aligning *shape* with *trajectory*.

When Keats, in "To Autumn," first sets Autumn "close" to the Sun before imagining the two of them loading and blessing "with fruit the vines that round the thatch-eves run," the word he uses is "conspiring," breathing together ("A," 2–4). As both Sun and season drop down to the sublunary zone of thatched roofs, that breath pumps in and out of Keats's first tightly modulated stanza, especially those seventh, eighth, and ninth lines with their wandering caesurae "lift[ing] the body of the stanza with deliberate leisure, and then allow[ing] it to subside[.]"[21] The two pairs of lines that frame this trio have the same unbroken structure, easing out the impression of some regular breath that quickens and grows uneven in the lines tucked in between, and that pauses with each break:

> To bend with apples the moss'd cottage trees,
>   And fill all fruit with ripeness to the core;
>   To swell the gourd, and plump the hazel shells
>   With a sweet kernel; to set budding more,
> And still more, later flowers for the bees,
> Until they think warm days will never cease,
>   For summer has o'er-brimmed their clammy cells. ("A," 5–11)

I wouldn't go so far as to say the poem's body is the poet's body is the reader's body, though people have. What moves me here is what moves the poem, which so carefully lays out a world whose strata—sky, sun, trees, earth—seem to be rotating toward one another. Everything in this poem is moving, sidling close to everything else inside the space that holds it all together. Even the words (to use Keats's term) swell, as if they long to touch their edges.

Here is another low-impact apostrophe, so subtle that not until the first line of the second stanza—"Who hath not seen thee oft amid thy store?"—does it become clear Keats is talking *to* Autumn and not just about it ("A," 12). That's partly thanks to the extremely unconventional route taken by the trope, even more unconventional than Cowper's blink-and-you'll-miss-it turn to his hare. The address to Autumn is dispersed across the entire first stanza, which comprises a single sentence and has nary an "O" nor even a pronoun in sight. If *The Task* is (as it were) tasked is to bring the world home, Keats's Great Odes each obey an impulse to stretch or dilate the world until it becomes impossible to parse discretely. The movement of "To Autumn" in particular is centrifugal, pulled outward by the apostrophic vector binding speaker to addressee with a golden cord. It blurs and bends and terminates in a hiss of animal sounds—of gnats and lambs and crickets and birds—that likewise seem to spill over the perimeter, until the distinction between speech and noise vanishes and even apostrophe, that figure of *standpoint*, has lost its bearings.

Whether it is Bush's hurtle through her big sky, Cowper's remarks to his hare, or Keats's slow girdling of the earth's zones, each of these lyric occasions tries to redesign social space, including the space of pets and weather. They test the possibilities of using grammar to open up metaphors of relation, and to charge them with the energy, incline, and pitch of some desiring movement. In preparation for Constable's clouds, I want to revisit that scene from *Hyperion* I brought up initially as a point of comparison and continuity with "The Big Sky." One thing I have not said about Hyperion's descent to earth is that it's precipitated by what might be called an experimental or avant-garde apostrophe, though we might at first receive it simply as a monologue. After all, this isn't the token scenario in which one person addresses an absent other. It's a scene with two characters—Hyperion and Coelus—in which one (Coelus) says something to which the other (Hyperion) does not respond but which he clearly hears, since he acts immediately on it. In other words, this moment in the poem is implicitly dialogic. So, why find an apostrophe in it? There are several clues, and one in particular:

> [T]he bright Titan, phrenized with new woes,
> Unus'd to bend, by hard compulsion bent
> His spirit to the sorrow of the time;
> And all along a dismal rack of clouds,
> Upon the boundaries of day and night,
> He stretch'd himself in grief and radiance faint.
> There as he lay, the heaven with its stars
> Look'd down on him with pity, and the voice
> Of Coelus, from the universal space
> Thus whisper'd low and solemn in his ear. (*H* 1.299–308)

Keats learned well from Milton how to highlight a thought by towing it over an enjambment. In *Paradise Lost*, enjambed lines typically apply themselves in the service of theological or moral paradoxes the poem then finds a way to unravel, but Keats's enjambments tend not toward the surprising resolution of contradictions but rather toward disjuncture.

In "Ode on a Grecian Urn," the urn's happy boughs are told they "cannot shed/[Their] leaves," and yet the line break yanks those leaves right off ("GU," 21–22). This passage from *Hyperion* amputates Coelus's voice from his body, which, it turns out, is not really a body but "universal space"— heaven, its stars, even the clouds on which Hyperion lies. If apostrophe usually "emphasizes that voice calls in order to be calling, to summon images of its power," this diremption of voice from its already disincarnated center underscores nothing so much as Coelus's impotence, as the Titan himself does in the speech that follows:

> —This is the grief, O Son!
> Sad sign of ruin, sudden dismay, and fall!
> Yet do thou strive; as thou art capable,
> As thou canst move about, an evident God;
> And canst oppose to each malignant hour
> Ethereal presence:—I am but a voice;
> My life is but the life of wind and tides,
> No more than winds or tides can I avail:—
> But thou canst. (*H* 1.335–43)[22]

Keats has Coelus build on a classical picture of the world, which was sliced into the sea, the sky, the air, and the earth. Saturn is still holding ground on earth—that's why Hyperion is being sent to see him—but Coelus seems to have melted into air and water, their primeval "life" unsettled by the more anthropomorphic Olympian gods. The downfall of the Titans, in other words, is also the downfall of an antecedent paganism that can tell the difference between planetary and cosmic elements without domesticating them, and that doesn't need to lump them together under the lank rubric of "nature." As we've seen in an earlier chapter, Keats will come back to this theme in his "Ode to Psyche," in which Psyche's exclusion from the Olympic pantheon enables her to guide the poet beyond culture, restoring him to a naked intimacy with the building blocks of existence: namely, bodies and brains. Here, Keats isn't so interested in what happens after all the gods are gone. He is interested, rather, in the poetic payoff of representing ontological primes like weight, size, volume, magnitude, and speed on a gargantuan scale.

Human beings lie on the ground and look at the clouds, but Titans lie on the clouds and look even further, all the way up to the stars. This is but one sign of Hyperion's vastness, which nearly every word in this passage does something to augment: he is so big when he lies down on the sky he looks like a man lying down on a rack, so spacious he covers the distance between night and day, so solid he can nudge time, so dense even his ether has presence. With a little help from another enjambment, Coelus even provides a visual for Hyperion's capacity to fend off "each malignant hour," a phrase against which the near-oxymoron of "ethereal presence" is pressed against or (as Coelus says) opposed. There is no resolution here, only struggle: time and space at war on a cosmic battlefield for which this poetics rolls out the map.

Coelus is nearly nothing and all voice; Hyperion is huge but speechless, "noiseless" even. Between the two of them they divide, deform, and reshuffle apostrophe's circuit of sender and recipient, as Coelus becomes the declamatory voice that is strangely absent or unlocatable and Hyperion the addressee who hears and responds, silently, by heading down to earth. If prosopopeia is "the fiction of an apostrophe" in which a conventionally speechless addressee is afforded the power of speech, the dialogue of the Titans is not apostrophe's fiction but its abstraction.[23] In the same way he breaks down the formal category of rhyme into the more basic element of sound, or the architectonic sinew of blank verse into the stooped and angled movement of bodies moving in space and against time, Keats is seeing what happens when you take the paradigmatic trope of relation and scramble the terms of its relationality. What if apostrophe is not a person addressing an entity that can't respond, but a voice without a body addressing a body without a voice?

It may seem like a leap, but much of what's going in this scene of an unfinished epic poem from two decades into the nineteenth century might be illuminated by Krauss's well-known essay on video and "the aesthetics of narcissism"—not because there is anything narcissistic about *Hyperion* or its aesthetics but because, for Krauss, video is defined by a similar upending of the dialogic postures of speaker or subject and addressee. If postwar painters like Jackson Pollock worked to decenter the pictorial field by involving the whole canvas in the seemingly random movement of the brush, video "renders nonsensical a critical engagement" with the idea of a center per se. "What would it mean to point to the center" of a video installation, when the piece so evidently relies on a somatic transaction between the beholder and the screen, on "the simultaneous projection and reception" of a relational field?[24] This is where the narcissism comes in—in the artist's insistence that the audience serve as an extension of her own body. It is also what makes video essentially satirical, thumbing its nose not just at the formal conventions of easel painting but at the whole idea of form as something static and contained.

It is quite explicitly the case that Hyperion is invited to become an extension of Coelus's body: Coelus, as he himself explains, lacks the muscle to take on the Olympians, and so it's Hyperion, the "evident God," whose body needs to stand in for both of them. Looking at this scene through the unlikely lens of Krauss's essay makes us see Coelus's projection of his own will onto Hyperion as a decentering of the usual logic of apostrophe, with its present, speaking subject and absent, silent auditor. The trick of video is to foist presence on the viewer, to loop her into the collapsed present of the screen or installation. The trick of Keats's unconventional apostrophe is to create a similar quagmire, freezing both Titans within the hour of their own incipient demise. Past and future fall away, and so does the easy iambic scaffold of the poem. Suddenly caesurae are laddering down the page, each one—I count six, maybe seven in the eight lines quoted above—a mute percussive tap on the infinite instant in which these figures find themselves. If this is, as Krauss says, a psychological situation, it is also a spatiotemporal one: two centers of consciousness are herded together by an uneven, unexpected redistribution of speech and movement, their patchy overlap flagged each time Keats takes a break (however miniature) from his meter.

If you buy this reading of *Hyperion*, we can say that for Keats apostrophe is the name for an interval of space and time ground nearly to a halt. Nearly, because it's important to this poem, and to the story of the Titans, that history is moving inexorably forward: the Olympians are going to win; the Titans are going to fall; revolutions cannot be stopped. Here, though, it is moving like a cloud, like the winds and tides to which Coelus compares his dim and aimless power. It is moving, that is, across a field without a frame, across an area where "the effects of temporality" are visible but "level[ed] out."[25]

Krauss's word for video's inhabitation of this field is *parody*, a pratfall of the easel picture that mocks its confidence in center and periphery. *Parody* is not the worst word to use for Keats, and it's not the worst word to use for Constable either. Both the poet and the painter inherit eighteenth-century prospect traditions that are heavily dependent on the representation of stable points of view, and both are committed to undermining those traditions through tactical dislocations and distensions of perspective. The next and final section turns to Constable's cloud paintings to take stock of their cognitive as well as their aesthetic situation, and to consider how these skyings approach "the horizontal"—which is to say, the domain of the cloud—"as the condition of defeating [orthodox] form."[26]

Clouds, Constable wrote, "ought not to come forward." They should be subtle, and that is why (he explains) they're so hard to paint, why "their brilliancy and consequence" is so difficult to render with the most expert degree of nonchalance.[27] The right tone for the cloud is the hum of the hardly thought about—to paraphrase Kramnick paraphrasing Cowper, less "O Cloud!" than "oh, hey, cloud." These wallflower clouds are always just there, never *for* something nor obviously opposed to the idea of being useful for contemplation. Unlike a Romantic ruin—and Constable painted or sketched plenty of those—clouds are not defunct; they do more than offer a picturesque reductio on the ideal of aesthetic autonomy. The trouble is, it's not clear what.

* * *

Constable's skyings are often referred to as studies, but none of them appear to have been used or adapted for other paintings. In this they bear a certain oblique resemblance to Howard's *Essay*, as least as far as Goethe's poem goes: the student of Howard's, whoever he is, can't apply his learning where it's needed most, that is, to the case of desire. On a similar note, studies are generally, if not by definition, for something, but Constable seems to have left his suspended in a state of relative independence, even inutility. To be clear, these are extraordinarily careful paintings, as shrewdly composed as a landscape by Poussin. And yet their self-governing energy implies a very different sort of freedom from the top-down, hierarchal and controlling posture leveraged by the prospect painting. As we've seen, there are both pre- and post-Romantic alternatives to this way of taking up space in the world, or rather of representing what it means to take up space. We see all those alternatives cruising about in Constable: a sense of casual proximity to clouds created by a flattening of the picture plane; a nonnarrative, antidramatic treatment of weather wrested from allegorical circumstance; and a playful needling of the prospect genre.

Quite a few people have suggested that Constable's cloud studies could and should be talked about in poetic and not just art-historical terms. Mary Jacobus calls them "a series of Romantic lyrics" that "evoke fleeting states of mind, feeling, and atmosphere" to conjure "a language for inner activity: darkening here, lightening here, here an ascent, there a fraying or an accumulation of intensity; a passage of calm before a storm or a glimpse of cerulean sky."[28] For Stanley Plumly they are "elegy landscapes," a therapeutic exercise for a painter whose wife, Maria, was chronically ill (she died in 1828, aged forty) and whose own temper had a melancholic lean.[29] To the extent that they've been taken as pictorial extensions of Howard's *Essay*, these paintings could also be connected to the didactic verse of Erasmus Darwin, and to a genre of natural-philosophical poetry that wouldn't long outlast the Romantic era.

Obviously I'm keen on these kinds of arguments, which allow for the conceptual shifts Romantic art obviously prizes. If the nineteenth century is a time when old hierarchies of classification begin to break down—when history painting loses out to still life and Darwin's expository couplets get lost in the ramble of the ode—it is also a time when a new deference to media specificity is matched by a greater terminological traffic between poetry, painting, dance, sculpture, and other arts. The development is unsurprising insofar as the vogue for spontaneity and ease of expression is apparent across Romantic culture, and because the emotional tenor of these values would seem to transcend distinctions of mode: a lyric poem and a self-portrait may use different tools and call on different senses, but when we say that they feel intimate or honest or natural we are naming the same effects in the same historically specific way.

Similarly, when art becomes something designed to make you feel, not teach or persuade you, it becomes easier to talk about it in a language that is highly generalized and portable, as emotional languages tend to be. In the 1760s, Gotthold Ephraim Lessing wrote that the doctrine of "ut pictura poesis" ought to be tossed aside in favor of a view of poetry and painting as "fair and friendly neighbors" ("billige freundschaftliche Nachbarn"), and the convivial drift of his metaphor is no accident. The context of media theory at this moment in time is preeminently social: it encourages a view of all works of art as engaged in the solicitation and management of human feeling and thus unified in their aims, if not in their particulars.[30] It is one small step from recognizing that unity to lending the technical vocabulary of one aesthetic modality to another, without question or qualm.

This is the set of circumstances that justifies calling Constable's work lyrical or elegiac. These proposals are reasonable enough, but they are also frustratingly subjective. It's easy and right to describe Gray's "Elegy Written in a Country Churchyard" as, well, an elegy, because it has all the trappings of one, but it's a little harder to say that the mood of the cloud studies is essentially mournful or downturned, since they are entirely devoid of narrative, allegorical, or indeed human content. Jacobus's suggestion that the studies show states of mind is more plausible. Still, her discussion likewise emphasizes psychological content at the expense of formal, technical, or generic markers: the studies are Romantic lyrics because they evoke the turmoil of one person's inner life. The implied mimesis between works of art and interior states is a telling extension of the principle of aesthetic generalization. Poetry and painting feel a lot alike, and feeling is a lot like poetry and painting.[31]

My own conviction is that the studies are emotionally illegible. Or, to put a finer point on it, they have a vested interest in the delay or denial of affective response. That's as far as the spectator goes, anyway. When it comes to the artist, Constable seems to be inhabiting something like the scientist's view from nowhere, perhaps (again) with a satirical edge. On the one hand, the place where the artist might be standing, or where he might be close to standing, is totally elided. Unlike in a prospect painting, we get no idea of what might lie to Constable's right or left, whether he is close to other people or far away from them, in a rural or urban environment, and so on. His bearings are nearly nonexistent, and in this he would seem to be the ideal observer of the natural world, his lack of appointment the expression of his impartiality. On the other hand, however, these paintings are obviously based on what is *di sotto in sù*, seen from below, from the bottom to the top, like the cloud-riddled ceiling frescos of the Italian Baroque. They thus foreground orientation while suppressing position—first, because they draw attention to the artist's frame of visual reference and second, because they anchor that frame to the very front of the picture, which tilts down toward him and also toward us.

It is not an emotional identification these studies are encouraging; it is a purely perceptual one, if by perceptual we understand grounded and gravitationally well moored. That is what might be called the universalizing thrust of the pictures, the aspect of them everyone must experience, as opposed to the cues to this or that feeling that might strike some and pass others entirely by. To some extent this might be true of all landscape painting, but Constable's originality lies in taking the generic expectation of being placed in the world and answering it in keenly corporeal terms. Unlike other contemporaneous sky studies—including J. M. W. Turner's—that suggest a viewing subject who is perpendicular to the horizon, Constable's force us to remember the sensation of a craned neck or (less painfully) what is feels like to lie down on your back and look up at the sky.

It is this emphasis on position and relation that encourages me to think of Constable's studies not as poems but as poetic devices, or—to be a bit more precise—as reinterpreting the work done by tropes in another medium and register. Again, this reinterpretation is enabled by a loosening of traditional expectations around genre and a cultural lean toward the sorts of values Romanticism would set as lyric's new foundation: a containment, narrowing, or huddling-up of focus, to be sure, but also a curiosity about what happens when the intimate becomes impersonal, or when experiences of impersonality, like being one reader of this poem or one viewer of this painting among any number of others, seem absolutely one's own, felt in the blood and along the heart.

Hyperion shows us that depreciating genres don't just slink off to die. They can be, and often are, repurposed into occasions for experimental practice. *Hyperion*, for its part, is an epic poem that is almost entirely eventless, more like an elasticated lyric whose center of consciousness

travels between inchoate characters. In that encounter of Hyperion and
Coelus at the end of book 1, the poem's loose joints allow for a more local
experiment with the characteristically lyric figure of apostrophe, reimag-
ined here as a speech made by a nearly absent being to a very present one
who does not or cannot talk back. What intrigues me about this particular deformation of both generic and tropological conventions is that it
is done, at least by Keats, in service of a poetics I've already described
(in my third chapter) as evacuative, lifting the burden of personality off
poetry so that it can better animate states of ecstatic blankness and, perhaps, their ethical extension.

Constable's cloud studies are engaged in a similar procedure. Like
Hyperion, they defy generic categories while playing on generic conventions. And, like *Hyperion*, they are interested in things coming apart.
Clouds are among these things, but so are the pictorial habits that gov-
ern eighteenth-century engagements with landscape, perspective, and
the notion of the prospect as something that is looked across and down
at. There is a distinctive leveling effect apparent across all of Constable's
work, and not just the cloud studies. In 1825, a critic complained of the
"sameness . . . of his disagreeable execution and coloring," with "plants,
foliages, sky, timber, stone, every thing . . . all contesting for individual attention" despite being offensively bland, "as if he had employed a dredg-
ing box" filled with white dust.[32] If the *London Magazine* could make such
a pronouncement about comparatively run-of-the-mill paintings like *The
Hay Wain* or *The Lock*, which do indeed crunch their elements together,
imagine what it might have said of the cloud studies, in which everything
strives for individual attention and everything is easily confused for nothing at all.

The flatness of Constable's images, their close quartering of depth and
breadth, is indispensable to their effect. It's especially marked in the cloud
studies, whose pictorial compression is enhanced by dint of their subject
matter. Clouds, as I've said, express surface without volume. Constable
fills his canvas with them, blending their edges into the sky and limiting
their colors to a small palette of whites, grays, and pale blues. A scrim
falls over our field of vision, but it also pushes out toward us. There is not
a single study in which the clouds seem to be seen from a safe distance;
in every case, they are hustling toward the viewer, the fancy that they
are coming for us boosted by the very visible brushstrokes used for these
paintings.

Constable always had a taste for showing his labor—even the glossy
landscapes of the 1810s show the swipe and press of tightly bound
bristles—but when it comes to the cloud studies the brush is truly out
in force. Tattered and ridged, strokes cluster where they don't belong,

or where their presence is least apt to what they're representing. It's one thing to lend a green lawn the suggestion of blades of grass or furrows, as in 1816's *Wivenhoe Park* (figure 5). It is quite another to stipple the edge of a cloud, or sweep raised lines at random intervals across the sky. Even several steps from a canvas like *Rainstorm over the Sea*—painted somewhere in the mid-1820s in Brighton—we see these marks for what they are, and the eye picks up on something not quite right: clouds aren't supposed to have texture; they don't break up into lines as hard and fine as these (figure 6).

It would be a mistake to read these brushstrokes as an assertion of the artist's personality via his virtuosic mark: that would be "to fall into one of two errors," either "mistaking self for process or confusing brushstrokes with picture."[33] In *Rainstorm over the Sea*, the brush seems to have been unhinged from any relationship either to the human hand or to the sea it is supposed to paint: all you see is a series of lashes running from the top to the near-bottom of the page, or from the near-bottom to the top. What is going on in the cloud studies is much stranger and more complex. By refusing to conceal the artificiality and, for that matter, the sheer eccentricity of how he paints clouds, Constable would seem to be celebrating the man behind the curtain and the authority of his gesture. However, because the paintings are pitched in an unaccountable zone between figurative and abstract representation—between, say, Haytley's portrait of the Montagus and Claude Monet's *Les meules à Giverny*—the status of the artist is uniquely up for grabs. Is he the dutiful observer of patrons and panoramas, or a visionary responsible only to his imagination?

The brushstrokes, I'd say, are the evidence and the performance of an embodied neutrality, the impersonal signature of a specific historical body that bore witness to something at a specific historical time: these clouds on that day doing this. The painter's body leaves its mark, but his character does not. This is what makes Constable's studies not just flat but flat-affected, or at least muted, soft-sold. To be sure, much has been made of Constable's remark that he considered the sky "the chief Organ of sentiment" in every landscape painting.[34] That phrase wasn't an unusual one in the long Romantic period and is mostly used to signify an innate capacity for feeling. The sky is to the landscape as the brain or the heart is to the body of a living creature; it enlivens it, keeps it going, gives it the capacity to feel and to express its feelings. This adds some to the claim that Constable's view of the landscape painting is fundamentally corporeal. It also hints at a belief that without the sky as its emotional motor, the landscape and its "objects" would remain inert, vegetation gone vegetable. Most importantly, however, it forces us to see something quite unexpected and a little bit grotesque, namely that when Constable

FIG. 5. John Constable, *Wivenhoe Park, Essex* (1816). Oil on canvas. Widener Collection. Photograph: Courtesy National Gallery of Art, Washington, DC.

FIG. 6. John Constable, *Rainstorm over the Sea* (ca. 1824–28). Photograph: © Royal Academy of Arts, London. Photography: John Hammond.

comes to paint only the sky, we should take this exercise for what it is: not an act of emoting but an act of dissection, an anatomical study of planetary tissue.

To paint just the sky thus represents an abstraction in the literal sense. The organ of sentiment is isolated or taken away from the body to which it belongs, while that body—which is to say, the ground, the earth, the rest of a surrounding ecosystem—is pushed aside and lopped off. Think of Coelus reminding Hyperion of his ethereal presence and its capacity for opposing the concentrated momentum of revolutionary time. The acute carnality of what is barely there is Constable's métier as well, and once we begin to consider his canvases not just as skyings but as shearings, cut out from a larger body, they become sinister, even macabre, more so for the drag of the brush across them like a suture or scar.

If this sounds like an overstatement, let's say instead that the erasure of the world beneath the sky, like the erasure of the artist's singularity from his singular stroke, is the sign of a loss each study tries to record. Painting the clouds and only the clouds gives weight to what is absent from them, and registers that absence as a palpable extension of the artwork's psychic field. Keats's description of his clouds as a "rack" is relevant here too. Skywatching isn't just woolgathering: it opens onto a scene of pain displaced from elsewhere, onto a tableau of obscure damage we wouldn't recognize were it closer to hand.

The simplest way to put it is this: the cloud studies take the *land* out of *landscape*, much as Turner's "abstractions of aerial perspective" send the sky crashing into the earth in a wash of grit and loam.[35] Their mechanism is essentially reductive, whittling the artist down to the work of his hand holding a tool, whittling the world down to a sky. And yet Constable's minimalism, if we want to call it that, is all about the force of nearly phantom things: the stand-up stiffness of paint scored by a brush, a tight vista of white straining forever forward. It's an effect that comes through most powerfully in those studies that hold on to just the tiniest sliver of landscape, like a shard of mirror that reflects the abundant austerity of clouds, clouds, and more clouds.

In late September 1821, Constable produced a cluster of cloud studies that, taken in sequence, show the steady erosion of trees and ground from the bottom of each canvas (usually paper laid on board), until terra firma dwindles to a proposition. On September 24, there was his *Study of Sky and Trees* (figure 7). Here, trees ruffle up from the bottom of the canvas, their topmost branches reaching about one-quarter of the way up the view. The bottom right corner hints at a hillside, but the bottom left is dizzyingly vacant, as if the trees might slide right off the paper into nothing. It seems, though, that the wind is blowing from left to right, "more to the north" (as Constable wrote on the back) as a storm begins to come on. Perhaps it is nothing itself that's going to swarm over and swallow the earth, not the earth that's going to dive off its own edge.

Three days later, *Cloud Study: Horizon of Trees* (figure 8) finds the sky in a domineering squat over hills and groves, the latter painted as a line of darker blue limping across the canvas like a sad caterpillar. Perhaps

FIG. 7. John Constable, *Study of Sky and Trees* (24 September 1821). Oil painting. Photograph: © Victoria and Albert Museum, London.

empty space won't swallow the earth after all; perhaps the heavens will simply crush it in a landslide of chalky shapes. A sneak preview of this possibility is offered on the right, where a stack of stratus clouds piles high, mimicking the "stratified bodies" in James Hutton's *Theory of the Earth*, layers of sand, gravel, shale, and schist "continually traveling" toward "the bottom of the sea." What if the sky were the earth? What if clouds could turn the land into their "lower country," composed of horizontal strata "among which . . . , besides coal, there are also found the relics of organized bodies"?[36] That is the prospect posed by *Horizon of Trees*, which splits its visual field between a blurry mass of soft-edged clouds and that more streamlined sheaf of long white ribbons, which seem at first to be the weaker of the formations but, on a longer viewing, reveal themselves as the fantastic threat of a world so overtaken by clouds that clouds have become the obdurate matter of geology.

The threat is brought home, finally, by the *Cloud Study* of September 28 (figure 9). There is almost no land here at all, and what is there is painted such a gray shade of blue that nothing definitive keeps us from saying that this is not land but sea. It's not sea—it's Hampstead Heath— but only the odd blurt of pale green offers that reassurance. It's not

FIG. 8. John Constable, *Cloud Study: Horizon of Trees* (27 September 1821). Photograph: © Royal Academy of Arts, London. Photography: John Hammond.

sea, but it's to the sea that this strip of darker color alludes, as if to state allegiance to a particular passage in a particular poem. On the back of this canvas Constable wrote "Sep.r 28. 1821/Noon—looking. North. West./ Windy from the S.W./large bright clouds flying rather fast/very stormy night followed." He says nothing of the birds swooping around in his sky, but these vividly recall Ovid's lines on avian life after the flood, on birds circling and circling, looking for land and finding only a vast expanse of blue, into which they will eventually drop, exhausted.[37]

I actually don't mean to imply that the tenor of the cloud studies is apocalyptic; to my mind, it isn't. The paintings are too committed to a certain degree of reduction and counterintuitive composition to allow any sort of narrative, much less such an overbearing one, to intrude upon their early-minimalist discipline. William Gilpin famously defined the picturesque as having an interest in cracked and broken things, like country walls or fence posts. Constable has taken that same curiosity about ordinary, minor, and nontraumatic instances of destruction and decay and used it in the service of his form rather than any particular theme. It's the same reason the cloud studies sometimes evoke only to spin away

FIG. 9. John Constable, *Cloud Study* (28 September 1821). Oil on paper laid on board. Photograph: Yale Center for British Art, Paul Mellon Collection.

from religious iconography, like those ceiling frescoes seen from below or the fantastical cupolas of Tiepolo, whose dazzling images of clouds overrun with gods and angels Constable has given the same treatment that Robert Rauschenberg gave Willem de Kooning's drawing in 1953, erasing any and all anthropomorphic figures from the canvas but leaving some blurred, billowing shapes behind.

"Our land," writes Hutton, "has two extremities," the tops of the mountains and the edge of the seashore. If these were to crumble, "there would remain an aqueous globe, in which the world would perish." But, he adds, remember that "in the natural operations of the world, the land is perishing continually." We have a front-row seat to this destruction, and, if we put the effort in, "we shall find the means of calculating what ha[s] passed on former occasion, as well as what will happen in the composition of a future earth."[38] Hutton's language harmonizes with Constable's studies: both allude to apocalypse while sidestepping its endgame, and both monitor the planet from within an accentuated present, which holds clues to past events and may help us anticipate future ones. Still, Hutton is a scientist and Constable a painter, and this makes a difference. The kinds of calculation proper to geology have an explanatory and predictive purview. For Hutton, the state of the earth as it is right now is a meaningful if partial expression of how it was, and a meaningful if partial indicator of how it will be. Nothing about Constable's studies can measure up to these standards, and nothing about them can provide these kinds of insights. As Hutton says of the Romans and the Greeks, you can look to their writings all you want trying to compare the size of coastlines then to the size of coastlines now, but you will be "disappointed"; "their works are not accurate enough for such a purpose."[39]

Nonetheless, the reception of Constable's work over the last few decades has been dogged by a well-meaning positivism, according to which the cloud studies are taken to be significant documents in the archive of climate change. Before then, and for much of the twentieth century, the cloud studies were hailed chiefly for prefiguring the modernism of the French Impressionists. Gillen D'Arcy Wood shrewdly observes that "it's difficult to imagine the recent curatorial and corporate investment in exhibiting the clouds studies without their being satisfyingly integrated, alongside Monet's haystacks, into a pre-history of twentieth-century painting." In place of this art-historical terminus, Wood imposes one of his own. "From our meteorological moment of the twenty-first century," he writes, "the processes of weather, as Constable observed them, now represent a specific climate history: the condition of the northern sky on the very brink of modern, man-made climate change." "With that," Wood decides, "all is changed utterly." All this is in service of dismissing "the conventional art-historical reading of the cloud studies" in favor of recognizing "their empirical, literal, documentary power." As an example of that power, consider the fact that "July, 2006, was the sunniest month in three hundred years of weather records in England and, were Constable on the Heath, he would have waited in vain for his clouds, his sketchbook filled with moribund Claudean blue."[40]

This is an impressive argument, not least in its positing of Romantic art as the summit of climate empiricism. Constable, on Wood's account, outstrips both neoclassical painting in his depiction of the Holocene and modernism in its self-consciously postindustrial response to environmental stress and shock. Now, to be clear, the sky study rose to prominence in the seventeenth century, and Claude's skies are never just blue (in fact they tend to be cloudy). But the real question Wood's discussion poses is, what kind of empiricism is this? A more fine-grained way of asking that question is, what is the antecedent of *that* in the sentence "With that, all is changed utterly"? Is it "man-made climate change"? Or the emergence of its "brink" as such?

Climate change, as Wood's language implies, doesn't just change the present, it interferes with the past; it sends us looking for the tipping point at which some ordinary thing, like the English sky, became the last of its kind. This is why it matters that when you look at Constable's puffy white cumuli of the 1820s, you should think about rain two hundred years later, and long past that point, to a time when summer rainfall in the south of England will likely decrease by up to 30 percent. Where I live, in Southern California, I could look at those clouds and ask how they do and do not remind me of the billows of smoke unleashed by the Thomas Fire of December 2017, or the Woolsey Fire of November 2018, or the broad ribbons of ash that on both occasions wrapped around the walls and hallways of the building where I work.

The trouble, as far as Constable goes, is that the perspective Wood wants us to take on the cloud studies is available only in retrospect. We don't have to go as far as our own meteorological moment; we could just go up to Ruskin's storm-cloud. Still, that's a good half century after Constable completed his skyings and, speaking in terms of sheer carbon output, much, much further along in the life of the current catastrophe. If these paintings have anything to say about climate change, it will be by virtue of their abstract and experimental character, not a documentary power they can't possibly have. To borrow Michel Serres's caution against reading Turner as a hard-charging modernist, "conjugat[ing]" Romantic painting "in the future anterior . . . constructs a story that makes sense and truth over the long term of history, but it is a story whose relationship" to its own contemporary moment is unavailable.[41]

The question of the brink is paramount: if Constable's work offers a correction to the apocalyptic sublime of Turner, whose vortices and biblical fires Wood finds offering little in the way of reflection on the end of human civilization, it ought to be in its very ignorance of that end as a climatological possibility. In other words, if you want to search these paintings for thoughts on climate change, you have to look, bizarrely, for their total incomprehension of its existence. But what would an empirical and (again) documentary ignorance look like?

From the start of this book, I've been pursuing the poetics of ne-science, the word Geoffrey Hartman uses to take stock of the epistemological leftovers of trauma. We are now in a slightly different register. We've left behind the harrowing events detailed in the first two books of *The Task*; we're no longer spinning our wheels with Wordsworth in the morass of an indispensable, inarticulable secrecy. We're partly back in Keats's wheelhouse, where everything terrible in human and historical existence has been absorbed and changed, distilled into a suite of pulsations that ask what life would be if history as we know it could come to an end. But we're also taking on a new orientation toward the passing of time, one that involves rotating the human toward the sky. This isn't just any sky: it's the sky happening now, this minute, in the collapsed and collapsing present of what Serres calls "the reign of heat":

> Because heat drove the mine machinery, propelled the locomotives, animated the propeller-driven or paddlewheel boats—those very things that gave England the temporary mastery of the seas—because, via the burning of coal, it stoked steel foundries—whence the forge masters drew their financial might—heat destroyed the agrarian, cool society of water mills and windmills. It created a new and burning society. Everywhere, fires unknown before that time were lit in such a way that a thousand things that had been stable for a long time disappeared, while others began to move. Then cities were smothered under blankets of unbreathable smoke, and London's streets, squares, and rooftops vanished under the haze from those fires.

Constable, Serres writes, avoids this reality, fiddling (while London burns) "at fields, meadows, and gardens still plunged in the old society of the eighteenth century and its agrarian, aristocratic world." He wants to stay cool, even as industrialization turns up the heat, and even as Turner— "the solar master"—runs headlong into the flames.[42] In sum, for Wood, Constable offers evidence of a world that no longer exists, and in showing that it no longer exists becomes part of a larger, scientific narrative of climatological rupture. For Serres, he misses out on the opportunity, masterfully seized by Turner, to exhibit the full scorching horror of the Industrial Revolution; his painting is artificially sealed, air-conditioned and out of touch.

Despite their differences of opinion, these narratives insist on all or nothing, and both demand a referent for every representation. The results are true but trivial. It is certainly right that Constable does not paint the Industrial Revolution or its attendant harms. If you're looking for Romantic art that has a documentary conscience, Turner is your man: even his "pictures of nothing" feature naval battles, slave ships, Napoleon at Elba, and other allegories of imperial hubris.[43] It is equally right that he does not paint climate change. When scholars propose that the cloud studies be taken seriously as meteorological documents, they invariably point to the notes Constable made on the back of his paintings ("Windy from the S.W./large bright clouds flying rather fast") and not the paintings themselves. This is understandable. As painted images, and without any supplementary notation, the studies contain as much information about climate change as Joseph Severn's 1857 painting *The Deserted Vil-*

lage does about an economic regime that siphons value from the country to the city, or about how it expands its frontiers by making migration a necessity and colonialism its consequence.

We've now arrived at something of a roadblock. The cloud studies do not make a good case for interdisciplinary collaboration, and there are certainly much better, more reliable and relevant ways to investigate cloud formation and its connection to specific meteorological events. They are works of environmental art but not of environmental science. And yet it seems right to say that Constable's clouds illuminate something about the world and our relation to it, that they have an insight or a prompt to offer that is distinctly of its time and no other. It also seems right to say that the specificity of that time matters, that these paintings are not just Romantic but Romantic annotations of recent history, a history marked by extremely violent and hardly surreptitious changes to existing social relations. If those changes are not yet written across the sky, as they would be by the time Ruskin identified his storm-cloud, they are certainly seen and felt and lived on the ground.

In the studies, that ground is gone. There are no social relations; there aren't even people. Sometimes there are birds, and trees, and there is the also the press and print of the artist's hand and the frame of his gaze, even if the artist himself is unimaginable against the backdrop of this disoriented world, with no robust sense of scale or distance or time of day. How far is Constable from the next village over? How big is he, compared to a cumulus? If the backward-bent-neck perspective of the studies reminds us that the artist has a body, and that having a body is uncomfortable, it also estranges us from any easy identification of our position with his, and this makes him even more of a cipher, more of a force field than a person. Stare hard enough at the clouds, and the whole earth will go out from under you. Attention is a game of managed losses: to see the clouds clearly, everything else will have to go.

The truth is, the cloud studies *are* like Monet's haystacks, or certain works of video art. Placing them in that lineage doesn't have to be facile; nor does it undermine their Romantic specificity. The corrosion of fixed perspective is exemplary of modernist and postmodernist painting, and Constable is tiptoeing toward it. That's important to notice, because he never quite gets there; nor should we assume that he wants to. *Someone was here*: the studies do insist on that phenomenological baseline; they do keep that much of a grip on figurative representation. Someone was here, he looked at the sky, he turned his face toward it; he gave shape to its silence, made recourse to form where there was no content, and painted surface where there was no depth. He froze this moment of impossible intimacy and put a frame around it, so that when we look at each painting we don't see a landscape, or even the sky, but rather the very idea of one-sidedness, a play of fidelity and withholding. Someone was here, watching the sky, and the sky would not watch him back.

This is the gesture I want to insist on calling an apostrophe, and not just because the upturned angle of the studies suggests that the paintings record a speaking to or looking toward. It is apostrophic, and the studies are apostrophes, because they score communication in an alien key, playing with generic as well as everyday expectations around embodiment and proximity, or what it means to feel near to a thing that is always far away. Apostrophe isn't a one-way street but a ring road of intimacy marked by pervasive strangeness, most obviously the fact that no one is really present to it. It may trope on a conversational circuit of give and take, but it also tropes on this: how paying close attention to something can make it assume "a graceful . . . kind of nonabsence," a spectral immediacy.[44] The more Constable looks at the sky, the further he falls from it, chin up, head back, hand out.

Each cloud study is about the loop of emphatic and ethereal presence, about straining so hard toward something in the world that it and we and the world attenuate. This is why the studies show so little of the land, and why the land always looks so beleaguered. You could say, Constable only cares about the sky; he doesn't paint the ground—or doesn't paint much of it—because the ground doesn't concern him. These aren't grass studies, and Constable isn't trying to get trees just right. In this case, however, we need to understand not painting the land positively, as an act of representation rather than omission, in the same way that poetic apostrophes allow silence to be heard as a response, distance to be felt as intimacy, absence to be occupied. Ignoring a thing can be an alternative form of attending to it, and an undercover expansion of our emotional field. When the land vanishes from beneath the picture plane, or when it barely grips its edge, we are covertly steered toward thinking about what is not there, toward wondering about this land that is perishing continually and the future earth that will come from its demise.

Treating the cloud studies poetically, though not as poems, goes some way toward making their apparent aversion to historical testimony legible in other terms. Constable's apostrophe, like Keats's, is actually twofold: the paintings are talking to the invisible land as much as they are talking to the silent sky. Both are its impossible addressees, entities with which he cannot make contact; both are places where human beings do not belong. Asking the painter to keep records of the sky as it's being poisoned, or of the earth as it's being cracked open for fuel, is to deny the displacement the studies are trying so hard to convey. That scrambling of a properly vertical and authoritative relation of human beings to their planet is Constable's best gift to the archive of industrialization, and it's not one that can be run through any meteorological algorithm or wheeled out as evidence for any lab. His work is about the unresponsiveness of the natural world to the questions we pose to it, and our irresistible urge to keep asking them anyway. That's not the stuff of history. As Goethe told us, it's the stuff of love—a love that, like all apostrophes, is edged by anger and grief.

In closing, I'd like to turn briefly to a contemporary work of art that harkens back to this poetics of unrequited address and tests it in yet another medium, one that combines lexical with pictorial and sculptural elements. This is Helen Mirra's *Sky-wreck* (figure 10), an installation at the Renaissance Society at the University of Chicago that ran for six weeks between May and June 2001. Based on the geodesic blueprints of Buckminster Fuller, the utopian-futurist architect and theorist, *Sky-wreck* involved 110 triangles of indigo cloth cut into polyhedral forms and spread out over large sections of the gallery's floor. The look is similar to that of Fuller's so-called Dymaxion maps, which he said he preferred to the more static projections of an ordinary world map.

Instead of mapping the planes of the earth, Mirra's shapes, with their rich blue color, represent the sky, appearing here as a piecemeal scaffold anchoring the space around it. Some of the triangles touch edges and some of them don't, and where there are gaps between discrete shapes they are sometimes wide enough for a person to stand in, heel to toe, and sometimes much thinner than that. Meanwhile, if the shape of the pieces and their arrangement on the floor call to mind the clear plastic forms of Magna-Tiles (the children's toy), the thick, rough-grained fabric they're made from gives the work a hand-crafted feel. The choice of fabric seems deliberately to invoke the history of mass production, and the fact that, even prior to the mechanization of textile mills, cloth was the first industrially manufactured material of early capitalist economies.

Cloth is not Mirra's only material, however. Here, as in much of her other work, the written or rather printed word operates as an additional medium. The title of the piece is taken from the first or—depending on how you count—the second line of Paul Celan's "Mit erdwärts gesungenen Masten," a poem in the late collection *Atemwende*, from 1967, the same year that Michael Fried published "Art and Objecthood," his infamous brief against minimalism. I say "first or second line" because the poem's title is syntactically continuous with the three words that lie beneath it. In its entirety, the poem reads:

FIG. 10. Installation view: Helen Mirra, *Sky-wreck* (2001). Courtesy of the artist. The Renaissance Society at the University of Chicago. Photograph: © The Renaissance Society at the University of Chicago. Photography: Tom Van Eynde.

| Mit erdwärts gesungenen Masten | *With masts sung earthward* |
| fahren die Himmelwracks | *the sky-wrecks drive.* |

| In dieses Holzlied | *Onto this woodsong* |
| beißt du dich fest mit den Zähnen | *you hold tight with your teeth* |

| Du bist der liedfeste | *You are the songfast* |
| Wimpel. | *pennant.*[45] |

We're back close to where we started, with remarks to some "you" pinned to the sky, as light and intractable as the clouds with which it shares the atmosphere. By that I don't mean that Mirra is thinking about Goethe (though Celan certainly is) but rather that *Sky-wreck* situates itself in a poetic lineage and an apostrophic one. If Fried's complaint about minimal and conceptual art—with which this piece is obviously also in dialogue—is that it is too theatrical, too focused on flagging down the spectator and cajoling her engagement, Mirra asks what happens if that theatricality is understood in poetic terms, less as solicitation and more as unpromising address. It's worth noting, on this score, that Fried might actually have a similar idea lurking in the back of his mind. Although "Art and Objecthood" insists that the spectator is as it were hailed into the objecthood of the work by the work itself (or by its "situation"), this dynamic does at one moment get flipped, and in language that exactly reproduces the standard view of apostrophe: being in the room with a sculpture by Donald Judd or Robert Morris is, Fried writes, "not entirely unlike being distanced, or crowded, by the silent presence of another person."[46]

Lineage implies a line of descent moving from past to present, but Mirra phrases the relation of her work's poetic to its visual elements differently. These terms are horizontal and also layered, recalling the clouds in Constable's *Horizon of Trees* and, like those clouds, the stratified bodies of geological representation. Photographs of *Sky-wreck* can't quite capture the way Mirra's triangles riff on the gallery space. Located on the top floor of a university building, the Renaissance Society has gabled ceilings that bring to mind Fuller's geodesic domes even more than *Sky-wreck* does; it also has brown linoleum floors cut into smallish squares, and it's on these squares that Mirra's triangles were laid. The effect is to turn floor and ceiling into additional layers of the piece, so that each layer—brown squares, blue triangles, the chalk-white polygons of the ceiling and walls—looks like part of an atmospheric cross-section. As in *Horizon of Trees*, we see the vocabulary of the geologist mapped onto a topography of the sky. Celan's poem is among these sedimentary layers, as is the medium of the word more generally: "Mit erdwärts gesungenen Masten" was printed along one wall of the gallery, and along another was a description of the mathematical parameters of the piece: "Given that the sight distance to the horizon is approx. five kilometers/If the sky is an eleven frequency icosahedral dome/Then 1/11th of the sky at a scale of 1:333" and so on.

When we say that the sky is the limit, what we really mean is that the limit does not exist, or at least that it doesn't exist for us and our endeavors. By representing the sky as a geological stratum, Mirra returns it to finitude, and to physical processes of deterioration and decay. She knows that human activity affects the atmosphere as it affects the earth, that we have invaded and mined and spoiled its once untouchable expanse. In the lush blue of her triangles, I see an ideal under threat, perhaps by the specter of geoengineering and the ways in which it will wreck the sky, shrouding it in a gray and orange haze in a last-ditch effort to keep the sun's rays from burning up our world. There's a reason why those triangles aren't suspended from the ceiling but spread out across the floor. We walk around them, treading carefully, but with an awareness that the sky—that once inaccessible, infinite space of imaginative projection—has been brought down to our level and broken there. Steering clear of the language of the Anthropocene, *Sky-wreck* nonetheless literalizes its core concept: the human species is on top now, alas.

Sky-wreck, then, is a special kind of address called an apology. It is an apostrophe in the classical sense, aimed at an entity who will never respond and never forgive. And yet Mirra's use of Celan leads the piece away from the weeping and wailing that might belong to this sort of tragic meditation. This is surprising, since Celan is the poet of human suffering on unimaginable scales. Still, his poetry dispenses with "emotional ebb and flow," disrupting sentimental routines of regret and struggling toward an aesthetic mode that "belongs to the future, one in which mimetic and mnemonic functions of language are broken, severed from a humanism to which we would desperately cling."[47]

Sky-wreck has the same idea. Giving us no choice but to stand in the mess we've made, it asks us to imagine what happens after the sky—which we now know and always say is falling—finally falls. You can look at the triangles like the pieces of a broken dinner plate, a precious heirloom, gift, or inheritance that can never be put back together. Or you can take comfort in the regularity of their size and shape and decide that, while the world will never be what it once was, there is still such a thing as order, as the laws of physics and chemistry, of the way things fit together. This doesn't have to be the cold comfort of a dream of a world without people, a popular idyll nowadays. It might, instead, be the emotional expression of a fundamentally political conviction, namely that life doesn't change but its forms do. This way of life, this present calamity, cannot and will not last forever. Something else will come in its place, and that something is not a given. By speaking to it, in the face of its silence, we give it the name we choose; we dream of its shape in the dark, whether it's fine or raining.

Epilogue

Sometime on the morning of March 4, 1969, Robert Barry walked into the Mojave Desert. It was cold, around 35°F. He had a camera and a large tank of helium gas. Opening the tank, he let the helium rise and expand into the dry air. There wasn't much to see because helium is odorless, invisible, and, as one of the seven noble gases, inert, nonreactive. Barry took a picture: of the tank at an angle in the sand, the blue sky, mountains in the distance and the desert sage. He would repeat this process four times, with measured volumes of neon, argon, krypton, and xenon, all released into space within driving distance of Los Angeles. "What I was trying to do, really," he would say, "was create something which really existed, and which had its own characteristics and its own nature, but which we couldn't really perceive." The posters for an exhibition of *Inert Gas Series* were nearly blank, some text at the bottom listing the address of a gallery and a phone number. The address was a Hollywood PO box; the phone number connected callers to an answering service. If you rang, you heard a taped message describing what Barry had done with his gases in the desert—a paraphrase given both in lieu and as an element of the artwork itself.

Where is *Inert Gas Series*? New York's Museum of Modern Art has one of those posters; the internet stores scans, cropped and discolored, of those photographs. But where is it pragmatically, on the ribbon road between language and the world? That is, when we say "Robert Barry's *Inert Gas Series*," to what do we refer? Surely not to those posters or pictures, nor to the gas, still out there fifty years later in one molecular shape or another. If I tell you about the piece, as I just did, do you know it? Do I?

Questions like these will be old hat to anyone familiar with the conceptual art movement, whose emphasis on the ephemerality and placelessness of the aesthetic event is usually framed in terms of art's postmodern dematerialization. *Inert Gas Series*, however, is not about the immaterial but about the invisible—about the threshold of minimal perceptibility over which things cross into our awareness or oblivion. What surrounds us, what do we inhale, absorb, secrete? The piece is candidly cerebral, flaunting its aim to prompt questions about the nature of representation and reference, mimesis and form, indices and parergons and supplements. It is also about environmental consciousness in the late 1960s. It is about California, and a regional preoccupation with unseen aerial poison and subtilized toxicity at what seems like the edge of the world.

This confluence is not accidental. Like all trauma, ecological crisis overloads the testimonial burden borne by the artworks that try to grapple with it. Chronicling the attenuation of planetary life is tough, and it's not surprising that the tropes of near-disappearance or partial erasure that scaffold environmental art often recall long-standing, big-picture questions about aesthetic representation: what it is, how it works, and the open question of its value. This is what it means to say poetry and trauma are a lot alike: both live in the disconnect between experience and expression. Barely perceptible, dimly imaginable, and absolutely real disturbances from atmospheric contamination to the prospect of an Earth several degrees warmer than this one are outstanding illustrations of why that disconnect is so hard to mend.

Strangely, the view that harm is difficult to represent is not a popular one among literary scholars whose work emphasizes environmental themes. Ecocriticism, in Margaret Ronda's careful assessment, "tend[s] to privilege an essentially observational and mimetic ethos," to think always in terms "of what *is*." This tendency is an odd match for the ever more proverbial paradigm of "the end of nature": the notion that, "under late capitalism . . . nature has been entirely vanquished, its cultural meanings depleted, its status as an 'independent force' destroyed." One would think, Ronda adds, that the "radical idea of nature's end demands an emphasis on what is not, on the negative workings of creative imagination in light of a concept's withering-away."[1] Instead, much of ecocriticism looks to literary texts to tell us something about the facts of environmental degradation and how we should feel about them. Its quarry is empirical and ethical. Going after it depends on a frank recapitulation of what used to be called the metaphysics of presence, as the ground of a seamless continuity between the substance of the text and the stuff of the world.

This book, like the historical period on which it focuses, is inseparable from the economic and ecological crises that beset it. What I have tried to show is that Romantic poetry has an earnestly indirect relationship to those crises, and that this indirection describes a failure to explain the ever more complex situation of social life under capital. A work like *Inert Gas Series* falls in the same genealogical line and has similar preoccupations; of course, where Romanticism belongs to the moment when agricultural society is giving way to its industrial successor, the conceptual tradition confronts downstream the early days of industry's obsolescence. And for certain, in Barry's outsourcing of his artwork's location to a PO box and a telephone answering service, there is plenty of evidence for the claim that his circumvention of nearly "any and all visuality" swaps out "an aesthetic of industrial production and consumption with an aesthetic of administrative and legal organization."[2]

Still, what I have tried to suggest in this book is that works of art are not robustly reducible to historically guided analyses of this sort, even as those analyses may be meaningful, significant, even indispensable. I have made that argument not to defend a notion of aesthetic autonomy but rather in response to philosophical insights regarding the ontological plurality of the world's contents. On a more local level, I have held to this basic premise because I think it is extremely important to eighteenth- and early nineteenth-century literature, for which it serves as both a long-standing, culturally sanctioned assumption about what art—especially poetry—is and does and a point of anguished continuity with the way things are in England and Europe around 1800. Romanticism, on my account, treats its inability to make sense of history as a means of making present, if only obliquely, the conditions under which history has become harder to make sense of. And yet to try to finesse that oblique representation into mimesis—to say, for example, that Keats's catachreses are good case studies in the labor theory of value, or that Cowper's use of parataxis demonstrates the perceptual derangement that comes with the commodification of life—is not just a losing proposition but a metaphysically untenable one.

The upshot of this view is that it allows us to look upon the apparent nescience, or ignorance, of Romantic poetry not as a mere absence or negation of understanding but as the material signature of the social experience of capital. I have located that signature in tropes and figures, as a way of joining the rhetorical theory of the early modern and Enlightenment period to this specific application of its claims. As we've seen, the prevailing wisdom inherited by the Romantics was that figurative language does not correspond exactly to anything in the world. That idea, as it happens, is equally influential in the art movements of the mid-twentieth century and particularly in conceptualism. This is explained not by any special affinity Romantic and conceptual art may have for one another but rather by conceptualism's embrace of analytic philosophy, particularly in the Anglophone lineage that has its roots in those very same early modern and Enlightenment discourses on rhetoric. When he collaborates with Donald Davidson, Robert Morris is tapping into the same set of ideas about denotation that Wordsworth had at his fingertips, on loan from luminaries like John Locke and David Hume, as well as the more quotidian Hugh Blair, George Campbell, or that sometime professor of rhetoric and belles-lettres Adam Smith.

Unlike poststructuralism, which insists on the disjuncture between all language and the reality to which it purports to refer, the rhetorical tradition I've been working with treats discrete instances of language use independently and pragmatically. In the special case of oblique or nonreferential uses of language, such as metaphor, it maintains that it is the *effect* of those uses that matters more than any deep ontological correlation between word and thing. By effect I don't mean something as straightforward as emotional impact, and to conflate the two would be a fairly serious mistake. To speak of the effectiveness of language is to suggest that it pushes materially into the world—that's all. In place of the insistently subtractive or attenuating logic of poststructuralist thought, which emphasizes nullification over conservancy, this way of thinking about rhetoric takes even absence to have a body of some sort. Hence, for example, Campbell's description of obscurity as "a flaw in the medium"— not a vacancy nor a void of understanding but a concrete complication of it. To confront obscurity, to take this one example, is not to grasp at nothing but to grasp at *something* that produces uneven, partial, or defective intelligence.

When Ronda encourages us to attend to the negative workings of the imagination, this might be what she has in mind: to find the material basis of negation in the objective existence of the poem or text. When Barry sets his gases loose in the Mojave Desert, this might be what he has in mind too. *Inert Gas Series* is a work of art, but it is also the performance of a method, an attempt to manifest the sort of attention that would be necessary to confront a crisis that is largely indiscernible. Indeed, Barry seems to be interested in teasing out an important distinction between materialism and empiricism, for where empiricism holds that things have to be experienced by the senses in order to be perceived, materialism does not. In fact, materialism, as Kant said of Newtonian physics, presents a unique epistemological challenge insofar as it asks us to commit our cognitive resources to phenomena that exceed perceptibility. This is the task of Marx's materialism as well, and in this book it has also been the ground for a criticism that treats literature as a unique (if not a privileged) technology for accounting for that which can't be brought to heel merely by looking at it.

The crisis relevant to *Inert Gas Series* is highly overdetermined. On the one hand, the historical fact of deindustrialization is plainly in the background here. On the other, so is environmental poisoning, as well as the covert threat of radiation. No analysis of *Inert Gas Series* can be complete without a recognition that the piece is set in Southern California, the part of the United States most associated with bad air. Just two years before Barry headed into the desert, the Mulford-Carrell Air Resources Act created the State Air Resources Board in response to California's horrific air quality. In a memorable episode twenty-five years earlier, the first documented instance of what we now casually call smog left the residents of Los Angeles unable to see more than three blocks around, eyes watering, lungs burning, panic-stricken that what was under way was nothing less than chemical warfare.[3] If the aesthetics of *Inert Gas Series* invokes administrative and legal organization, the organizations in question are not just the art gallery or the museum but the regulatory agency, the government body, and even the health-care systems through which the human casualties of our unbreathable atmospheres might pass.

On this reading, Barry's piece concerns the imperceptible accumulation of nitrogen and sulfur oxides, smoke, ozone, and various kinds of particulate matter before they hit a tipping point and become smog, before smog hits a tipping point and becomes plainly toxic, before toxic air hits a tipping point and becomes all air, all the time. This is a man-made disaster whose threat lies in being unseen until it is too late. Such a threat, and the predicament it implies, cannot be displayed head-on. They are part of *what is* as much as a metaphor, or an apostrophe, or climate change, or a social relation. Like each of those things, they are hard to see, but that doesn't mean that they don't exist, nor that their ways of existing ought to be corralled into a single mode of presentation.

One of the things *Inert Gas Series* does is remind us of the omnipresence of invisible things. It pulls us away from the naïve positivism of everyday experience and encourages, or at the very least gestures toward, more varied habits of noticing and naming. I see a similar impulse at work in a passage from Dorothy Wordsworth's Grasmere journal, in which she finds herself, as she often does, in conditions of limited visibility. The passage comes from an entry dated Sunday, June 1, 1800, and the entry in full is as follows:

> *Sunday June 1st.* Rain in the night—a sweet mild morning—Read Ballads, went to church. Singers from Wytheburn. Went part of the way home with Miss Simpson. Walked upon the hill above the house till dinner-time—went again to church—a Christening & singing which kept us very late. The pewside came down with me. Walked with Miss Simpson nearly home. After tea went to Ambleside, round the lakes—a very fine warm evening. I lay upon the steep of Loughrigg my heart dissolved in what I saw when I was not startled but recalled from my reverie by a noise as of a child paddling without shoes. I looked up and saw a lamb

close to me—it approached nearer & nearer as if to examine me & stood a long time. I did not move—at last it ran past me & went bleating along the pathway seeming to be seeking its mother. I saw a hare in the high road. The post was not come in—I waited in the Road till John apprentice came with a letter from Coleridge & 3 papers. The moon shone upon the water—reached home at 10 o clock—went to bed immediately. Molly brought Daisies &c which we planted.[4]

One of the hallmarks of Wordsworth's style in her journals is to drop short declarative statements one after another like single beads onto the floor and then turn her prose over to a sudden and self-consciously lyrical acceleration, the whole bag suddenly dumped out. Thus the firm raps of "the pewside came down," "walked with Miss Simpson," "went round the lakes," and "a fine warm evening" give way to the rush of unconnected clauses that begins "I lay upon the steep of Loughrigg my heart dissolved in what I saw." Syntax too undergoes a dissolution here, as if those punctuating dashes and dots are a track on Wordsworth's pulse, receding from the page as she recedes from the world around her. William will make similar moves in *The Prelude*, using enjambment to generate the speed that also lends the enjambed lines a twinkle of special authority and authenticity: these are the lines to which you pay attention, not just because they seem to be unloading a thought so passionate it won't break for endstops but also because that passion seems to promise something revelatory, intimate, in contrast to the rhopographic mise-en-scène that precedes and follows after them.

And, in fact, that is what those middle lines of the passage do. Wordsworth liked to insist on her attachment to "the evidence of [the] senses," but here there is a fairly clean break between a straightforward narration of events and an emotionally freighted turn inward, which is itself scaffolded by the language of conjecture.[5] "Not startled but recalled," Wordsworth starts down a path of hypotheses and retractions, that first fitful self-correction—I was not *this* but *that*—setting the tone for each little shift in her understanding of what she actually hears and sees.

The governing figure here is the simplest of them all, which is to say, it's simile. Although there is only one explicit simile in this passage—the noise Wordsworth hears is "as of a child"—its unobtrusive logic of comparison sponsors the rush of inferences that take us from the noise that is like a child to the lamb that acts as if it wants to examine her to the lamb running away seeming to be seeking its mother. *As, as if, seeming*: each of these words or phrases is a counterfactual marker that gently unbraids the actual from the possible. Between the scrupulous reportage that begins Wordsworth's journal entry and the equally scrupulous reportage that concludes it, this intermediate zone acts as a wedge between what has definitely happened and what might only be perceptible using the resources of figuration and other means of noting a departure from fact—at least where *fact* implies what has obviously and conclusively been or been done.

The significance of this break from an inventory of the day's stuff (rain, books, church, tea, walks, mail) has to be considered within the historical context of the journal, which is preoccupied by trying to determine exactly what its own historical context is. This preoccupation is most evident in Wordsworth's first several entries, which record tantalizing bits and pieces of talk about "these hard times" and their alarming "alteration" (*GJ*, 1, 3). In an entry dated Sunday, May 18 (really May 19), Wordsworth speaks with her neighbor John Fisher, who "observe[s] that in a short time there would be only two ranks of people, the very rich & the very poor, for those who have small estates says he are forced to sell, & all the land goes into one hand" (*GJ*, 3). The next and last sentence of the entry is "Did not reach home till 10 o clock," a veer away from topical matters as abrupt as the one that ties off Wordsworth's account of her ecstatic misery on the occasion of William's marriage to Mary Hutchinson: "I kept myself as quiet as I could, but when I saw the two men running up the walk, coming to tell us it was over, I could stand it no longer & threw myself on the bed where I lay in stillness, neither hearing nor seeing anything. . . . As soon as we had breakfasted we departed" (*GJ*, 126).

These are only a few examples, but they all partake of the dynamic impulse Wordsworth obeys in her journal, namely to go fast when she is talking *either* about current events *or* her own excitation and to go slow when she is giving us the rundown of a day. When Wordsworth needs speed she also tends to lean on an elevated form of what her brother calls diction: after the usual tick-tock litany of "W went to Ambleside—John walked out—I made tarts &c—," an entry from Tuesday, June 24, ends by trilling over an "old woman" who presents "an affecting picture of patient disappointment suffering under no particular affliction." This last sentence wouldn't be out of place in Austen: it is theoretical, spinning a generalization out of a specific case and delivering it with a quiet, confident flourish somewhere between fireside chat and philosophical essay.

Outbreaks of ardor; misgivings about the state of the world; highhanded assessments of characters who, like this old woman, embody the intersection of feeling and newscasting in a way that is deliberately imprecise and exemplary of "no particular." These are the kinds of discursive situations that hasten Wordsworth out of her almost satirically prosaic prose and onto the exit ramps of almost satirically stylized style. Sometimes that style belongs, as it does here, to the graceful novelistic sentence; more often it is the affiliate of what Rachel Feder identifies as an experimental poetics in the long range.[6] Ultimately, however, it's not a question of whether Wordsworth is dealing with psychological experiences or national concerns: it's a question of how one person's joy and pain are bound, excruciatingly, to "these hard times," and how they together seem unassimilable to the bookkeeping or itemization of a daily life that not so secretly sustains them. The Grasmere journal, after all, is a record of one woman's unwaged labor and many people's domestic servitude. It is part of a much bigger story than Wordsworth lets on, a much bigger story than she would know how to tell.

Accordingly and everywhere in the journal, the intimate and the political struggle to shake loose from the *this happened* statements of fact that dominate Wordsworth's writing. This does not mean, by any measure, that Wordsworth's *vie sentimentale* is of the same magnitude as the widening gap between the very rich and the very poor, or the "sad ravages in the woods" at the southern end of Grasmere (*GJ*, 74). Rather, the twining together of these various predicaments through recourse to an exalted, breathless, distended, and hurrying idiom suggests something like the opposite. It suggests, that is, that emergencies have a way of becoming singular, that extraordinary and yet entirely common dramas of personal experience and extraordinary and entirely uncommon disruptions of the social and metabolic order hitch a ride on the same language and, in so doing, lose sight of the contradictions that shape them both.

This is not a complaint. It is a way of thinking about how Wordsworth sets up a problem in her writing, and how the Loughrigg passage might offer a way to step aside from it. There is something quite strange about the phrase "I was not startled but recalled"—from, as Wordsworth says, her reverie, but to what? The recollection is partial, returning Wordsworth not *to* herself or *to* her surroundings but to a space midway between fantasy and observation. That space, as we've seen, belongs to the work of timid figuration and cautious hypotheticals. It is the space of a time-out, a break from the paradoxical dissolving and confinement of the self or its heart by what, in another register, might be called depersonalization. To make her way out of this state of self-loss, Wordsworth has to decide what *something else is*. This is where the lamb comes in. As she allows figuration to reconjugate her reality—to make the move from child to lamb, from a lamb that seems to examine her to a lamb that simply stands, from a lamb that seems to be seeking its mother to a hare seen, just seen, in the high road—she eases back into her body and eases her body back into the world, with all its beauty and all its cascading harms.

The rhetoric of crisis is highly absorptive. Anyone can melt into it, and when she does, she might find that her own difficulties bleed too easily into other, bigger problems, until it's hard to know which is which. In this scenario, figuration becomes a lifeline that unexpectedly disrupts the euphoric collapse of person into place into plight. To see the lamb confusedly and then clearly is, for Wordsworth, to use poetry to start to recover the difference between reverie and resentment, between dissociation and refusal. Waiting on the other side of that recovery is a dailiness at once well ordered and tumultuous, filled with disappointments and small mercies, moons that shine, beds to make and sleep in, flowers to plant, love and grief but mostly grief, rest and toil but mostly toil. It is not a radical vision, but it is what she has. It is not a good life, but it will have to be lived. If it is going to be changed, some of it will have to be lost.

Throughout this book Romantic poetry has been linked to the failure or inability to grasp the causal structure of hard times in terms that might begin to challenge it. As I have said, this is not intended as a characterization of all poetry, and yet it is meant nonetheless as a check on the overinflated power too often attributed to the work of writing. What this parting glance at both Wordsworth and Barry might offer is a more measured view of figuration as companion and goad, staying with us in a world in which we would rather not exist. We come back to what is unbearable; we cannot pretend that it is otherwise if we are to make our home there. The figurative grammar that organizes our return does not tell us what to do once we arrive. It makes only one slender promise: if you could stop caring what this is like, you might know, finally, what it must no longer be.

Acknowledgments

While I was writing this book, some good things happened and some very terrible things too. Josh and Lila Armstrong have celebrated with me and made shelter when it was needed. There is no way to thank them in full, but I will keep trying.

Alan Thomas took an early interest in my manuscript, and it has been a pleasure to work under his gentle, generous watch. Randolph Petilos helped me out of the weeds on several occasions; I'm happily obliged to him, and to everyone at the University of Chicago Press, for their support.

Many thanks to the National Gallery of Art in Washington, DC, the Renaissance Society at the University of Chicago, the Victoria and Albert Museum, the Wellcome Collection, and the Yale Center for British Art, which have made some of the images that appear here open-access and available for reproduction free of charge, and to Helen Mirra. Thanks, too, to Phil Chang.

For their enthusiasm, skepticism, and good company, I am grateful to colleagues and friends like Ali Behdad, Lauren Berlant, Charles Bernstein, Felix Bernstein, Bill Brown, Marshall Brown, Miranda Burgess, Allison Carruth, Jim Chandler, Joshua Clover, Kris Cohen, Sarah Cole, Jonathan Crimmins, Fred D'Aguiar, Nan Z. Da, Nicholas Dames, Jenny Davidson, Arne De Boever, Patricia Dailey, Helen Deutsch, Jeff Dolven, Craig Dworkin, Mary Favret, Rachel Feder, Frances Ferguson, Anne-Lise François, Paul Fry, Billy Galperin, Steven Goldsmith, Amanda Goldstein, Kevis Goodman, Jonathan Grossman, Lily Gurton-Wachter, Elaine Hadley, Martin Harries, Olivia Harrison, Matthew Hart, Megan Heffernan, Ursula Heise, Daniel Hoffman-Schwartz, Joe Howley, Turkuler Isiksel, Claire Jarvis, Virginia Jackson, Eleanor Johnson, Scott Juengel, A.J. Julius, Sarah Tindal Kareem, Evan Kindley, Joshua Kotin, Jonathan Kramnick, David Kurnick, Celeste Langan, Marjorie Levinson, Eric Lindstrom, Deidre Lynch, Anthony Madrid, Saree Makdisi, Sara Marcus, Sharon Marcus, Annie McClanahan, Brian McGrath, Maureen

McLane, Jon Mee, Tobias Menely, Jonathan Mulrooney, Molly Murray, Felicity Nussbaum, Jerry Passannante, Jessica Rett, Christa Robbins, Michael Robbins, Margaret Ronda, Emily Rohrbach, Michael Rothberg, David Russell, Jonathan Sachs, Jennifer Scappettone, Roy Scranton, David Simon, Caleb Smith, Danny Snelson, Juliana Spahr, Rebecca Spang, Emily Sun, Andrew Stauffer, Keston Sutherland, Hamza Walker, Michael Warner, Tristram Wolff, Daniel Wright, Abigail Zitin, Yasemin Yildiz, and Christina Zwarg.

Audiences at Columbia University, the Graduate Center at the City University of New York, Harvard University, Indiana University Bloomington, New York University, the University of Oxford, Princeton University, the University of California's Berkeley, Irvine, and Los Angeles campuses, the University of Chicago, Vanderbilt University, and Yale University engaged various pieces of the book as it was coming together, and the finished product is worlds better for it.

Joshua Clover needs to be thanked twice for reading the manuscript way more than once, and for fixing whatever I wasn't determined to leave broken. I'm very happy to be on this road with him, even if I can rarely keep up.

My love lies always with Lauren Beck, Naela El-Hinnawy, Liz Harris, Cassie Kaufmann, Kristian Kerr, Kelly Kleinert, and Marie McDonough, and more lately though no less joyfully with Saba Harouni and Lexsea Mann. I am also grateful to Marcella Kroll, who helped me come back.

Thank you, Zoe; welcome, Alma.

This book is offered in memory of Hannah Frank, an artist and scholar of tremendous power and a very large-souled human being. I hope it's possible to find in here some of what she taught me, not least that "looking is laborious. But looking is also dreaming."

Notes

INTRODUCTION

1. Or had to be, more literally, the first pitch, with the sense of a first recourse or port of call.

2. Raymond Williams, *The Country and the City* (New York: Oxford University Press, 1973), 141.

3. Karl Marx, *Capital*, vol. 1, trans. Ben Fowkes (London: Penguin, 1990), 165. Hereafter cited in the text as *C*, followed by volume and page numbers.

4. Joshua Clover, "*Value | Theory | Crisis*," *PMLA* 127.1 (2012): 107–14; 108.

5. Geoffrey Hartman, "On Traumatic Knowledge and Literary Studies," *New Literary History* 26.3 (1995): 537–63; 537.

6. Hartman, "Retrospect 1971," in *Wordsworth's Poetry, 1787–1814* (New Haven: Yale University Press, 1971), xvi.

7. Philip Sidney, *An Apology for Poetry (or The Defence of Poesy)*, ed. Geoffrey Shepherd and R. W. Maslen (Manchester: Manchester University Press, 2002), 103.

8. Ecclesiastes 1:8, KJV.

9. William Wordsworth, letter to Charles James Fox, in *The Letters of William and Dorothy Wordsworth*, vol. 1, *The Early Years, 1787–1805*, ed. Ernest de Selincourt, rev. Chester Shaver (Oxford: Oxford University Press, 1967), 312–15; 312.

10. Huey P. Newton, "Huey Newton Speaks from Jail," *Motive* 29 (October 1968): 8–16; 8.

11. Fredric Jameson, *The Political Unconscious: Narrative as a Socially Symbolic Act* (Ithaca: Cornell University Press, 1981), 148.

12. The reference is to Tertius Lydgate's ill-formed and ill-fated ambition "to pierce the obscurity of those minute processes which prepare human misery and joy, those invisible thoroughfares which are the first lurking-places of anguish, mania, and crime, that delicate poise and transition which determine the growth of happy or unhappy consciousness." George Eliot, *Middlemarch*, ed. David Carroll (Oxford: Clarendon Press, 1986), 162. Eliot's reference to the happy or unhappy consciousness likely alludes to Hegel's use of the same categories in his *Phenomenology of Spirit*.

13. As Andreas Malm points out, the hostile takeover of the steam engine is not nearly as precipitous as we might assume. See his *Fossil Capital: The Rise of Steam Power and the Roots of Global Warming* (London: Verso, 2016), 56.

14. Geoffrey Hartman, "Tea and Totality," in *Minor Prophecies: The Literary Essay in the Culture Wars* (Cambridge, MA: Harvard University Press, 1991), 67, 58.

15. Eve Kosofsky Sedgwick, "Paranoid Reading and Reparative Reading, or, You're So Paranoid You Probably Think This Essay Is about You," in *Touching Feeling: Affect, Pedagogy, Performativity* (Durham: Duke University Press, 2003), 123–51; 123.

16. John Dupré, *The Disorder of Things: Metaphysical Foundations of the Disunity of Science* (Cambridge, MA: Harvard University Press, 1993) 6–7.

17. J. B. S. Haldane, preface to Friedrich Engels, *Dialectics of Nature*, trans. C. P. Dutt (London: International Publishers, 1940), xv. Friedrich Engels, *Anti-Duhring: Herr Eugen Dühring's Revolution in Science* (Moscow: Progress Publishers, 1947), 12. For a lively account of Haldane's career and the fortunes of dialectical materialism among mid-twentieth-century scientists, see Helena Sheehan, *Marxism and the Philosophy of Science: A Critical History* (London: Verso, 2018).

18. Sidney, *An Apology for Poetry*, 96.

19. David Hume, "Of the Standard of Taste," in *Essays Moral, Political and Literary* (New York: Cosimo Classics, 2006), 236, 246.

20. Alexander Baumgarten, *Reflections on Poetry*, trans. Karl Aschenbrenner and William B. Holther (Berkeley and Los Angeles: University of California Press, 1954), 39. The full Latin title of Baumgarten's 1735 text is *Meditationes philosophicae de nonnullis ad poema pertinentibus*, with the word *nonnullis*—not nothing— suggesting that the kinds of philosophical renumeration afforded by poetry can only be paid out in small bills.

21. Tzvetan Todorov, *Theories of the Symbol* (Ithaca: Cornell University Press, 1984), 109.

22. John Guillory, *Cultural Capital: The Problem of Literary Canon Formation* (Chicago: University of Chicago Press, 1993), 221.

23. César Chesneau Du Marsais, *Des tropes ou des diférens sens dans lesquels on peut prendre un même mot dans une même langue*, 2nd ed. (Paris: David, 1757), 6–7.

24. Dénis Diderot, *Oeuvres complètes de Diderot*, ed. J. Assézat [and Maurice Tourneux], 20 vols. (Paris: Garnier, 1875–77), 14.444. My translation.

25. Hugh Blair, lecture 6, "Rise and Progress of Language," in *Lectures on Rhetoric and Belles Lettres*, ed. Linda Ferreira-Buckley and S. Michael Halloran (Carbondale: Southern Illinois University Press, 2005), 61.

26. Pierre Fontanier, *Les figures du discours*, with an introduction by Gerard Genette (Paris: Flammarion, 1968), 66. Fontanier's treatise was originally published between 1821 and 1830. My translation.

27. Annie McClanahan, *Dead Pledges: Debt, Crisis, and Twenty-First-Century Culture* (Stanford: Stanford University Press, 2017), 94; Blair, "Rise and Progress of Language," 61. For Blair the capacity to use metaphor is, at least for early humans, a matter of basic survival:

Mankind never employed so many Figures of Speech, as when they had hardly any words for expressing their meaning. . . . For, first, the want of proper names for every object, obliged them to use one name for many; and, of course, to express themselves by comparisons, metaphors, allusions, and all those substituted forms of Speech which render Language figurative. Next, as the objects with which they were the most conversant, were the sensible, material objects around them, names would be given to those objects long before words were invented for signifying the dispositions of the mind, or any sort of moral or intellectual ideas. Hence, the early Language of men being entirely made up of words descriptive of sensible objects, it became, of necessity, extremely metaphorical.

28. Donald Davidson, "What Metaphors Mean," *Critical Inquiry* 5.1 (1978): 31–47; 46–47.

29. Jean-Baptiste le Rond d'Alembert, *Oeuvres complètes de D'Alembert*, 5 vols. (London: Martin Bossange and Co., 1822), 4.1.326–27. My translation.

30. Plato, *Ion*, trans. Penelope Murray and T. S. Dorsch, in *Classical Literary Criticism*, ed. Murray (New York: Penguin, 2000), 1–14; 5 [534].

31. John Keats, *The Fall of Hyperion*, in *Complete Poems*, ed. Jack Stillinger (Cambridge, MA: Harvard University Press, 1982), 1.167–68, 1.148–49.

32. William Wordsworth, *The Thirteen-Book Prelude*, ed. Mark L. Reed, 2 vols. (Ithaca: Cornell University Press, 1991), 1.3.492–93.

33. Wordsworth, letter to Fox, 313; Keats, *Isabella; or, The Pot of Basil*, in *Complete Poems*, 118.

34. William Cowper, *The Task*, in *Poetical Works*, ed. H. S. Milford (London: Oxford University Press, 1967), 129.

35. Christopher Nealon, "Infinity for Marxists," *Mediations* 28.2 (2015): 47–64; 54.

36. Sidney, *An Apology for Poetry*, 103.

37. Susan Stewart, "Garden Agon," *Representations* 62 (1998): 111–43, 111.

38. William Blake, *Jerusalem; or, The Emanation of the Giant Albion*, in *The Complete Poetry and Prose of William Blake*, ed. David V. Erdman (New York: Anchor Books), 1.10.24, 153.

CHAPTER ONE

1. Lyn Hejinian, *My Life* (Copenhagen and Los Angeles: Green Integer, 2002), 96.

2. Andrew Marvell, "Upon Appleton House," in *The Poems of Andrew Marvell*, ed. Nigel Smith (London: Routledge, 2006), 761–62, 767–68.

3. Alexander Pope, letter to Martha Blount dated 22 June 1724, in *The Major Works*, ed. Pat Rogers (Oxford: Oxford University Press, 2008), 179–83; 181.

4. John Dixon Hunt, *The Figure in the Landscape: Poetry, Painting, and Gardening during the Eighteenth Century* (Baltimore: Johns Hopkins University Press, 1989), 67. Without forcing the analogy beyond advantage, there are intriguing similarities between Dixon Hunt's line on gardens and Jonathan Crary's celebrated story about fin-de-siècle visual technologies and early modernist art, which likewise evolves

from a historically specific transformation in the physiological capacities of the spectator and artist. As a particular "organization of the visible," the garden arrays experience digressively, at once mimicking and enhancing the perturbations of a "modernity . . . [that] coincides with the collapse" of extant models of thought and sensation. In moving through the garden, the body is subject to an environment whose immediacy and instantaneity create the feeling that whatever lies around the bend is almost utterly concealed, even as we wander right through it. See Crary, *Techniques of the Observer: On Vision and Modernity in the Nineteenth Century* (Cambridge, MA: MIT Press, 1992), 23–24.

5. Derek Jarman, *Modern Nature* (Woodstock: Overlook Press, 1994), 35. Hereafter cited in the text as *MN*, followed by page numbers.

6. Joshua Clover, *Riot. Strike. Riot: The New Era of Uprisings* (London: Verso, 2016), 175.

7. Adorno, "Parataxis: On Hölderlin's Late Poetry," in *Notes to Literature*, vol. 2, ed. Rolf Tiedemann, trans. Shierry Weber Nicholsen (New York: Columbia University Press, 1992), 109–49; 128, 131. Hereafter cited in the text as "P," followed by page numbers.

8. Pindar, Nemean V, in *The Odes of Pindar*, trans. C. M. Bowra (New York: Penguin, 2015), 2.18–21.

9. Incidentally Hölderlin himself seems to have connected Ciceronian cadences with an undesirable emotional lability, writing to a friend, "If only Man were not so periodic! Or at least that I weren't among the worst in this regard!" ("Wenn nur der Mensch nicht so periodisch wäre! oder ich wenigstens nicht unter die ärgsten gehörte in diesem Punkt!") See Hölderlin, letter to Christian Ludwig Neuffer dated October 1793, in *Sämtliche Werke und Briefe 1: Gedichte*, ed. Jochen Schmidt, 3 vols. (Frankfurt am Main: Deutscher Klassiker Verlag, 1992), 3.112. My translation.

10. Friedrich Hölderlin, "Andenken," in *Hyperion and Selected Poems*, ed. Eric Santner (New York: Continuum, 1994), 266. My translation.

11. Hölderlin, "Andenken," 267.

12. Katrin Pahl, *Tropes of Transport: Hegel and Emotion* (Evanston: Northwestern University Press, 2012), 127, 136. Thanks to Daniel Hoffman-Schwartz for this citation and also for wonderfully generous and helpful discussion on the point of translation here.

13. Bob Perelman, "Parataxis and Narrative: The New Sentence in Theory and Practice," in *The Marginalization of Poetry: Language Writing and Literary History* (Princeton: Princeton University Press, 1996), 59–78; 70. In the version of this essay originally published in the journal *American Literature*, Perlman does in fact use the phrase "unresolved pressure for social narrative" in his discussion of the poetry of Ron Silliman; the version of the essay collected in *The Marginalization of Poetry* mysteriously leaves out "social," though the rest of the sentence is unchanged. See Perelman, "Parataxis and Narrative: The New Sentence in Theory and Practice," *American Literature* 65.2 (1993): 313–24; 321.

14. Perelman, "Parataxis and Narrative,", 60–61.

15. Hugh Blair, lecture 11, "Structure of Sentences," in *Lectures on Rhetoric and*

Belles Lettres, ed. Linda Ferreira-Buckley and S. Michael Halloran (Carbondale: Southern Illinois University Press, 2005), 110–20; 111.

16. François Guillaume Jean Stanislaus Andrieux, *Cours de gramme et de belles-lettres*, in *Journal de l'École polytechnique* 10.4 (November 1810): 69–279; 107. On the democratic or (minimally) collaborative possibilities of style coupé, see Julie Candler Hayes's discussion of Diderot and parataxis in *Reading the French Enlightenment: System and Subversion* (Cambridge: Cambridge University Press, 2004), 145.

17. Samuel Taylor Coleridge, letter to Thomas Poole dated 9 October 1809, in *Collected Letters of Samuel Taylor Coleridge*, ed. Earl Leslie Griggs, 6 vols. (Oxford: Clarendon Press, 1956–71), 3.234. Coleridge goes on to say that Bacon modeled his prose on Seneca's. This is curious, since the accusation that the French have "rejected all the cements of language" is likely invoking Caligula's reported remark that Seneca's writing was "harena sine calce," sand without lime, i.e., bad cement. This is one of many instances in the *Biographia* where Coleridge seems perched somewhere between irony and inattention.

18. Samuel Taylor Coleridge, *The Collected Works of Samuel Taylor Coleridge*, vol. 14, pt. 2, *Table Talk*, 233. Cf. Aristotle's characterization of parataxis as λέξις εἰρομένη, literally "words strung like beads" in his *Art of Rhetoric*, ed. and trans. J. H. Freese, Loeb Classical Library (Cambridge, MA: Harvard University Press, 1926), 1409a24.

19. Edmund Burke, *Reflections on the Revolution in France*, ed. L. G. Mitchell (Oxford: Oxford University Press, 2009), 191.

20. William Wordsworth, *The Prelude, 1798–1799*, ed. Stephen Maxfield Parrish (Ithaca: Cornell University Press, 1977), 58–60.

21. Hölderlin, letter to Johann Gottfried Ebel dated 10 January 1797, in *Sämtliche Werke und Briefe 1: Gedichte* 3.253–55; 254. My translation.

22. Susan Bernofsky, *Foreign Words: Translator-Authors in the Age of Goethe* (Detroit: Wayne State University Press, 2005), 125.

23. See Hegel's "remark" at the end of the discussion of real measure in Georg Wilhelm Friedrich Hegel, *The Science of Logic*, ed. and trans. George di Giovanni (Cambridge: Cambridge University Press, 2010), 320–23.

24. Hölderlin, letter to Ebel, 3.254.

25. Friedrich Hölderlin, translation of Pindar's second Olympian, quot. and trans. with lines from the original Greek, in Bernofsky, *Foreign Words*, 126.

26. Hölderlin, letter to Ebel, 3.254.

27. Samuel Johnson, "Life of Cowley," in *Lives of the Poets: A Selection* (Oxford: Oxford University Press, 2009), 5–53; 40.

28. Sylvia Adamson, "The Breaking of Hypotaxis," entry 7.4 in the section "Literary Language," in *The Cambridge History of the English Language*, vol. 4, *1776–1997*, ed. Suzanne Romaine (Cambridge: Cambridge University Press, 1998), 630–46; 639.

29. George Woodward, "The English Pindarick," in *Poems on Several Occasions* (Oxford: Clarendon Printing-House, 1730), 24.

30. John Hamilton, *Soliciting Darkness: Pindar, Obscurity, and the Classical Tradition* (Cambridge, MA: Harvard University Press, 2004), 306.

31. Joseph Addison, *Spectator* 477, Saturday, September 6, 1712, in *The Works of the Right Honourable Joseph Addison, Esq.*, 4 vols. (London: Jacob Tonson, 1721), 3.588–91; 589.

32. Thomas Whatley, *Observations on Modern Gardening, Illustrated by Descriptions* (London: T. Payne, 1770), 151.

33. Miriam Bratu Hansen, *Cinema and Experience: Siegfried Kracauer, Walter Benjamin, and Theodor W. Adorno* (Berkeley and Los Angeles: University of California Press, 2011), 150.

34. Hannah Frank, *Frame by Frame: A Materialist Aesthetics of Animated Cartoons*, ed. Daniel Morgan (Berkeley and Los Angeles: University of California Press, 2019), 28.

35. William Cowper, *The Task*, in *Poetical Works*, ed. H. S. Milford (London: Oxford University Press, 1967), 2.2. Hereafter cited in the text as *T*, followed by book and line numbers. Where the reference is to the prose sections of the poem, such as its Advertisement or Arguments, I've given page numbers instead.

36. See Kevis Goodman, *Georgic Modernity and British Romanticism: Poetry and the Mediation of History* (Cambridge: Cambridge University Press, 2004).

37. Coleridge, *Biographia Literaria* 1.16. See also William Hazlitt, *My First Acquaintance with Poets*, in *The Complete Works of William Hazlitt*, ed. P. P. Howe, 21 vols. (London: J. M. Dent, 1930–34), 17.120.

38. Coleridge, *Biographia Literaria* 2.72.

39. Hegel, *Phenomenology of Spirit*, trans. A. V. Miller (Oxford: Oxford University Press, 1977), 131.

40. György Lukács, "The Tasks of Marxist Philosophy in the New Democracy," speech delivered to the Congress of Marxist Philosophers in Milan, Italy, December 20th 1947, and quoted in István Mészáros, *Lukács' Concept of Dialectic* (London: Merlin Press, 1972), 63–64.

41. J. G. A. Pocock, "Virtues, Rights, and Manners: A Model for Historians of Political Thought," in *Virtue, Commerce, and History: Essays on Political Thought and History, Chiefly in the Eighteenth Century* (Cambridge: Cambridge University Press, 1985), 37–40; 49.

42. Cowper, "Yardley Oak," in *Poetical Works*, 101–2; For the Romantic period as an era of world war, see Mary Favret, *War at a Distance: Romanticism and the Making of Modern Wartime* (Princeton: Princeton University Press, 2009).

43. Phillis Wheatley, "On Being Brought from Africa to America," in *Complete Writings*, ed. Vincent Carretta (New York: Penguin, 2001), 13 (lines 6–7). See my essay "Romantic Difficulty" for a discussion of Wheatley's "mirthless play on the biblical Cain and the husking, peeling, grinding, boiling, and drying of sugarcane until its blackness is diabolically 'refin'd.'" Anahid Nersessian, "Romantic Difficulty," *New Literary History* 49.4 (2018): 451–466; 463.

44. Ruth Jennison, *The Zukofsky Era: Modernity, Margins, and the Avant-Garde* (Baltimore: Johns Hopkins University Press, 2012), 31–2.

45. Jennison, *The Zukofsky Era*, 32.

46. Jane Austen, *Mansfield Park*, ed. Kathryn Sutherland (Oxford: Oxford University Press, 2003), 53.

47. Austen, *Mansfield Park*, 184. See also Edward Said, "Jane Austen and Empire," in *Culture and Imperialism* (New York: Vintage, 1994), 80–96.

48. Sergei Eisenstein, "Dickens, Griffith, and the Film Today," in *Film Form: Essays in Film Theory*, ed. and trans. Jay Leyda (New York: Harcourt, 1949), 195–255; 236.

49. Christina Sharpe, *In the Wake: On Blackness and Being* (Durham: Duke University Press, 2016), 20–21.

50. Both Cowper and Turner are thinking, among other things, about the Zong massacre of 1781. *The Task* also makes an explicitly topical reference to *Somerset v. Stewart* (98 ER 499), often referred to as Somerset's Case, the 1772 judgment known for birthing the avoidant maxim that, in Cowper's words, "Slaves cannot breathe in England; if their lungs/Receive our air, that moment they are free,/ They touch our country and their shackles fall" (2.40–42). For a thorough unfolding of this trope, see Anthony John Harding, "Commerce, Sentiment, and Free Air: Contradictions of Abolitionist Rhetoric," in *Affect and Abolition in the Anglo-Atlantic, 1770–1830*, ed. Steven Ahern (Farnham: Ashgate Publishing, 2013), 71–88; for recent, fascinating work on other examples of Cowper's abolitionist poetics, see Ivan Ortiz, "Lyric Possession in the Abolition Ballad," *Eighteenth-Century Studies* 51.2 (2018): 197–218.

51. Christopher T. Fan, "Animacy at the End of History in Changrae Lee's *On Such a Full Sea*," *American Quarterly* 69.3 (2017): 675–96; 680.

52. Karl Marx and Friedrich Engels, *The Communist Manifesto* (New York: Penguin, 2002), 5.

53. Cowper, letter to the Rev. William Unwin dated 7 September 1783, in *William Cowper: Selected Letters*, ed. James King and Charles Ryskamp (Oxford: Oxford University Press, 1989).

54. Cowper, "The Rose," in *Poetical Works*.

55. Paul de Man, *The Rhetoric of Romanticism* (New York: Columbia University Press, 1984), ix.

56. Walter Hughes, "In the Empire of the Beat: Discipline and Disco," in *Microphone Fiends: Youth Music and Youth Culture*, ed. Andrew Ross and Tricia Rose (London: Routledge, 1994), 147–57; 154–55.

57. Steven Dillon, *Derek Jarman and Lyric Film* (Austin: University of Texas Press, 2004), 229. Brion Gysin is another important influence here. See especially the account of Jarman's involvement in The Final Academy project by Genesis Breyer P-Orridge (then Genesis P-Orridge) in "Thee Cinema," quoted in Jack Sargeant, *Naked Lens: Beat Cinema* (Berkeley: Soft Skull Press, 2008), 181–89; 186.

58. Dillon, *Derek Jarman and Lyric Film*, 230.

59. Jarman, *At Your Own Risk: A Saint's Testament* (Minneapolis: University of Minnesota Press, 2010), 125.

60. Hölderlin, "Brod un Wein," in *Hyperion and Selected Poems*, 182. My translation.

61. Raoul Vaniegem, *Traité de Savoir-Vivre à l'Usage des Jeunes Générations* (Paris: Gallimard, 1967), published online at http://arikel.free.fr/aides/vaneigem/traite-6 .html (accessed October 14, 2018). My translation.

CHAPTER TWO

1. Geoffrey Hartman, "Blessing the Torrent," in *The Unremarkable Wordsworth* (Minneapolis: University of Minnesota Press, 1987), 75–89, 84.

2. Nan Shepherd, *The Living Mountain* (Edinburgh: Canongate Books, 2011), xliii.

3. This is Wordsworth's infamous assessment of *Endymion*, made to Keats's face no less; on Wordsworth's hebetude see William Hazlitt, "Mr Wordsworth," in *The Spirit of the Age: or, Contemporary Portraits*, in *The Complete Works of William Hazlitt*, ed. P. P. Howe, 21 vols. (London: Dent, 1930–34), 11: 86–95, 86.

4. William Wordsworth, "Michael, A Pastoral Poem," in *Lyrical Ballads and Other Poems, 1797–1800*, eds. James A. Butler and Karen Green (Ithaca: Cornell University Press, 1992) 1–8. Hereafter cited in the text as "M," followed by line numbers.

5. David Bromwich, *Disowned by Memory: Wordsworth's Poetry of the 1790s* (Chicago: University of Chicago Press, 1998), 2.

6. William Empson, "Obscurity and Annotation," in *Argufying: Essays on Literature and Culture*, ed. John Haffenden (London: Hogarth Press, 1988), 70–87, 72.

7. Hartman, "On Traumatic Knowledge and Literary Studies," *New Literary History* 26.3 (1995): 537–563; 537.

8. Hartman, "On Traumatic Knowledge and Literary Studies," 552. The previous sentence reads: "[I]t is possible to move from Wordsworth to the present."

9. Wordsworth, *The Fourteen-Book Prelude*, ed. W. J. B. Owen (Ithaca: Cornell University Press, 1985), 14.286.

10. George Gordon, Lord Byron, *Don Juan*, in *The Complete Poetical Works*, vol. 5, *Don Juan*, ed. Jerome J. McGann (Oxford: Clarendon Press, 1986), 10.41.321–26. Thanks to Jerry McGann for discussion on this point.

11. Dorothy Wordsworth, entry dated 19 May (actually 18 May) 1800, in her Grasmere journal, published in *The Grasmere and Alfoxden Journals*, ed. Pamela Woof (Oxford: Oxford University Press, 2008), 26.

12. Titus Lucretius Carus, *Of the Nature of Things, in Six Books, Translated into English Verse*, trans. Thomas Creech, 6th ed., 2 vols. (London: T. Warner and J. Walthoe, 1722), 1.4.53–54.

13. Geoffrey Hartman, "Retrospect 1971," in *Wordsworth's Poetry, 1787–1814* (New Haven: Yale, 1971), xvi.

14. Wordsworth, letter to Charles James Fox, in *The Letters of William and Dorothy Wordsworth*, vol. 1, *The Early Years, 1787–1805*, ed. Ernest de Selincourt, rev. Chester Shaver (Oxford: Oxford University Press, 1967), 312–15.

15. Wordsworth, *The Thirteen-Book Prelude*, ed. Mark L. Reed, 2 vols. (Ithaca: Cornell University Press, 1991), 1.3.492–93. Unless otherwise indicated, all quotations from *The Prelude* are from this edition and are cited in the text as *P* followed by volume, book, and line numbers.

16. Francis Jeffrey, review of *The Excursion*, originally published in the *Edinburgh Review* 24 (Nov. 1814): 1–30, reprinted in *Romantic Bards and British Reviewers: A*

Selected Edition of the Contemporary Reivews of the Works of Wordsworth, Coleridge, Byron, Keats and Shelley, ed. John O. Hayden (Lincoln: University of Nebraska Press, 1976), 39–52, 43; 52.

17. John T. Hamilton, *Soliciting Darkness: Pindar, Obscurity, and the Classical Tradition* (Cambridge, MA: Harvard University Press, 2003), 7.

18. Hamilton, *Soliciting Darkness*, 11.

19. Jeffrey, review of *The Excursion*, 52.

20. Quintilian, *Institutio oratoria*, published as *The Orator's Education* by Loeb Classical Library, 5 vols. (Cambridge, MA: Harvard University Press, 1980), 3.8.2.17. My translation.

21. Denis Diderot, *Salon de 1767*, in *Oeuvres complètes*, ed. Jules Assézat and Michel Tourneux, 20 vols. (Paris: Garnier Frères, 1875–1877), 11.143. In his *Infidel Poetics*, Daniel Tiffany translates *soyez ténébreux* as "be obscure," but a more literal, possibly richer rendering would be "be shadowy." Besides, in the passage Tiffany has in mind Diderot has already used the word *obscur* twice to describe the poet's ideal scenery or prospect; the shift to *ténébreux* suggests the desire to make distinctions or to add gradations to a general term. See Tiffany, *Infidel Poetics: Riddles, Nightlife, Substance* (Chicago: University of Chicago Press, 2009), 17.

22. George Campbell, *The Philosophy of Rhetoric*, 2 vols. (London: W. Strahan and T. Cadell, 1776), 2.81–2. The object of Campbell's scorn here is Abraham Cowley, the eighteenth-century critic's favorite malum exemplum.

23. 1 Corinthians 13:12, KJV.

24. Erich Auerbach, "*Figura* (1938)," trans. Jane O. Newman, in *Time, History, and Literature: Selected Essays of Erich Auerbach*, ed. James I. Porter (Princeton: Princeton University Press, 2013), 65–113; 96.

25. Augustine, *De trinitate* 15.9.15. My translation.

26. Augustine, *De trinitate* 15.9.16. My translation. See the discussion of Augustine in Eleanor Cook's invaluable *Enigmas and Riddles in Literature* (Oxford: Oxford University Press, 2006), esp. 39–47, and in Päivi Mehtonen, *Obscure Language, Unclear Literature: Theory and Practice from Quintilian to the Enlightenment*, trans. Robert MacGilleon (Helsinki: Academia Scientiarum Fennica, 2003), 88–90.

27. Augustine, *Enarrationes in Psalmos; De trinitate* 15.9.15; *De civitate dei*, published as *City of God* by Loeb Classical Library, 7 vols. (Cambridge, MA: Cambridge University Press, 1972), 7.22.29. My translations.

28. Salvador A. Oropesa, "*Obscuritas* and the Closet: Queer Neobaroque in Mexico," *PMLA* 124.1 (2009), 172–179; 173; Alexander Baumgarten, *Reflections on Poetry (Meditationes philosophicae de nonnullis ad poema)*, trans. (with original text) by K. Aschenbrenner and W. B. Holter (Berkeley: University of California Press, 1954), §12.

29. See John Guillory's still devastating account in "Mute Inglorious Miltons: Gray, Wordsworth, and the Vernacular Canon," the second chapter of *Cultural Capital: The Problem of Literary Canon Formation* (Chicago: University of Chicago Press, 1993), 85–133.

30. Wordsworth, *The Excursion*, ed. Sally Bushell, James Butler, and Michael C. Jaye (Ithaca: Cornell University Press, 2007), 1.136–138.

31. J. H. Prynne, "Resistance and Difficulty," *Prospect* 5 (Winter 1961): 26–30; 28.

32. William Wordsworth, Preface to the 1800 edition of *Lyrical Ballads*, in *Wordsworth's Poetry and Prose*, ed. Nicholas Halmi (New York: Norton, 2014), 76–96; 92.

33. Edmund Burke, *A Philosophical Enquiry into our Ideas of the Sublime and Beautiful*, ed. Paul Guyer (Oxford: Oxford University Press, 2015), 2.4.49–50.

34. Burke, *A Philosophical Enquiry* 2.4.49.

35. Paul H. Fry, *The Reach of Criticism: Method and Perception in Literary Theory* (New Haven: Yale University Press, 1983), 84.

36. David Hume, *An Enquiry Concerning Human Understanding*, in *An Enquiry Concerning Human Understanding and Other Writings*, ed. Stephen Buckle (Cambridge: Cambridge University Press, 2007), 7.2.29.

37. Hume, *An Enquiry Concerning Human Understanding* 7.2.29.

38. Wordsworth, entry dated 11 October 1800, *The Grasmere and Alfoxden Journals*, 26.

39. Daniel Wright, "George Eliot's Vagueness," *Victorian Studies* 56.4 (Summer 2014): 625–648; 625.

40. George Eliot, "Notes on Form in Art," in *Essays of George Eliot*, ed. Thomas Pinney (New York: Columbia University Press, 1963), 431–36; 433.

41. John Clare, "The Fallen Elm," 55, 57; "The Lament of Swordy Well," 23–24; "Trespass," 11–14; all published in *"I Am": The Selected Poetry of John Clare*, ed. Jonathan Bate (New York: Farrar, Straus and Giroux, 2003).

42. Georgi Plekhanov, "Dialectic and Logic," in *Fundamental Problems of Marxism*, trans. Eden Paul and Cedar Paul, ed. David Riazanov (New York: International Publishers, 1929), 113. Hereafter cited in the text as "DL," followed by page numbers.

43. Samuel Taylor Coleridge, *Biographia Literaria*, ed. James Engell and Walter Jackson Bate, 2 vols. (Princeton: Princeton University Press, 1985), 1.18–19. Hereafter cited in the text as *BL*, followed by volume and page numbers.

44. Entry 4822 in *The Notebooks of Samuel Taylor Coleridge*, vol. 4, *1819–1826*, ed. Kathleen Coburn and Merton Christensen (Princeton: Princeton University Press, 1957). Coleridge's "grammatical metaphor" may also be playing on Pope's fondness for the classical theme of concordia discors.

45. For Kenneth Johnston, these aspects of the Wordsworthian character are plainly post-traumatic, the fallout from William Pitt's reign of alarm and the suppression of even the most benign dissent. *The Prelude*, Johnston writes, displaces the ordeal of the 1790s into its tripartite structure, "in which the young Wordsworth's imagination is portrayed as meeting and surmounting one challenge after another" from antagonistic cultural forces represented by Cambridge, London, and a revolutionary ideology that proves inhospitable to the growth of the poet's mind. If the "details" of Wordsworth's own life remain, in this autobiographical poem, "factually real . . . if not literally represented," they are first preserved by their inflation into structure and belied by being serially overcome.

This is a solid reading, though perhaps too confident in the poet's ability to vault himself up and over the refractory matter of histories personal, political, and everything in between. It also takes the bait that *The Prelude*'s epic architecture sets out. Because this is a big, baggy, retrospective but nonetheless forward-hurtling poem that comes to land, with enviable poise, on a vow to teach others how and what to love, it can seem like it accomplishes what it set out to achieve: thousands of lines on the page and the promise of more to come. *The Prelude*, in other words, succeeds because it ends; the poet's mind cannot grow backward, not after this test of endurance. In his emphasis on the poem's mountaineering, its determined drama of conflict and conquest, Johnston buys what Wordsworth appears to be selling. The question, for me anyway, is what else is on offer? And what is its cost? See Kenneth R. Johnston, *Unusual Suspects: Pitt's Reign of Alarm and the Lost Generation of the 1790s* (Oxford: Oxford University Press, 2013), 252.

46. Wordsworth, "Note" to *The Thorn* (1800), in *Wordsworth's Poetry and Prose*, 38–39; 39. The discussion of "an accompanying consciousness of . . . the deficiencies on language" that immediately follows this passage hews closely to the section of tautology in Campbell's *Philosophy of Rhetoric*. Tautology, Campbell writes, is acceptable when

> the language of the passions is exhibited. Passion naturally dwells on its objects; the impassioned speaker always attempts to rise in expression; but when that is impracticable, he recurs to repetition and synonymy, and thereby in some measure produces the same effect. The hearer, perceiving him, as it were, overpowered by his subject, and at a loss to find words adequate to the strength of his feelings, is by sympathy carried along with him, and enters into all his sentiments. There is in this case an expression in the very effort shown by recurring to synonyms, which supplies the deficiency in the words themselves (*PR* 2.275).

47. Wordsworth's January 1804 letter to John Thelwall is the locus classicus of this claim. See *The Letters of William and Dorothy Wordsworth* 1:434–35; 434.

48. Bromwich, *Disowned by Memory*, 75.

49. Wordsworth, *Lyrical Ballads and Other Poems, 1797–1800*, 755.

50. Wordsworth, "Concerning the relations of Great Britain, Spain, and Portugal, to Each Other, and to the Common Enemy, at this Crisis; and Specifically as Affected by the CONVENTION OF CINTRA: The whole brought to the test of those Principles, by which alone the Independence and Freedom of Nations can be Preserved or Recovered," in *The Prose Works of William Wordsworth*, ed. W .J. B. Owen and J. W. Smyser, 3 vols. (Oxford: Oxford University Press, 1974), 1.221–343; 224.

51. *14P* has "I crossed the square (an empty area then!)/Of the Carrousel, where so late had lain/The dead, upon the dying heaped[.]" This suggests that the comma after "cross'd" in MS A is an error, and that the revision protects the verb's intended transitivity.

52. Wordsworth, *The Fourteen-Book Prelude* 10.55.

53. John Rice, *An Introduction to the Art of Reading with Energy and Propriety* (London: J. and R. Tonson, 1765), 176.

54. Brennan O'Donnell, *The Passion of Meter: A Study of Wordsworth's Metrical Art* (Kent, OH: Kent State University Press, 1995), 233.

55. Wordsworth, letter to Thelwall, 434.

56. John Walker, *Elements of Elocution: Being the Substance of a Course of Lectures on the Art of Reading; delivered at Several Colleges in the University of Oxford*, 2 vols. (London: Printed for the author, 1781), 1.332. In his *Illustrations of English Rhythmus,* Thelwall complains that Walker's distinctions—in this case, between various kinds of pauses—are not fine-grained enough, that they produce "perplexing contradictions," and in their stead proposes this tripartite taxonomy: "a suspensive quantity, an interruptive pause, and an accentual close," each of which should be "well-defined, and orally illustrated." See Thelwall, *Illustrations of English Rhythmus* (London, 1812), xxiii.

57. Wordsworth, "Concerning the relations of Great Britain, Spain, and Portugal," 224.

58. Wordsworth, *The Fourteen-Book Prelude* 10.63–5.

CHAPTER THREE

1. William Wordsworth, Advertisement to the first edition of *Lyrical Ballads*, in *Lyrical Ballads and Other Poems, 1797–1800*, ed. James A. Butler and Karen Green (Ithaca: Cornell University Press, 1992), 738.

2. Quintilian, *Institutio oratoria*, published as *The Orator's Education*, vol. 3, *Books 6–8*, ed. and trans. Donald A. Russell (Cambridge, MA: Harvard University Press, 2002), 8.6.34; Joseph Priestley, "Lecture XXII: Of the Nature of Metaphors," in *A Course of Lectures on Oratory and Criticism* (London: J. Johnson, 1777), 185.

3. John Keats, "Ode to Psyche," 60, and *Endymion: A Poetic Romance* 3.388–90, both in *Complete Poems*, ed. Jack Stillinger (Cambridge, MA: Harvard University Press, 1978). All quotations from Keats's poems are taken from this edition and are hereafter cited in the text with an abbreviated title followed by line numbers or, as relevant, book and line numbers.

4. Keats, letter to Benjamin Bailey dated 22 November 1817, in *The Letters of John Keats*, ed. Hyder Edward Rollins, 2 vols. (Cambridge, MA: Harvard University Press, 1958), 1.185. All quotations from Keats's letters are taken from this edition, hereafter cited in the text as *L* followed by volume and page numbers.

5. Karl Marx, *Capital*, vol. 1, trans. Ben Fowkes (New York: Penguin, 1990), 164. Hereafter cited in the text as *C*, followed by volume and page numbers.

6. Dudley Fenner, *The Arte of Rhetorike*, in *The artes of logike and rethorike plainelie set foorth in the English tounge, easie to be learned and practised: togither vvith examples for the practise of the same for methode, in the gouernement of the familie, prescribed in the word of God, and for the whole in the resolution or opening of certayne partes of Scripture, according to the same* ([Middelburg: R. Schilders,] 1584), [chap. 1, unpaginated], at http://name.umdl.umich.edu/A00630.0001.001; John Hoskyns, *Directions for Speech and Style*, in *The Life, Letters, and Writings of John Hoskyns*, ed. Louise Brown Osborn (New Haven: Yale University Press, 1937), 125. Hoskyns's *Directions* was first published around 1599.

7. [Anon.], *The Art of Rhetorick Laid Down in an Easy Entertaining Manner, and*

Illustrated with Several Beautiful Orations from Demosthenes, Cicero, Sallust, Homer, Shakespear, Milton, &c. (London: J. Newbery, 1746), 30.

8. Alexander Pope, *Peri Bathous; or, The Art of Sinking in Poetry*, in *The Major Works*, ed. Pat Rogers (Oxford: Oxford University Press, 2008), 195–239; 215. An oft-cited example of catachresis comes from Milton's *Lycidas*, in St. Peter's despairing assessment of the unskilled shepherds he calls "Blind mouths! that scarce themselves know how to hold/A sheep-hook"—likewise a use of the figure that highlights the simultaneous impairment of the poetic and social order. See John Milton, *Lycidas*, in *Complete Poems and Major Prose*, ed. Merritt Y. Hughes (New York: Macmillan, 1957), 119–20.

9. Gayatri Chakravorty Spivak, "French Feminism Revisited," in *Outside in the Teaching Machine* (New York and London: Routledge, 1993), 141–172; 161. See also Jacques Derrida, *Margins of Philosophy*, trans. Alan Bass (Chicago: University of Chicago Press, 1982), 255–57.

10. Danielle Allen writes of the bee topos as a working-through of the relationship between social organization, labor, and value from Hesiod to Mandeville in "Burning the Fable of the Bees: The Incendiary Authority of Nature," in *The Moral Authority of Nature*, ed. Lorraine Daston and Fernando Vidal (Chicago: University of Chicago Press, 2004), 74–99.

11. Matthew Arnold, "John Keats," in *The Complete Prose Works of Matthew Arnold*, ed. R. H. Super, 11 vols. (Ann Arbor: University of Michigan Press, 1976–77), 9.207.

12. Keston Sutherland, "Marx in Jargon," in *Stupefaction: A Radical Anatomy of Phantoms* (Calcutta: Seagull Books, 2011), 26–90; 43.

13. Sutherland, "Marx in Jargon," 40–42. That satire is generically dependent on its own formal immanence and inscrutability—in the meaning of a tone that doesn't reliably track a point of view—is part of the rationale Sutherland uses to call *Capital* satiric, in the sense that it is irreconcilable with the positivist "standards of truth maintained in the interests of bourgeois realism" (57). The other part of the rationale is that satire, since it is always at someone's expense, operates as a "literary exposure of social contradiction":

> The worker reduced to *Gallerte* meets with the most horrible fate available in Marx's satire on wage labor but he is not for that reason the object of the satire. His suffering can hardly be increased by literature, and it is precisely in emphasis of that fact that Marx allocates to him the most repulsive fate in the drama. . . . The object of Marx's satire on abstract human labour is not the worker reduced to a condiment but the bourgeois consumer who eats him for breakfast. It is the bourgeois consumer who suffers by the influence of Marx's satire on abstract human labour, because the satire makes his unavoidable daily acts and his very survival disgusting. (46–47)

14. Wilhelm Busch, *Max und Moritz* and *Der Eispeter*, in *Gesammelte Werke* (München: Braun & Schneider, 1959). I am hugely grateful to Cordula Grewe for

bringing Busch's cartoons to my attention with her talk "The Arabesque from Kant to Comics," presented at "Romanticism, Now and Then," a workshop sponsored by the journal *New Literary History* and held at the University of Virginia, in Charlottesville, VA, April 20–21, 2019.

15. Marx, *Das Kapital, Bd. I*, in Marx and Friedrich Engels, *Werke*, 43 vols. (Berlin: Dietz, 1956–90), 23.603. My translation. A standard English translation of *Zwickmühle* is "alternating rhythm," but the proper meaning of the term is preserved in French as *double moulinet* and has come to have some significance to theories of communization. For a recent reassessment of the *moulinet* paradigm, see Endnotes, "Crisis in the Class Relation," in *Endnotes II: Misery and the Value Form*, available at https://endnotes.org.uk/issues/2/en/endnotes-crisis-in-the-class-relation (accessed April 22, 2019).

16. Mariarosa Dalla Costa, "Women and the Subversion of the Community," in *Women and the Subversion of the Community: A Mariarosa Dalla Costa Reader*, ed. Camille Barbagallo (Oakland: PM Press, 2019), 17–50; 28. Dalla Costa's next sentence clarifies that she means "autonomy" not in any general but in a highly specialized sense, while also reveling in the seemingly awkward fit—which it is this essay's task to make less awkward—between the sexual context and the revolutionary one: "The working class organizes as a class to transcend itself as a class; within that class we organize autonomously to create the basis to transcend autonomy."

17. [George] Bernard Shaw, "Keats," in *The John Keats Memorial Volume* (London: John Lane, 1921), 173–78; 175.

18. Shaw, "Keats," 174–76. The expression "down to tin tacks," which we now commonly hear as "down to brass tacks," is likely military in origin; see Anatoly Liberman, "The Oxford Etymologist Gets Down to Brass Tacks and Tries to Hit the Nail on the Head," published at the Oxford University Press blog and available at https://blog.oup.com/2015/04/get-down-to-brass-tacks-idiom-origin/ (accessed April 22, 2019).

19. Like the brothers' employees, the "little victims" of the Industrial Revolution "breathe the deadly fumes of fires and metals," while "instead of the birds, they hear nothing but the click of combs or the grinding of engines." Leigh Hunt, "On the Employment of Children in Manufactories," *Examiner* 536 (April 1818): 209–12; 210.

20. [John Scott,] *London Magazine* 2 (September 1820): 315–21; 316.

21. Marjorie Levinson, *Keats's Life of Allegory* (Oxford: Basil Blackwell, 1988), 3. For a long time following his death Keats was cast as a poet of limpid sensuality whose feeble life was snuffed out, as Byron had it, by an article. In the mid-twentieth century, largely thanks to Walter Jackson Bate's landmark biography, this picture was amended to bring Keats in line with more normatively masculine values tied to a certain brand of class consciousness. If the old Keats was frail and oversexed, the new Keats was at least as much fighter as lover, a working-class kid from the London suburbs who punched bullies at school, drank, and made jokes about the c-word with his politically radical friends. To some extent, all writing about Keats is still forced to navigate these variously limited characterizations of his personality, which—in an almost comically extreme contradiction of his own wishes—is seldom treated as distinct from his poems. Levinson's book is still the best and most rigor-

ous attempt to move from biography to poetics without isolating Keats from his reception, which is, she makes clear, so powerfully and unpredictably diagnostic.

22. Levinson, *Keats's Life of Allegory*, 6.

23. Quintilian, *Institutio oratoria* 8.6.34.

24. Levinson, *Keats's Life of Allegory*, 9.

25. Raymond Williams, *Marxism and Literature* (Oxford: Oxford University Press, 1978), 96–97.

26. Wordsworth, "A Slumber Did My Spirit Seal," in *Lyrical Ballads and Other Poems, 1797–1800*, ed. James A. Butler and Karen Green (Ithaca: Cornell University Press, 1992), 1–2, 7–8. Paul Fry's reading of the poem comes closest to describing its harrowing insentience: "In Wordsworth's shockingly minimal vision, or lack of vision, the spirit is never *un*sealed. The elemental world slumbers with Lucy slumbering in its bosom, just where the speaker . . . has always slumbered also." If the Lucy figure was once, as she is in the other poems in this cluster, "a figure of brightness," she is so no more: "Lucy Gray is now light gray." See Paul H. Fry, *Defenses of Poetry: Reflections on the Occasion of Writing* (Stanford: Stanford University Press, 1995), 199.

27. Félix Guattari, *Les trois écologies* (Paris: Galilée, 1989), 38.

28. Keats, "In drear nighted December," in *Complete Poems*, 21.

29. Craig Dworkin, *No Medium* (Cambridge, MA: MIT Press, 2013), 22.

30. Coleridge, *The Collected Works of Samuel Taylor Coleridge*, vol. 7, *Biographia Literaria*, ed. Walter Jackson Bate and James Engell, 2 vols. (Princeton: Princeton University Press, 1983), 2.55. The reference is to Coleridge pouncing on Wordsworth's phrase "the real language of men" to describe the diction of *Lyrical Ballads*. ("I object," he writes, "in the very first instance, to an equivocation in the use of the word 'real.'")

31. Dworkin, *No Medium*, 5–7.

32. George Gordon, Lord Byron, letter to John Murray dated 20 November 1820, in *Byron's Letters and Journals*, ed. Leslie A. Marchand, 12 vols. (Cambridge, MA: Harvard University Press, 1973–81), 7.225; Kenneth Burke, *A Rhetoric of Motives* (Berkeley: University of California Press, 1969), 204.

33. Byron, letter to Murray, 7.346. Cf. Dworkin's discussion of Tom Friedman's *11 x 22 x .0005*, a blank sheet of paper with the same dimensions as a *Playboy* centerfold:

> On the one hand, (or with one hand, as the case may be), the masturbatory *mise-en-scène* of Friedman's work theatricalizes the solitary and presumably private process that result in the erased page: an obsessive repetitive manual frottage. By doing so, it literalizes the vernacular phrase "to rub one off" and anticipates the popular criticism that presenting something like a blank piece of paper as art is, *prima facie*, 'masturbatory' in the figurative sense of "self-absorbed or self-indulgent." On the other hand, the work performs a sly reversal of cultural clichés. Rather than staining, Friedman's activity in this case cleans up a dirty picture, rendering what he has identified elsewhere as an "obscenely white, empty space." (Dworkin, *No Medium*, 20)

34. Anne-Lise François, "'The feel of not to feel it,' or the Pleasures of Enduring Form," in *A Companion to Romantic Poetry*, ed. Charles Mahoney (Oxford: Wiley-Blackwell, 2011), 445–66; 446.

35. Marx, [Private Property and Communism. Various Stages of Development of Communist Views. Crude, Equalitarian Communism and Communism as Socialism Coinciding with Humaneness], in *Economic and Philosophic Manuscripts of 1844*, trans. Martin Milligan (Amherst, NY: Prometheus Books, 1988), 99–114; 107. Hereafter cited by page numbers in parentheses and abbreviated *EPM*.

36. "Vom Standpunkt einer höhern ökonomischen Gesellschaftsformation wird das Privateigentum einzelner Individuen am Erdball ganz so abgeschmackt erscheinen, wie das Privateigentum eines Menschen an einem andern Menschen." Marx, *Das Kapital, Bd. III*, in *Werke* 25.784.

37. Williams, *Marxism and Literature*, 151.

38. James Chandler, *England in 1819: The Politics of Literary Culture and the Case of Romantic Historicism* (Chicago: University of Chicago Press, 1998), 425.

39. [Thomas Taylor], *The Fable of Cupid and Psyche, Translated from the Latin of Apuleius* (London: Leigh and Sotheby, 1795), 8.

40. See my *Utopia Limited: Romanticism and Adjustment* (Cambridge, MA: Harvard University Press, 2015), 199–204.

41. Hermione de Almeida, *Romantic Medicine and John Keats* (Oxford: Oxford University Press, 1991), 97.

42. Gaius Valerius Catullus, Catullus 5 ("Vīvāmus mea Lesbia, atque amēmus"), in *Poems of Catullus*, ed. G. A. Williamson (Bristol: Bristol Classical Press, 1991), 7–9.

43. [Taylor], *The Fable of Cupid and Psyche*, vi.

44. Giorgio Agamben, *Means without End: Notes on Politics*, trans. Vicenzo Binetti and Cesare Casarino (Minneapolis: University of Minnesota Press, 2000), 57.

45. Marx, *Comments on James Mill*, excerpted in *Karl Marx: A Reader*, ed. Jon Elster (Cambridge: Cambridge University Press, 1986), 31–35; 34.

46. Percy Bysshe Shelley, *Laon and Cythna; or, The Revolution of the Golden City*, ed. Anahid Nersessian (Peterborough, ON: Broadview Press, 2016), 5.511–13.

47. Shelley, *A Philosophical View of Reform*, ed. T. W. Rolleston (Oxford: Oxford University Press, 1920), 5. Of *Laon and Cythna*, Keats remarked slyly, "Shelley's poem is out & there are words about it being objected to as much as Queen Mab was. Poor Shelley I think he has his Quota of good qualities, in sooth la!!." See *Letters* 1.194.

48. Edmund Burke, *A Philosophical Enquiry into the Origin of Our Ideas of the Sublime and Beautiful*, ed. Paul Guyer (Oxford: Oxford University Press, 2015), 2.12.63.

49. I refer here to Charles Cowden Clarke's account of lending Keats his copy of *The Faerie Queene*, which Keats apparently "went through . . . as a young horse would through a spring meadow—ramping! Like a true poet, too—a poet 'born, not manufactured,' a poet in grain, he especially singled out epithets, for that felicity and power in which Spenser is so eminent. He *hoisted* himself up, and looked burly and dominant, as he said, 'what an image that is—*sea-shouldering whales!*'"

Quoted in Walter Jackson Bate, *John Keats* (Cambridge, MA: Harvard University Press, 1963), 33. This reaction, as Bate notes, "has passed into legend," at least among Keats scholars.

50. From Keats's notes in his copy of *Paradise Lost*, quoted in Bate, *John Keats*, 246.

51. Nicholas Roe, *John Keats: A New Life* (New Haven: Yale University Press, 2012), 16.

52. Bate, *The Stylistic Development of Keats* (New York: Modern Language Association of America, 1945), 42.

CHAPTER FOUR

1. Johann Wolfgang von Goethe, "Du Schüler Howards," in *Goethes Werke—Hamburger Ausgabe in 14 Bänden, Band I: Gedichte und Epen I*, rev. 16th ed., ed. Erich Trunz (Munich: C. H. Beck, 1996).

2. Mary Jacobus, *Romantic Things: A Tree, a Rock, a Cloud* (Chicago: University of Chicago Press, 2012), 10.

3. Jonathan Culler, *Theory of the Lyric* (Cambridge, MA: Harvard University Press, 2015), 187. Culler believes that all lyric poems are triangulated in this way; apostrophe is only the most "blatant" device for achieving the effect.

4. Lorraine Daston, "Cloud Physiognomy," *Representations* 135.1 (2016): 45–71. As Daston explains, the analogy is chosen advisedly:

> The physiognomic analogy between the human face and clouds is an old one, and oft-repeated. When in 1663 Robert Hooke proposed a scheme for making weather observations to the Royal Society, one of the eight categories was the "face of the sky," by which Hooke mostly meant cloud configurations: "if thick after what manner wth a thin white, long hairy racks or . . . looking almost like the waves in a map or like those on the back of a mackerel." [Luke] Howard had defended the regularity of his cloud genera by interpreting them as the visible signs of the "general causes" of variation in the atmosphere, just "as is the countenance of the state of a person's mind or body." This analogy between facial physiognomy and cloud configurations stressed the underlying regularity of both phenomena; the same analogy could however also be enlisted to accent individuality and variability—like human faces, no two clouds were identical. But whichever way the analogy was turned, it made the recognition of cloud types into a skill as reliable as facial recognition. Clouds, the analogy implied, were genuinely physiognomic: the details that composed them gelled into a whole, just as eyes, nose, cheekbones, and mouth gelled into a face. (65)

5. Hugh Blair, lecture 16, "Hyperbole—Personification—Apostrophe," in *Lectures on Rhetoric and Belles Lettres*, ed. Linda Ferreira-Buckley and S. Michael Halloran (Carbondale: Southern Illinois University Press, 2005), 170–183; 177. "All strong passions," adds Blair, "have a tendency to use [apostrophe,] not only love, anger, and indignation, but even those which are seemingly more dispiriting, such as grief, remorse, and melancholy." All passions, in other words, "struggle for vent" regard-

less of their relative velocity, and if apostrophe is, as it seems to be, something of a rhetorical projectile—a speaking propulsively into the air—its arc need not be high but might also droop, decline, diminish.

6. William Wordsworth, *The Excursion*, ed. Sally Bushell, James Butler, and Michael C. Jaye (Ithaca: Cornell University Press, 2007), 1.507–13.

7. Anne-Lise François, "Unspeakable Weather; or the Rain Romantic Constatives Know," in *Phantom Sentences: Essays in Linguistics and Literature Presented to Ann Banfield*, ed. Robert S. Kawashima, Gilles Philippe, and Thelma Sowley (Bern: Peter Lang, 2008), 147–61; 161. For a fascinating comparative perspective on the morphology of giving evidence about the weather, see Sarah Murray's "Evidentiality and Illocutionary Mood in Cheyenne," *International Journal of American Linguistics* 82.4 (October 2016): 487–517; thanks to the author for instruction on this point.

8. Rosalind Krauss, "The Crisis of the Easel Picture," in *Jackson Pollock: New Approaches*, ed. Kirk Varnedoe and Pepe Karmel (New York: Museum of Modern Art, 1999), 155–79. I am grateful to Christa Robbins for drawing this essay to my attention, and for conversation about Krauss more generally.

9. Lisa Robertson, "The Weather: A Report on Sincerity," *Chicago Review* 51.4/52.1 (2006): 28–37; 32.

10. John Ruskin, "The Storm Cloud of the Nineteenth Century: Two Lectures Delivered at the London Institution, February 4th and 11th, 1884" (Orpington, Kent: George Allen, 1884), 42.

11. Ruskin, "The Storm Cloud of the Nineteenth Century," 48.

12. Krauss, "Agnes Martin: The /Cloud/," in *Bachelors* (Cambridge, MA: MIT Press, 1999), 75–89; 82.

13. Hubert Damisch, *A Theory of Cloud: Toward a History of Painting*, trans. Janet Lloyd (Stanford: Stanford University Press, 2002), 14–15.

14. Kate Bush, "Not This Time," *The Big Sky (Special Single Mix)*, EMI Records, 1986. All quotations from both "Not This Time" and "The Big Sky" cite tracks on this recording, which scarcely differs from the official single except that the bass is a tiny bit quieter.

15. John Keats, *Hyperion*, in *Complete Poems*, ed. Jack Stillinger (Cambridge, MA: Harvard University Press, 1982), I.35–7. All quotations from Keats's poems are taken from this edition and are hereafter cited in the text with an abbreviated title followed by line numbers or, as relevant, book and line numbers.

16. Allison Carruth, "The Digital Cloud and the Micropolitics of Energy," *Public Culture* 26.2 (2014): 339–64. On Carruth's definition, the micropolitics of her title refer to "the planetary ramifications of minute individual practices that are fueled by cultural values of connectivity and speed and that rely, above all, on the infrastructure of server farms," which require (among other things) "concrete warehouses, endless racks of servers, a morass of electrical circuitry, and water-hungry cooling systems."

17. John Barrell, *The Idea of Landscape and the Sense of Place, 1730–1840: An Approach to the Poetry of John Clare* (Cambridge: Cambridge University Press, 1992), 24–25. See also Barrell's long essay "An Unerring Gaze: The Prospect of Society

in the Poetry of James Thomson and John Dyer," in *English Literature in History, 1730–80: An Equal, Wide Survey* (London: Hutchinson, 1983), 51–109. Steve Hindle discusses this painting in detail, and notes its "unfortunate omission" from Barrell's 1983 book *The Dark Side of the Landscape*, in his "Representing Rural Society: Labor, Leisure, and the Landscape in an Eighteenth-Century Conversation Piece," *Critical Inquiry* 41.3 (2015): 615–54.

18. David Fairer, "'Where Fuming Trees Refresh the Thirsty Air': The World of Eco-Georgic," *Studies in Eighteenth-Century Culture* 40 (2011): 201–18. I allude here to the title of Ursula K. Heise's *Sense of Place and Sense of Planet: The Environmental Imagination of the Global* (Oxford: Oxford University Press, 2008).

19. Jonathan Kramnick, *Paper Minds: Literature and the Ecology of Consciousness* (Chicago: University of Chicago Press, 2018), 83. Hereafter cited in the text as *PM*, followed by page numbers.

20. William Cowper, Advertisement to *The Task*, in *Poetical Works*, ed. H. S. Milford (London: Oxford University Press, 1967), 128.

21. Walter Jackson Bate, *The Stylistic Development of Keats* (New York: Modern Language Association of America, 1945), 184.

22. Jonathan Culler, "Apostrophe," in *The Pursuit of Signs: Semiotics, Literature, Deconstruction* (Ithaca: Cornell University Press, 1981), 135–54; 142.

23. Paul de Man, "Autobiography as De-Facement," in *The Rhetoric of Romanticism* (New York: Columbia University Press, 1984), 67–82; 75.

24. Krauss, "Video: The Aesthetics of Narcissism," *October* 1 (Spring 1976): 50–64; 50.

25. Krauss, "Video: The Aesthetics of Narcissism," 55.

26. Krauss, "Crisis of the Easel Picture," 161.

27. John Constable, letter to John Fisher dated 20 September 1821, quoted in John E. Thornes, *John Constable's Skies: A Fusion of Art and Science* (Edgbaston: University of Birmingham Press, 1999), 82.

28. Jacobus, *Romantic Things*, 14.

29. See Stanley Plumly, *Elegy Landscapes: Constable and Turner and the Intimate Sublime* (New York: Norton, 2018), 112–13.

30. Gotthold Ephraim Lessing, *Laokoon oder Über die Grenzen der Malerei und Poesie*, ed. Friedrich Vollhardt (Stuttgart: Reclam, 2012), 115.

31. For Daston, the prospect of reading clouds for their affective content is a dicey one. There may be such a thing as cloud physiognomy, but at the Romantic moment of its inception "there were huge lacunae in the vernacular vocabulary of clouds" where no such gaps existed in the vocabulary of faces. Actors' manuals, oratorical treatises, and scientific writings on facial expressions and what they signify are plentiful in the eighteenth century and persist well into the nineteenth (think of Charles Darwin's *The Expression of the Emotions in Man and Animals*, from 1872), suggesting that, in this case, "the continuum of experience had already been pre-parsed into types" available for both vernacular and technical usages. See Daston, "Cloud Physiognomy," 61.

32. [Anon.,] "The British Institution—No. 11," *London Magazine* 3 (September–December 1825): 49–69; 67.

33. James D. Herbert, *Brushstroke and Emergence: Courbet, Impressionism, Picasso* (Chicago: University of Chicago Press, 2015), 85.

34. Constable, letter to Fisher, 57.

35. William Hazlitt, "On Imitation," in *The Round Table: A Collection of Essays on Literature, Men, and Manners* (Edinburgh: Archibald Constable, 1817), 2.11–20; 19.

36. James Hutton, *Theory of the Earth, with proofs and illustrations; in four parts*, 2 vols. (Edinburgh: William Creech, 1795), 1.422.

37. Ovid, *Metamorphoses*, vol. 1, *Books 1–8*, trans. Frank Justus Miller, rev. G. P. Goold, Loeb Classical Library (Cambridge, MA: Harvard University Press, 1916), 1.292, 1.307–8. Constable had a fondness for classical as well as modern poetry. The introduction to his 1833 collection of plates *Various Subjects of Landscape, Characteristic of English Scenery, principally intended to display the Phenomenon of the Chiar'oscuro of Nature* (London: Constable, 1833) is prefaced by quotations from Wordsworth and Thomson as well as Ovid and Virgil.

38. Hutton, *Theory of the Earth* 1:185–86.

39. Hutton, *Theory of the Earth* 1:190.

40. Gillen D'Arcy Wood, "Constable, Clouds, Climate Change," *Wordsworth Circle* 38.1/2 (Winter/Spring 2007): 25–33.

41. Michel Serres, "Science and the Humanities: The Case of Turner," *subStance* 26.2 (1997): 6–21, 6.

42. Serres, "Science and the Humanities," 6–7.

43. Hazlitt, "On Imitation," 20.

44. John Ashbery, "Clepsydra," in *Selected Poems* (New York: Penguin, 1986), 63–70; 63.

45. Paul Celan, "Mit erdwärts gesungenen Masten," in *Breathturn into Timestead: The Collected Later Poetry: A Bilingual Edition*, ed. and trans. Pierre Joris (New York: Farrar, Straus and Giroux, 2014), 8. This is the translation Mirra uses; see figure 10 above.

46. Michael Fried, "Art and Objecthood," in *Art and Objecthood: Essays and Reviews* (Chicago: University of Chicago Press, 1998), 148–72; 155.

47. Hamza Walker, "Thread-skies," in Helen Mirra, Jen Bervin, Ben Marcus, and Walker, *Sky-wreck* (Chicago: Renaissance Society, 2002), [6].

EPILOGUE

1. Margaret Ronda, "Mourning and Melancholia in the Anthropocene," Post45, June 2013, at http://post45.research.yale.edu/2013/06/mourning-and-melancholia-in-the-anthropocene/ (accessed May 4, 2019).

2. Benjamin H. D. Buchloh, "Conceptual Art 1962–1969: From the Aesthetic of Administration to the Critique of Institutions," in *October: The Second Decade, 1986–1996*, ed. Rosalind E. Krauss, Yve-Alain Bois, et al. (Cambridge: MIT Press, 1997), 117–55; 131.

3. See Chip Jacobs and William J. Kelly, *Smogtown: The Lung-Burning History of Pollution in Los Angeles* (New York: Harry N. Abrams, 2008), esp. 15–41.

4. Dorothy Wordsworth, Grasmere journal, entry for June 1 (1800), in *The Gras-*

mere and Alfoxden Journals, ed. Pamela Woof (Oxford: Oxford University Press, 2002), 6–7. Hereafter cited in the text as *GJ*, followed by page numbers.

By "the pewside came down with me" Wordsworth seems to mean that everyone except the preacher left the church at the same time she did, although whenever I read this sentence I'm tempted to think she means that she tripped and took a pew down with her.

5. This is Wordsworth describing the educational method she and her brother are using to educate their friend Basil Montagu's son, directing his "insatiable curiosity" to "everything he sees, the sky, the fields, trees, shrubs, corn, the making of tools, carts, &c &c &c." Wordsworth, letter to Jane Marshall dated 19 March 1797, in *The Letters of William and Dorothy Wordsworth*, vol. 1, *The Early Years, 1787–1805*, ed. Ernest de Selincourt, rev. Chester Shaver (Oxford: Oxford University Press, 1967), 180.

6. Rachel Feder, "The Experimental Dorothy Wordsworth," *Studies in Romanticism* 53.4 (2014): 541–59. As she puts it, Feder does not intend "to crown Dorothy Wordsworth the fairy godmother of experimental verse" but "to illuminate a history of poetic experiments that manipulate their marginal status, that activate generic innovation and invention grounded in questions of materiality" (544), such as the unique status of the Romantic chapbook.

Index

Wordsworth, Dorothy: experimental poetics of, 176; Grasmere journal, 74–75, 173–77; historical commentary of, 61, 175–76; Jarman on, 27, 51

Wordsworth, William: character of, 20, 57–58, 80–81, 90, 93; Coleridge on, 39, 78–79; egotistical sublime of, 20, 80, 111; and French Revolution, 80–81, 86–91; *Lyrical Ballads*, 3, 39, 62–63, 78, 80, 83, 107; "Michael," 4, 20, 59, 62–64, 72–82, 84–85, 97; poetics of, 20, 85, 89–90; Preface to *Lyrical Ballads*, 69, 83, 85; *The Prelude*, 16, 58, 62, 64, 66, 72, 80–91, 107; secrecy and, 59–60, 64, 88,

90, 160; "A slumber did my spirit seal," 107; "The Thorn," 83, 89; use of obscurity, 20, 59, 62–64, 72–82, 84–85; on versification, 69, 83, 85, 88, 93, 191n46; "The World is Too Much With Us," 104

work: and catachresis: 97; in Keats's poetry: 94, 97, 121; of lyric: 132; in "Michael," 74–75, 80–81; poetry as, 142. *See also* labor

workers: under capitalism, 94, 98–99, 102, 107, 193n13; in prospect painting: 141

Wright, Daniel, 75

Zwickmühle, 102, 194n15